Sexual Harassment in the Workplace

Perspectives, Frontiers, and Response Strategies

Edited by
Margaret S. Stockdale

Volume 5

Women and Work

SAGE Publications
International Educational and Professional Publisher
Thousand Oaks London New Delhi

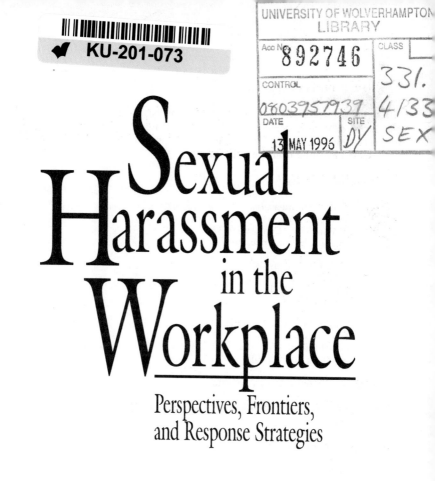

For information address:

SAGE Publications, Inc.
2455 Teller Road
Thousand Oaks, California 91320
E-mail: order@sagepub.com

SAGE Publications Ltd.
6 Bonhill Street
London EC2A 4PU
United Kingdom

SAGE Publications India Pvt. Ltd.
M-32 Market
Greater Kailash I
New Delhi 110 048 India

Printed in the United States of America

Library of Congress Cataloging-in-Publication Data

ISBN 0-8039-5793-9 (cloth)
ISBN 0-8039-5794-7 (paper)
ISSN 0882-0910

This book is printed on acid-free paper.

96 97 98 99 10 9 8 7 6 5 4 3 2 1

Sage Project Editor: Christina M. Hill

Sexual Harassment in the Workplace

Women and Work: A Research and Policy Series

The Sage series **Women and Work: A Research and Policy Series** brings together research, critical analysis, and proposals for change in a dynamic and developing field—the world of women and work. Cutting across traditional academic boundaries, the series approaches subjects from a multidisciplinary perspective. Historians, anthropologists, economists, sociologists, managers, psychologists, educators, policy makers, and legal scholars share insights and findings—giving readers access to a scattered literature in single, comprehensive volumes.

Women and Work examines differences among women—as well as differences between men and women—related to nationality, ethnicity, social class, and sexual preference. The series explores demographic and legal trends, international and multinational comparisons, and theoretical and methodological developments.

Contents

Acknowledgments ix

Series Editors' Introduction xi
BARBARA A. GUTEK, LAURIE LARWOOD, and ANN STROMBERG

Section I: Introduction

1. What We Know and What We Need to Learn About Sexual Harassment 3
MARGARET S. STOCKDALE

Section II: Perspectives on Sexual Harassment in the Workplace

2. Sexual Harassment in the Academy: The Case of Women Professors 29
ELIZABETH GRAUERHOLZ

3. Sexual Harassment and Women of Color: Issues, Challenges, and Future Directions 51
AUDREY J. MURRELL

4. Men's Misperceptions of Women's Interpersonal Behaviors and Sexual Harassment 67
FRANK E. SAAL

5. The Implications of U.S. Supreme Court and Circuit Court Decisions for Hostile Environment Sexual Harassment Cases 85
RAMONA L. PAETZOLD and ANNE M. O'LEARY-KELLY

6. Sexual Harassment as a Moral Issue: An Ethical Decision-Making Perspective 105
LYNN BOWES-SPERRY and GARY N. POWELL

Section III: Research Frontiers

7. Organizational Influences on Sexual Harassment 127
CHARLES L. HULIN, LOUISE F. FITZGERALD, and FRITZ DRASGOW

8. Sexual Harassment Types and Severity: Linking Research and Policy 151
JAMES E. GRUBER, MICHAEL SMITH, and KAISA KAUPPINEN-TOROPAINEN

9. An Integrated Framework for Studying the Outcomes of Sexual Harassment: Consequences for Individuals and Organizations 174
KATHY A. HANISCH

10. The Real "Disclosure": Sexual Harassment and the Bottom Line 199
DEBORAH ERDOS KNAPP and GARY A. KUSTIS

Section IV: Responding to Harassment: Strategies for Change

11. Understanding Sexual Harassment: Contributions From Research on Domestic Violence and Organizational Change 217
JEANETTE N. CLEVELAND and KATHLEEN MCNAMARA

12. Dealing With Harassment: A Systems Approach 241
MARY P. ROWE

13. Sexual Harassment at Work: When an Organization Fails to Respond 272
BARBARA A. GUTEK

Index 291

About the Authors 297

To seven remarkable women,
Caryl, Denise, Marji, Robin, Rose, Shawna, and Suzanne;
to my husband and daughter, Michael and Sarah Heck;
and to my parents, Pat and Tom Stockdale,
With love, Peg

Acknowledgments

I owe a debt of gratitude to all the contributors to this book for the seriousness with which they approached their work and for their willingness to make their scholarly work accessible to researchers, practitioners, and others in the various disciplines interested in the field of women and work broadly, and sexual harassment specifically. The editorial board members, whose names appear on the inside cover of this book, graciously volunteered their time to provide thorough and careful reviews of each of the chapters. Series editors Laurie Larwood and Ann Stromberg merit special recognition for reviewing *every* chapter (often more than once) and providing excellent, constructive advice not only to the contributors but also to me for keeping the book tightly focused. Vicki Staebler-Tardino provided invaluable editorial assistance helping me with correspondence and creating the indexes. Les Sellers rescued me more than once with his word processing and graphics assistance. Finally, this book could not have been produced without Barbara Gutek. She refused to be listed as a coeditor, but it's a distinction she deserves. She was the shepherd of this volume of *Women and Work,* and she worked very closely with me through all its stages. She reviewed every chapter at least twice, integrated the other series editors' comments to help me focus on the salient issues, worked directly with some of the contributors, and extended her shoulder from Arizona to Illinois for me to lean on. Thank you Barbara.

Series Editors' Introduction

The widespread entry of women into the paid labor force represents one of the major social changes of the last quarter of the twentieth century. The *Women and Work* series is designed to bring together research from a variety of disciplines focusing on this quiet revolution, more specifically on women's paid and unpaid work experiences. With the inaugural volume in 1985 and in two subsequent volumes, authors were chosen to represent current thinking in one of the many disciplines in which research on women and work is found. Many chapters summarized a significant stream of research while others presented unusual perspectives or unique departures that deserved broader recognition.

The series is based on the notion that a multidisciplinary approach is essential to a full understanding of the situation of working women. Progress will be made more readily if economists understand what historians have learned, for example, or if psychologists learn about the findings of management professors. As editors, we have attempted to be sure that the various disciplines researching women and work are represented in the series and that the contributions are both up to date and written for, and understandable by, a multidisciplinary audience. Our hope is that together the contributions will cross-fertilize the emerging area of women and work. Thus Volume 1 included chapters representing economics, sociology, psychology, history, and education; Volume 2 contained a health symposium with contributions from medicine, public health, economics, and law; and the international issues symposium in Volume 3 represented sociology, political science, anthropology, and psychology.

Research on women and work seems to be coming together rapidly. Ideas are widely shared and broadly understood across disciplines, moving the field much more swiftly than any of us might have believed possible a decade ago. The phenomenon has also brought us a broader colleague base than any traditional discipline allowed and has in fact allowed our thinking to become more widely accepted in our parent disciplines.

Beginning with Volume 4 published in 1993, the series changed in some important ways. While maintaining a commitment to a multidisciplinary focus, each volume has focused on a specific theme. When we began, it was difficult to identify topics on women and work in which there was sufficient current research to support an entire volume. That is no longer the case. Thus, beginning with Volume 4, each volume focuses on a specific topic and each has a guest editor. Volume 4, edited by Ellen Fagenson on the topic of "women in management," was the first in the new format. Management was well suited to be the topic for the first volume in our new format, as it is symbolic of the newly available opportunities for professional women over the past few decades. The history of women in management, in numbers as well as in importance, has been closely connected with the rhythm and health of the women's movement. That substantial progress has been made is easily seen. That there is much more progress needed and work to be done is indisputable. Women have moved up but have not reached the top, and women of color have been underrepresented in this field.

Volume 5 focuses not on an area of progress, such as management, but on a problem that has, as Hulin, Fitzgerald, and Drasgow (this volume) note, "a long past but a short history." The topic is sexual harassment. About 15 years after journalists and scholars first began writing about sexual harassment, we have accumulated a fair amount of data (despite very little research funding), and *sexual harassment* is now a household term and a topic of concern for employers as well as employed women.

In 1979, law professor Catharine MacKinnon wrote a book, *Sexual Harassment of Working Women,* which sought a legal mechanism for handling sexual harassment and compensating its victims. In a strong and compelling argument, MacKinnon contended that sexual harassment was primarily a problem for women, that it rarely happened to men, and that it therefore should be viewed as a form of sex discrimination. Viewing sexual harassment as a form of sex discrimination would make available to victims the same legal protection available to victims of sex discrimination. A worker who is sexually harassed is placed at a disadvantage relative to other workers and therefore does not have equal opportunity with other, nonharassed employees.

The first legal guidelines were developed in 1980 by the Equal Employment Opportunity Commission (EEOC), the agency responsible for assuring that all employees have equal opportunity in the workplace. Their guidelines were consistent with MacKinnon's position and defined sexual harassment under Title VII of the 1964 Civil Rights Act as a form of unlawful sex-based discrimination. Several states have passed their own increasingly strong laws aimed at eliminating sexual harassment, and legal scholars have sought additional avenues to recover damages incurred from sexual harassment. Various public and private agencies as well as the courts have seen a steady if uneven increase in sexual harassment complaints since the early 1980s.

The various guidelines and regulations define sexual harassment broadly. For example, the updated EEOC guidelines state that unwelcome sexual advances, requests for sexual favors, and other verbal or physical conduct of a sexual nature constitute sexual harassment when (a) submission to such conduct is made either explicitly or implicitly a term or condition of an individual's employment or academic advancement, (b) submission to or rejection of such conduct by an individual is used as the basis for employment decisions or academic decisions affecting such individual, or (c) such conduct has the purpose or effect of reasonably interfering with an individual's work or academic performance or creating an intimidating, hostile, or offensive working or academic environment.

Volume 5 of the *Women and Work* series provides a comprehensive look at what we know about sexual harassment. Our guest editor, Margaret Stockdale, has contributed substantially to the emerging knowledge base. Each of the chapters of the volume was reviewed by

Professor Stockdale, at least two of the series editors, and one or more members of the editorial board. Our goal has been to produce a volume that is grounded in theory, research, and practice but is accessible to researchers, advanced students, and practitioners in multiple disciplines.

—Barbara A. Gutek
Laurie Larwood
Ann Stromberg

REFERENCE

MacKinnon, C. (1979). *Sexual harassment of working women.* New Haven, CT: Yale University Press.

SECTION I

Introduction

1

What We Know and What We Need to Learn About Sexual Harassment

MARGARET S. STOCKDALE

A complete understanding of sexual harassment requires a multidisciplinary, multi-level synthesis. Two models are provided to help sort through the various concepts and theories that have guided past sexual harassment research so as to provide direction for future research and practice. The first model focuses on factors that explain the occurrence of sexual harassment; the second focuses on processes that connect targets' experiences of sexual harassment with outcomes suffered. The chapter ends with an overview of this volume of *Women and Work*.

Over the past 15 years, we have learned much about the range of ways that people can experience sexual harassment (SH), the frequency with which workers and students experience these events, its effects on lives, and its costs to society (Fitzgerald & Shullman, 1993; Gutek & Koss, 1993). We are now learning about the perpetrators of SH and the situations in which it occurs (Pryor, 1987; Pryor, LaVite, & Stoller, 1993). Furthermore, theoretical models addressing both cultural, social, and individual processes are developing (e.g., Fain & Anderton, 1987; Gutek, Cohen, & Konrad, 1990; Ragins & Scandura, 1992; Stockdale,

1993). Although further development and refinement are needed, a solid foundation of sexual harassment scholarship is established upon which to build integrative, theory-driven programs of research. In this chapter, I present general frameworks to guide this activity.

THE IMPORTANCE OF INTEGRATIVE RESEARCH ON SEXUAL HARASSMENT

The accumulated evidence from research activities in the past decade and a half demonstrates that sexual harassment is prevalent in organizations and that the consequences have been potentially serious (e.g., Fitzgerald et al., 1988; Gutek, 1985; Martindale, 1990; U.S. Merit Systems Protection Board [MSPB], 1981, 1988). Gutek and Koss (1993) recently delineated evidence of sexual harassment consequences to individuals and organizations. Noting that epidemiological studies have not been conducted, Gutek and Koss, nonetheless, summarized surveys indicating that substantial numbers of harassed individuals leave their jobs, withdraw from work in the form of absenteeism and lowered productivity, change career intentions, experience lower job satisfaction and deteriorated interpersonal relationships with coworkers, as well as a host of other negative attitudinal and emotional changes. Particularly poignant is the emerging evidence that harassment experiences, even those that have been labeled "less serious," such as gender harassment, are correlated with posttraumatic stress disorder and depression (Kilpatrick, 1992, cited in Gutek & Koss, 1993).

Gutek and Koss (1993) noted that we need to have a better understanding of the processes connecting experiences of harassment with psychological and organizational outcomes. Such research will need to incorporate multiple levels of analysis to examine impacts of personal, interpersonal, group, organizational, and societal characteristics. Beginning with this introductory chapter, this volume of *Women and Work* synthesizes sociological, psychological, legal, organizational, and multicultural research and theoretical perspectives on SH.

Social science disciplines can lend considerable expertise in helping to define, measure, and untangle critical processes. For example, perception is central to most sexual harassment definitions (Equal Employment Opportunity Commission [EEOC], 1980) and has been the focus of much research (e.g., Baker, Terpstra, & Larntz, 1990; Gutek, Morasch, & Cohen, 1983; Kenig & Ryan, 1986; Padgitt & Padgitt, 1986; Popovich, Licata, Nokovich, Martelli, & Zoloty, 1986; Pryor, 1985). In addition to characteristics of observers (e.g., gender) and of situations (e.g., severity), attribution processes have been found to explain observers' perceptions of harassment (Pryor & Day, 1988), and may be important for victim's perceptions as well (Stockdale & Vaux, 1993; Stockdale, Vaux, & Cashin, 1995). Finally, SH has been explained in terms of sex role stereotyping (Deaux, 1995). Comprehensive research on individual or "micro" issues should continue.

Contributions from disciplines with a "macro" orientation would be particularly valuable to sexual harassment scholarship. Most sexual violence literature in psychology discusses personal correlates and mechanisms of sexual abuse and ignores other levels of analyses (e.g., Burt, 1980; Koss & Dinero, 1988; Malamuth, 1986; Rapaport & Burkhart, 1984). It is organization-related phenomena that distinguish sexual harassment from other forms of sexual violence. That is, SH is illegal because it violates workers' rights to nondiscriminatory employment or students' rights to study in a nondiscriminatory environment. The status relationship between perpetrators and targets of SH is an organization-related variable that has been studied. We know, for example, that people harassed by supervisors are more likely to experience more serious forms of harassment than those harassed by peers or coworkers (U.S. MSPB, 1981). Grauerholz (this volume) provides an interesting discussion of the severity of harassment perpetuated by students toward female faculty. Recently, we have begun to learn about the role of occupational culture (e.g., Ragins & Scandura, 1992; Yount, 1991), workplace climate (e.g., Hulin, Fitzgerald, & Drasgow, this volume), and leader attitudes (e.g., Pryor et al., 1993). We have only begun to systematically assess the influence of cultural phenomena (see Kauppinen-Toropainen & Gruber, 1993). The theories and practices of organizational behavior, sociology, and anthropology should continue to inform these endeavors.

The following section presents two models of sexual harassment processes in organizations: one that focuses on antecedents and theories of sexual harassment, and a second that focuses on outcomes of sexual harassment experiences. These models were developed from the existing literature to provide a framework for organizing existing knowledge and to guide future research and intervention activities.

ORGANIZING MODELS

The first model (Figure 1.1) organizes explanations for sexual harassment occurrences and the important factors that tend to be associated with SH. It is important to separate the *experience* of harassing and nonharassing events from the *perception* of sexual harassment because research finds that people have different interpretations of the same kinds of experiences. The first model helps provide an understanding of the variables that explain or predict the occurrence of sexually harassing experiences, and the second model helps untangle the psychological, social, and organizational processes that connect these experiences with emotional, work-, or school-related consequences. How individuals interpret their experiences may be one such process.

Types of Sexual Harassing Experiences

Sexual harassment is both a legal and a psychological phenomenon (Fitzgerald, 1990). The EEOC (1980) as well as the courts (e.g., *Meritor Savings Bank FSB v. Vinson et al.,* 1986) have recognized two broad categories of SH: (a) quid pro quo, that is, exchange of work-related benefits or consequences for sexual favors through the use of bribery or threat, and (b) hostile work environment, that is, unwanted actions of a sexual nature that have the "purpose or effect of unreasonably interfering with an individual's work performance or creating an intimidating, hostile, or offensive working environment" (EEOC, 1980, p. 74677). Although various schemas have been offered (see Gruber, 1992; Gutek, 1985), Fitzgerald and her colleagues (Fitzgerald, Gelfand, & Drasgow, 1994; Fitzgerald & Hesson-McInnis, 1989) have conducted extensive research to understand the psychological dimensions of SH. They have determined that a scheme of three broad categories of harassment succinctly capture the range of SH experiences. *Gender harassment* involves generalized sexist comments and behavior that convey insulting, degrading, and/or sexist attitudes. *Unwanted sexual attention* ranges from unwanted, inappropriate, and offensive physical or verbal sexual advance to gross sexual imposition, assault, or rape. *Sexual coercion* implies the solicitation or coercion of sexual activity by promise of reward or threat of punishment. Fitzgerald's scheme has been adopted in the first model presented here to describe the types of experiences that occur to women and men. I chose the psychological over the legal dimensions because many people have experiences that

Examination of Factors Affecting the Occurrence of Sexual Harassment

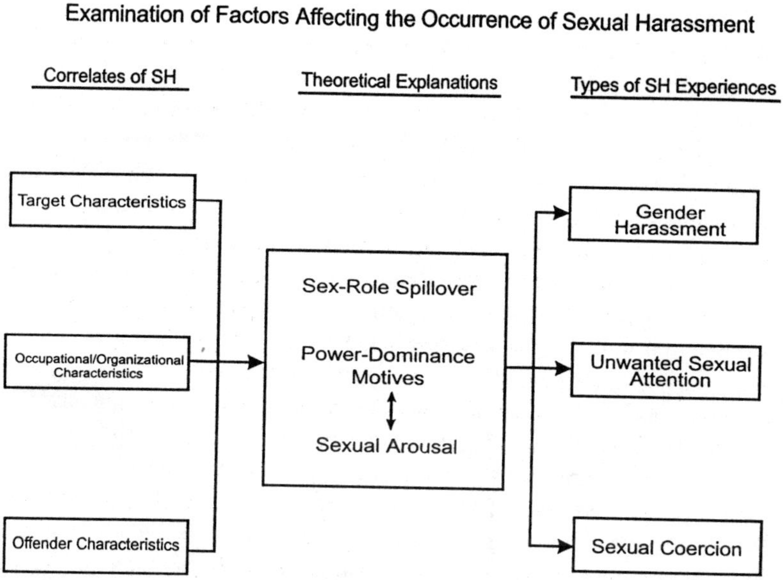

Figure 1.1. Examination of Factors Affecting the Occurrence of Sexual Harassment

may not meet stringent legal criteria, but are, in fact, sexually harassed (see Fitzgerald, Swan, & Fischer, 1995).

policies - legal criteria, just cos type of SH not listed does not mean you are not sexually harassed

Correlates of SH Experiences

Target characteristics, such as gender, age, and marital status, have been found to be associated with sexual harassment reports. Most notably, young, unmarried women are the most likely group of people to be sexually harassed (Fain & Anderton, 1987; Gutek, 1985; U.S. MSPB, 1981, 1988), but older individuals, married people, and men have not been immune. There is still little information to determine whether whites and nonwhites differ in rates of experiencing various forms of SH, in their interpretations of SH, or in their responses to SH. Murrell (this volume) provides a thorough theoretical discussion about this, but, to date, the data are inconclusive (see Fain & Anderton, 1987). Reports of SH also tend to be related to *occupational and organizational* characteristics. Several studies have found that women in occupations in which the number of women is disproportionate to the number of men tend to be sexually harassed more than women in gender-balanced occupations. For example, women in nontraditional occupations (e.g., Gruber & Bjorn, 1982; U.S. MSPB, 1981, 1988; Yount, 1991) or those in traditionally female occupations experience more sexual harassment than others (e.g., Gutek & Morasch, 1982). Sheffey and Tindale (1992) found that ambiguous social-sexual behaviors occurring in a traditionally feminine occupation are much less likely to be viewed as sexually harassing compared with the same behaviors occurring in an integrated or male-dominated occupation, suggesting that women in traditional occupations may have to put up with significantly more flagrant acts before anyone notices them as SH.

Gutek et al. (1990) found that the more that women and men came in contact with members of the opposite sex, the more likely they were to report sexual harassment experiences. Obviously, women are more likely to encounter men if they work in traditionally male occupations. Ragins and Scandura (1992) found, however, that cross-gender contact only predicted accounts of sexual harassment for women in "blue-collar" occupations where a physical, "macho" culture pervaded compared with "white-collar," managerial occupations. Finally, people whose supervisors tolerate or condone SH are more likely to report experiencing SH, which suggests that supervisor attitudes help establish a climate in which SH may or may not flourish (Pryor et al., 1993). Although sexual harassment has been reported in most organizational and occupational sectors, cross-gender contact, occupational culture, and leader attitudes may prove to be useful markers for identifying potentially risky, "hostile" environments.

Finally, *characteristics of offenders* cannot be ignored in a discussion of factors predicting the occurrence of SH. Tinsley and Stockdale (1993) informally questioned whether sexual harassment could be explained by a few "scuzzy oafs"—deviant individuals who could be held responsible for the lion's share of harassing experiences. If so, sexual harassment would be a manifestation of pathology, and explanations involving other social variables would not be needed. Research on sexual violence has demonstrated, however, that rape offenders are often normal individuals who, instead of holding deviant personality characteristics, have traditional, patriarchal sex role attitudes characterized by acceptance of rape myths and negative attitudes toward women. The constellation of these characteristics has been described as a rape-supporting belief system (Koss, Leonard, Beezley, & Oros, 1985).

A similar portrait of perpetrators of sexual harassment emerges, although SH perpetrators have not been examined as extensively as rapists (Stockdale, 1993). Because sexual harassment has been construed as a form of sexual aggression, like rape (Grauerholz & Solomon, 1989), it is likely that sexual harassers, like rapists, can be distinguished from others on the basis of sexist attitudes and sexual assault-supporting belief systems. The following discussion describes these traits as represented by the "Likelihood to Sexually Harass" construct.

The most systematic and theoretically driven examination of offender characteristics has come from Pryor (1987; Pryor et al., 1993). Drawing from research on sexual assault perpetrators, Pryor (1987) hypothesized that men with negative attitudes toward women and who ascribed to traditional sex role beliefs might demonstrate a willingness to sexually harass women. An instrument developed to measure this propensity, called the Likelihood to Sexually Harass (LSH) scale, correlated with measures of a sexual violence belief system (e.g., adversarial sexual beliefs, rape myth acceptance, and likelihood to rape as well as negative attitudes toward feminists; Pryor, 1987).

Using a social psychological Person × Situation framework, Pryor et al. (1993) hypothesized that high-LSH men (i.e., men with a harassing disposition) sexually harass women under certain circumstances. Specifically, when norms for sexual contact exist, high-LSH men engage in more sexually harassing acts than low-LSH men. Pryor (1987), for example, found that high-LSH men touched a female confederate more sexually than low-LSH men when they were teaching her how to play golf—a task requiring physical contact. No differences were found between high- and low-LSH men when they taught the female confederate how to play poker—a task not requiring physical contact. Similarly, Pryor et al. found that high-LSH men acted in a more sexually harassing manner than low-LSH men toward a female confederate when the male experimenter modeled similar behavior. Again, no differences were found among these men when the male experimenter did not model such behavior. The conditions that distinguished high- and low-LSH men on sexually harassing behaviors were those that permitted norms of sexual contact. These norms permit men with sexually harassing characteristics to act out these tendencies.

Thus Pryor's (1987; Pryor et al., 1993) hypothesis, that personal characteristics of offenders and characteristics of situations interact to produce sexually harassing occurrences, was supported. Offender personality characteristics interact with organizational or situational characteristics. For example, people may be particularly vulnerable to SH if they work with men with hostile attitudes toward women or with a tendency to sexually aggress and if they work in organizations with gender-skewed work role sets or climates that are tolerant of SH. Currently, we lack theoretical precision to explain why high-LSH men in certain situations sexually harass women. It may be that under such conditions, power and dominance motives, sexual-erotic motives, or sex role spillover perceptions are primed in high-LSH men (see Bargh & Raymond, 1995). Preliminary evidence by Pryor et al. indicates that high-LSH men relate power and sexual cues together more than low-LSH men. Further research and theory are needed to delineate the mechanisms that mediate high-LSH men's sexually harassing actions.

Theoretical Explanations for SH

Researchers have tried to explain SH from many different but interrelated perspectives. These theories are listed in Figure 1.1, but possible relations between them are not delineated in the model because neither research nor theory provides adequate guidance. A sequential discussion of these theoretical concepts may illuminate pathways among them and stimulate research activity.

Sex role spillover has been described by Gutek and her colleagues (e.g., Gutek & Morasch, 1982) as the transference of gender roles to the work role. The female sex role stereotype contains a "sexual-object" component. When this sex role characteristic is expected in a work domain (i.e., when an implicit work requirement is to be "sexy," such as for a receptionist), sex role spillover occurs. Gutek (e.g., Gutek & Morasch, 1982; Gutek et al., 1990) has argued that the sexual objectification of women increases probabilities that women in such circumstances will experience sexual harassment. Sex role spillover has been shown to occur when the gender composition of the work group or work role set is either predominantly male or female, as opposed to gender balanced. Women in traditionally female or male occupations have been found to experience more sexual harassment than women in gender-neutral occupations (Gutek & Morasch, 1982). Gender skew is theorized to make "femaleness" more salient (e.g., Kanter, 1977), which then facilitates sex role spillover. Other factors affecting gender salience need to be examined in relation to their influences on sex role spillover and sexual harassment. Heilman and her colleagues (e.g., Heilman, 1984; Heilman & Stopeck, 1985) have examined factors that influence sex-biased judgments of work role competence (e.g., female attractiveness, information relevance). Furthermore, it appears that these factors influence sex-biased ratings by priming feminine stereotypes (see also McKenzie-Mohr & Zanna, 1990). This work may provide useful insights for continued examination of factors affecting sex role spillover.

The role(s) of *power and dominance* have long been considered important in explaining sexual harassment (Farley, 1978; MacKinnon, 1979; Tangri, Burt, & Johnson, 1982). MacKinnon (1979) summarized sexual harassment as the "unwanted imposition of sexual requirements in the context of a relationship of unequal power" (p. 1). A major component of the EEOC's (1980) definition of quid pro quo harassment concerns the use of organizational control systems to gain sexual compliance. Cleveland and Kerst (1993) recently sorted through power concepts and definitions and provided a multi-level (societal, organizational, and personal) analysis that should help researchers gain precision in delineating power-related causal processes.

There are many ways that theories of power can explain SH. Individuals with strong needs for personal power (control over others) or who have strong dominance needs coupled with hostile attitudes toward women have been found to be likely perpetrators of sexual violence (Koss & Dinero, 1988; Koss et al., 1985; Malamuth, 1986; see also Cleveland & McNamara, this volume). Unbalanced power distributions in interpersonal relationships are also important in understanding SH. Kipnis (1990), for example, has shown how individuals with disproportionate power over others begin to view the others as weak, lazy, and worthless and deserving to be treated at the whim and fancy of the power holders. Such processes may be used to explain why some supervisors and teachers sexually harass their employees or students. Finally, a discussion of power cannot ignore patriarchy. In our society as well as in many (if not most) others, men are accorded greater status and power simply because they are men. Growing up in a culture of privilege may create a sense of entitlement to sexually harass women. This perspective on power may help to explain why male coworkers sexually harass their female peers or why male subordinates and students sexually harass their bosses and teachers (again, I refer you to Grauerholz, this volume, for further discussion). Furthermore, coupled with the disproportionately lower power and status accorded to members of nonwhite racial and ethnic groups, nonwhite women may be especially targeted for sexual harassment. As mentioned before, however, the data are inconclusive and certainly more research is needed.

The model presented in Figure 1.1 suggests that victim characteristics (e.g., being young, unmarried, and female) and organizational factors (e.g., gender-skewed work groups or occupations) may influence or prime such power-related motives, which may also be influenced by perpetrator and other situational characteristics. For example, young, unmarried women may be viewed as being easier than others to dominate, especially by those with personally aggrandizing power needs. Power has been used as an organizing framework for sexual harassment (e.g., Tangri et al., 1982) but has received very little research attention and theoretical scrutiny. Social science scholars are called upon to provide guidance for this important issue.

The role of *sexual arousal* is included in this model because it may be intertwined with other explanations of SH previously described, especially in connection with certain perpetrator characteristics. For example, factors influencing power and dominance motives may simultaneously prime sexual arousal. Lips (1991) documented evidence that power and dominance are important themes in men's sexuality. Some men may have a particular propensity to connect sexual stimuli and power motives. Pryor et al. (1993) reported a study by Pryor and Stoller that found that men scoring high on the Likelihood to Sexually Harass (LSH) construct perceived a schematic connection between social dominance and sexuality. Similarly, McKenzie-Mohr and Zanna (1990) found that pornography was much more likely to prime sexual motives in men who had stereotypical views of women and men than in men with less stereotypical perceptions.

Bargh and his colleagues (Bargh & Raymond, 1995; Bargh, Raymond, Pryor, & Strack, 1995) have been developing and researching a theory that links power and sex-related motives. They argue that men who have a propensity to sexually harass are more likely to automatically associate power cues with sexual cues. Bargh et al. measured male college students' likelihood to sexually harass or aggress and found that those scoring high on these measures were more likely than other men to associate sex cues with power cues. Furthermore, they found that men with these propensities were more sexually attracted to a woman when power themes had been primed than when they were not. Men who did not have sexually harassing propensities were not affected by the power manipulations. Bargh and Raymond argue that sexually aggressive men chronically associate power and sexual-related cues to the extent that they are not even aware that they may be abusing their own positions of power. Therefore, sexual arousal, especially in connection with theories addressing personal characteristics of perpetrators and theories of power, should not be dismissed in future examinations of causal influences on sexual harassment.

To summarize, the first model presents a framework for organizing current knowledge and theory on antecedents and causes of sexual harassment. Although this model is broad, it helps sort issues that have been confused previously in the literature. I would like to encourage researchers and others to use the model to guide their research and practice and to develop interventions that could interrupt these causal sequences, thereby reducing the amount of sexual harassment. The next section presents the second half of the picture—the processes connecting sexual harassment experiences to individual and organizational outcomes.

DIRECT AND INTERVENING PROCESSES AFFECTING SEXUAL HARASSMENT CONSEQUENCES

As mentioned earlier in this chapter, there are serious consequences associated with sexual harassment experiences to both individuals and organizations (Gutek & Koss, 1993). There is much variability, however, in self-reported consequences, with many victims reporting no negative effects (Cashin, Stockdale, & Shearer, 1993). Because victims vary widely in their responses, the American Psychological Association (APA), in its *amicus curiae* brief to the U.S. Supreme Court, argued that psychological consequence should not be used as a basis for establishing claims of sexual harassment (APA, 1993). The Court found the APA's brief convincing and ruled that psychological consequences are not a requirement for establishing claims of sexual harassment.

It appears that the connection between sexual harassment experiences and negative outcomes of that experience may be mediated by many factors. Figure 1.2 outlines a process model that connects sexual harassment experiences to these outcomes. This model does not, however, focus on the outcomes of reporting sexual harassment or going to court to seek redress. Several chapters in this volume explore these issues in more depth (see chapters by Gutek; Paetzold & O'Leary-Kelly; Rowe). As with Figure 1.1, this model represents a framework for organizing existing knowledge and guiding future investigations. It is important to first point out that sexual harassment may lead to serious consequences despite victims' appraisal of their experiences and their manner of response. Thus the model includes a direct path from experiences to consequences. Appraisal and responses are themselves important phenomena and may have causal influences on the outcomes associated with the experiences. Attention to these processes may help guide efforts to improve coping as well as increase active responding to harassment.

Mental Appraisal

The *perception* that an act constitutes sexual harassment is explicit in its definition. Therefore, much research attention has examined factors believed to influence sexual harassment judgments (see Stockdale & Vaux, 1993, for a review). Most of this research has examined laypersons' or observers' perceptions of harassment. A common design is to gather a sample of people (e.g., college students), have them read one or more scenarios, and ask them to judge the degree to which each scenario constitutes sexual harassment (e.g., Gutek et al., 1983). This work helps us understand how the public, in general, views harassment and how we might expect management, coworkers, juries, and so forth to respond to accusations of sexual harassment.

As shown in Figure 1.2, the extent to which targets of harassment appraise their experience as sexual harassment may be a function of characteristics of both the situation and themselves. Previous research on *observers'* appraisal of sexual harassment-type scenarios has examined the influence of many personal characteristics, such as *observer gender* (e.g., Gutek et al., 1983; Padgitt & Padgitt, 1986; but cf. Baker, Terpstra, & Cutler, 1990), *observer gender role* (e.g., Ryan & Kenig, 1991; Valentine-French & Radtke, 1989), *observer sensitivity* (e.g., Brooks & Perot, 1991; Powell, 1983), as well as situational characteristics, such as *frequency and severity of experience* (Baker, Terpstra, & Larntz, 1990; Padgitt & Padgitt, 1986; Pryor, 1985), *harasser status* (e.g., Reilly, Carpenter, Dull, & Bartlett, 1982; but cf. Grauerholz, this volume), and *organizational climate* (e.g., Hulin et al., this volume).

There is reason to believe, however, that victims (targets) of SH and passive observers (e.g., participants in an experiment) may view harassment very differently. Koss (1990) speculated that SH victims, like victims of rape or domestic violence, have a special motivation to remain silent about their experiences—even to themselves. This motivation is rooted in the "just-world hypothesis." People like to believe that the world is fair and that we get what we deserve. To the extent that we can deny that a bad thing has happened (e.g., sexual harassment),

SH victims deny it.

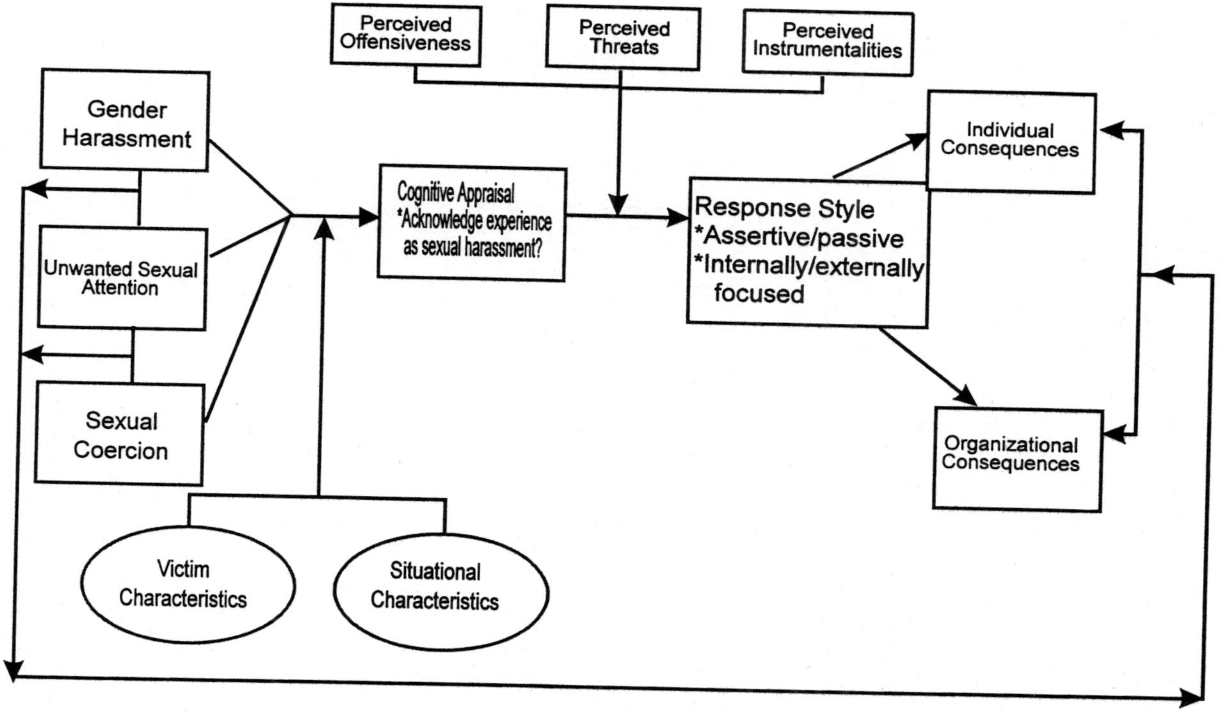

Figure 1.2. Factors Influencing Connections Between Sexual Harassment Experiences and Outcomes

we can maintain our belief in a just world. Alternatively, we can blame ourselves (e.g., "I should not have led him on like that") to maintain our belief in a just world. Acknowledging that one has been victimized shatters the belief in a just world. Our sense of control over the matter is lost. Furthermore, victims of sex-based crimes may be particularly silent about their experiences because of the very personal, shameful aspects of such crimes. Thus "victims" of SH are motivated to deny that they have been sexually harassed.

One study (Stockdale & Vaux, 1993) found that people who experienced more severe harassment were not more likely than those experiencing less severe harassment to acknowledge that they had been harassed. In a replication and extension of this study, Stockdale, Vaux, and Cashin (1995) found that women were more likely than men to acknowledge being sexually harassed as were people who experienced more frequent sexual harassment, were sexually harassed by an organizational superior (versus coworker or peer), and who suffered more negative emotional consequences.

There is evidence that cognitive-appraisal processes may affect targets' willingness to acknowledge their victimization. Kahn, Mathie, and Torgler (1994) found that targets of acquaintance rape who did not acknowledge their experience as rape held a much more typical "stranger-rape" mental representation of rape than did acknowledged victims of acquaintance rape. To the extent that a stranger-rape schema is maintained, victims of other forms of rape can deny experiencing rape. Future research should examine the cognitive processes affecting SH targets' appraisals of their experiences and the conditions under which these processes will be altered.

Response Style

Targets can respond to sexual harassment in various ways, ranging from ignoring the offense to direct confrontation with the perpetrator to filing official grievances and lawsuits. Fitzgerald et al. (1995) discussed the connections between the ways that SH targets' mentally appraise their experiences and the ways they respond to the offenses. The first appraisal that targets make concerns whether their experience is stressful or threatening. I have shown previously that targets may be motivated to not acknowledge their experiences as sexual harassment to maintain "just-world" beliefs. However, gender differences in appraisal of sexually harassing experiences are important to understand. Because women are more likely to be targets of sexual harassment as well as targets of other forms of sexual violence and to experience more serious consequences from these crimes, women are more likely than men to see sexual harassment as a threat. The second appraisal that targets make concerns how to psychologically respond to or cope with the offense. Internally focused strategies, according to Fitzgerald et al. (1995), are characterized by attempts to manage the psychological impact of the event. By ignoring, denying, enduring, or redefining the event, targets may believe they are reducing the amount of stress they could experience. Externally focused strategies entail attempts to change the circumstances or solve the problem, for example, by avoiding the perpetrator, assertively trying to stop the perpetrator, or seeking institutional redress. Other researchers have categorized response strategies on active (most assertive) to passive (least assertive) dimensions (Gruber, 1989; Stockdale, Cashin, & Tardino, 1995).

Several researchers have speculated about why victims are reluctant to report or take other active measures (Brooks & Perot, 1991; Gwartney-Gibbs & Lach, 1992; Koss, 1990; Riger, 1991; Stockdale & Vaux, 1993). I suggest, in Figure 1.2, that victims' perceptions of the offensiveness of the harassing event, as well as perceptions of threats and advantages associated with potential forms of responding, may influence how they may, in fact, respond. Brooks and Perot (1991), for example, found that perceived offensiveness of an event was positively associated with willingness to actively respond to it. Gruber (1989) also found that women were more likely to actively respond to more offensive treatment. Koss (1990) suggested that sexual harassment victims, like rape victims, may be reluctant to report harassment for fear of retaliation or other forms of harm. The perceived instrumentality of active (or passive) responding for obtaining desired outcomes has not been formally examined but seems intuitively reasonable. Expectancy theories of motivation (e.g., Vroom, 1964) predict that individuals would not choose a course of action that is perceived to yield undesirable consequences. If many victims feel threatened by active responding or believe that such actions are futile, the instrumentality of active responding, by definition, would be low. Alternatively, targets may highly evaluate the benefits of passive forms of responding such as avoiding the perpetrator, making light of the situation, or simply ignoring the offense. Even if targets acknowledge the experience as SH, passive responding may help reduce the perceived seriousness of the offense and help maintain just-world beliefs.

Consequences

The final portion of the second model addresses connections between response styles and consequences to the individual and organization. Noting, again, that consequences such as job loss and emotional distress may occur regardless of victims' manner of response, it is important to demonstrate the nature of relations between victims' responses and subsequent outcomes. A recent study, for example, asked survey respondents who had indicated experiencing at least one legally defined form of sexual harassment how they responded to the event and what the consequences were, if any, of their experience (Stockdale, Cashin, & Tardino, 1995). Responses were categorized as avoiding, defusing (i.e., joking), and confronting. Psychological (negative emotions) and work- or school-related (e.g., being less productive, changing jobs or majors) consequences were measured. More distressing forms of sexual harassment were related to the seriousness of the outcomes. Furthermore, respondents who used confrontational response styles reported more serious outcomes than did others. Further analyses revealed, however, that the consequences for women were exacerbated when they responded confrontationally (assertively) to their sexual harassment compared with women who did not respond in such a manner. This did not happen to men, however. In fact, men who joked (defused) about being sexually harassed experienced less severe emotional consequences than men who did not joke about it. Thus the utility of active and passive responding for reducing psychological and work-related consequences may be quite different for women and men. These processes need to be better understood, but institutional policies that permit only one type of response (e.g., formal complaints) are likely to be ineffective in curtailing sexual harassment.

IMPLICATIONS FOR RESEARCH AND INTERVENTION

Research

The models described in this chapter are not theories of sexual harassment processes. They do, however, help to organize existing knowledge and disentangle concepts and processes that have been obscured in the literature. For example, the model separates the experience of sexual harassment from the perception or labeling of the experience as sexual harassment. Fitzgerald's (1990) work on developing objective measures of sexual harassment has been instrumental in clarifying these distinctions. The model also separates theoretical constructs used to explain sexual harassment experiences from the factors that help predict outcomes of these processes. For example, sex role spillover, a theoretical construct, is separated from factors thought to influence it, such as skewed work group composition.

I strongly urge social scientists and practitioners to lend their expertise to build greater understanding of sexual harassment and its consequences. The models provided in this chapter can be used as guides. Specification and measurement of important elements that encompass the spectrum of sexual harassment-related phenomena are necessary first activities to which psychometricians and other measurement specialists can lend considerable expertise. Theories that build on the connections suggested by these models should be developed and tested. Moreover, research on organizational and cultural phenomena, such as work group or organizational climate, ethnicity, and power dynamics (especially vis-à-vis minority issues) is needed (see Kauppinen-Toropainen & Gruber, 1993; Murrell, this volume).

Finally, these processes need to be examined from multi-level perspectives. Multi-level consequences should be more carefully explicated and examined. We have studied consequences to victims and skimmed the surface in our examination of consequences to organizations. Yet we know little about the effects of sexual harassment on the climate or culture of the workplace in which it occurs. We also know little, if anything, about the consequences of sexual harassment for female labor force participation. In addition to effects of direct harassment on victims' career decisions, awareness of sexual harassment might have a substantial impact on female labor force participation in general. That is, women may choose not to pursue nontraditional careers, especially those likely to place them in "macho, physical cultures," because they do not want to experience sexual harassment and other forms of sexist treatment. More generally, sexual harassment may be one of the many means for the oppressive management of women in a patriarchal culture. Theory and research are clearly needed at this level.

Two chapters in this book provide an excellent discussion of organizationwide consequences. Knapp and Kustis (this volume) show how cost-accounting procedures can be applied to calculate the wide-ranging expenses of SH to an organization. Their model incorporates costs incurred by the victim (e.g., financial loss due to absenteeism, job loss, medical and/or psychological expenses, and so forth) and the organization (e.g., productivity loss, recruiting and training loss to replace the victim and/or the perpetrator, and so forth). Hanisch (this volume) embeds the experience of SH in the broader context of organizational and personal stressors and examines the various ways that organizational members may respond to these stressors.

Practice and Intervention

With a clear understanding of factors affecting sexual harassment processes, practitioners are called upon to develop and evaluate courses of action that may curb, if not eliminate, this offensive phenomenon. With a greater understanding of perpetrator characteristics, personnel selection instruments can be developed to help weed out potential perpetrators (see Pryor et al., 1993). Given the success of biographical data and personality traits for general personnel selection purposes (see Muchinsky, 1993), it seems reasonable to ascertain applicants' propensities to engage in harassing activity.

Training programs abound, but with a clearer understanding of the spectrum of sexual harassment processes, training can be fine-tuned to target the specific sequences in these models. For example, organizational leaders need to understand what circumstances create particularly risky environments (e.g., nontraditional male-dominated occupational sectors), and the role they can take in buffering potential consequences to individuals adversely affected by these situations. Training for supervisors and employees is needed to help raise awareness of the instrumentality of active responding to sexual harassment. Of course, sound policy and enforcement are needed to make sure that active responding *is* related to positive outcomes. Rowe (this volume) provides a thorough discussion of the factors that should be considered when developing organizational policies on SH. She advocates a "pro-choice" approach to policies so that targets can choose the response they feel will lead to the most effective outcomes for themselves. These are a few examples of organization-related interventions that may pay big dividends (see also Cleveland & McNamara, this volume).

CONCLUSION AND OVERVIEW OF THE BOOK

This chapter has attempted to bring some clarity to a heated issue that is shrouded in controversy and ambiguity. The remaining chapters in this book elaborate and extend many of the theoretical and practical issues raised in this review. The first section examines various perspectives on sexual harassment. Elizabeth Grauerholz provides a sociological perspective and explores the societal-based power dynamics that may explain the sexual harassment of female faculty members. Audrey Murrell examines the oft-neglected impact of race and ethnicity on sexual harassment experiences and response patterns. Frank (Skip) Saal debunks the popular opinion that perpetrators of sexual harassment may only be misperceiving women's friendly behaviors as signs of a sexual come-on. Ramona Paetzold and Anne O'Leary-Kelly provide an analysis of higher court decisions to describe the emerging legal theory on hostile work environment SH. Lynn Bowes-Sperry and Gary Powell delineate an ethical perspective on sexual harassment that may help explain how observers or bystanders make judgments about and respond to sexual harassment. The second section of the book explores specific research issues in sexual harassment. Chuck Hulin, Louise Fitzgerald, and Fritz Drasgow not only delineate an organizational climate perspective on sexual harassment but also describe efforts to develop a valid and reliable instrument to measure a work unit's climate for tolerating sexual harassment. Jim Gruber, the late Michael Smith, and Kaisa Kauppinen-Toropainen discuss issues and controversies surrounding how the severity of sexual harassment should be determined. They also provide evidence from a cross-cultural program of research showing that women from different geopolitical cultures and from different occupational sectors have similar views of the severity of their experiences. As discussed above, chapters by Debbie Knapp and Gary Kustis and by Kathy Hanisch examine the consequences of sexual harassment and its costs to victims and organizations. The final section of the book takes a forward look to providing guidance for constructing effective interventions against sexual harassment. After reviewing the links between domestic violence and sexual harassment, Jan Cleveland and Kathleen McNamara highlight organizational development techniques that may prove useful for training purposes. Mary Rowe provides a thorough discussion of issues to consider for designing effective institutional policies against sexual harassment. Finally, Barbara Gutek describes an actual case of sexual harassment and the institution's response to it. In addition to describing the consequences of institutional inaction, this case ties together many of the themes and issues raised throughout the book.

REFERENCES

American Psychological Association (APA). (1993). *A brief for amicus curiae,* in *Teresa Harris v. Forklift Systems, Inc.,* 114 S. Ct. 367 (1993).

Baker, D. D., Terpstra, D. E., & Cutler, B. D. (1990). Perceptions of sexual harassment: A re-examination of gender differences. *Journal of Psychology, 124,* 409-416.

Baker, D. D., Terpstra, D. E., & Larntz, K. (1990). The influence of individual characteristics and severity of harassing behavior on reactions to sexual harassment. *Sex Roles, 22,* 305-325.

Bargh, J. A., & Raymond, P. (1995). The naive misuse of power: Nonconscious sources of sexual harassment. *Journal of Social Issues, 51,* 85-96.

Bargh, J. A., Raymond, P., Pryor, J., & Strack, F. (1995). The attractiveness of the underling: An automatic power → sex association and its consequences for sexual harassment and aggression. *Journal of Personality and Social Psychology, 68,* 768-781.

Brooks, L., & Perot, A. R. (1991). Reporting sexual harassment. *Psychology of Women Quarterly, 15,* 31-47.

Burt, M. R. (1980). Cultural myths and support for rape. *Journal of Personality and Social Psychology, 38,* 217-230.

Cashin, J., Stockdale, M. S., & Shearer, V. (1993). *The 1993 Survey of Sexual Harassment at Southern Illinois University at Carbondale* (Technical report). Carbondale: Southern Illinois University, Department of Psychology.

Cleveland, J. N., & Kerst, M. E. (1993). Sexual harassment and perceptions of power: An under-articulated relationship. *Journal of Vocational Behavior, 42,* 49-67.

Deaux, K. (1995). How basic can you be? The evolution of research on gender stereotypes. *Journal of Social Issues, 51,* 11-20.

Equal Employment Opportunity Commission (EEOC). (1980). Guidelines on discrimination because of sex. *Federal Register, 45,* 74676-74677.

Fain, T. C., & Anderton, D. L. (1987). Sexual harassment: Organizational context and diffuse status. *Sex Roles, 17,* 291-311.

Farley, L. (1978). *Sexual shakedown: The sexual harassment of women on the job.* New York: McGraw-Hill.

Fitzgerald, L. F. (1990). Sexual harassment: The definition and measurement of a construct. In M. Paludi (Ed.), *Ivory power: Sexual harassment on campus.* Albany: SUNY Press.

Fitzgerald, L. F., Gelfand, M. J., & Drasgow, F. (1994, April). *Measuring sexual harassment: Theoretical and psychometric advances.* Paper presented at the Ninth Annual Conference of the Society for Industrial and Organizational Psychology, Nashville, TN.

Fitzgerald, L. F., & Hesson-McInnis, M. (1989). The structure of sexual harassment. *Journal of Vocational Behavior, 35,* 309-326.

Fitzgerald, L. F., & Shullman, S. L. (1993). Sexual harassment: A research analysis and agenda for the 1990s. *Journal of Vocational Behavior, 42,* 5-27.

Fitzgerald, L. F., Shullman, S., Bailey, N., Richards, M., Swecker, J., Gold, Y., Ormerod, A. J., & Weitzman, L. (1988). The incidence and dimensions of sexual harassment in academia and the workplace. *Journal of Vocational Behavior, 32,* 152-175.

Fitzgerald, L. F., Swan, S., & Fischer, K. (1995). Why didn't she just report him? The psychological and legal implications of women's responses to sexual harassment. *Journal of Social Issues, 51,* 117-138.

Grauerholz, E., & Solomon, J. C. (1989). Sexual coercion: Power and violence. In K. McKinney & S. Sprecher (Eds.), *Human sexuality: The societal and interpersonal context.* Norwood, NJ: Ablex.

Gruber, J. E. (1989). How women handle sexual harassment: A literature review. *Sociology and Social Research, 74,* 3-9.

Gruber, J. E. (1992). A typology of personal and environmental sexual harassment: Research and policy implications for the 1990s. *Sex Roles, 26,* 447-463.

Gruber, J. E., & Bjorn, L. (1982). Blue-collar blues: The sexual harassment of women autoworkers. *Work and Occupations, 9,* 271-298.

Gutek, B. A. (1985). *Sex and the workplace.* San Francisco: Jossey-Bass.

Gutek, B. A., Cohen, A. G., & Konrad, A. M. (1990). Predicting social-sexual behavior at work: A contact hypothesis. *Academy of Management Journal, 33,* 560-577.

Gutek, B. A., & Koss, M. P. (1993). Changed women and changed organizations: Consequences of and coping with sexual harassment. *Journal of Vocational Behavior, 42,* 28-48.

Gutek, B. A., & Morasch, B. (1982). Sex-ratios, sex-role spillover, and sexual harassment of women at work. *Journal of Social Issues, 38,* 55-74.

Gutek, B. A., Morasch, B., & Cohen, A. G. (1983). Interpreting social-sexual behavior in a work setting. *Journal of Vocational Behavior, 22,* 30-48.

Gwartney-Gibbs, P. A., & Lach, D. H. (1992). Sociological explanations for failure to seek sexual harassment remedies. *Mediation Quarterly, 9,* 365-375.

Heilman, M. E. (1984). Information as a deterrent against sex discrimination: The effects of applicant sex and information type on preliminary employment decisions. *Organizational Behavior and Human Performance, 33,* 174-186.

Heilman, M., & Stopeck, M. (1985). Being attractive, advantage or disadvantage? Performance-based evaluations and recommended personnel actions as a function of appearance, sex, and job type. *Organizational Behavior and Human Decision Processes, 35,* 202-215.

Kahn, A. S., Mathie, V. A., & Torgler, C. (1994). Rape scripts and rape acknowledgement. *Psychology of Women Quarterly, 18,* 53-66.

Kanter, R. (1977). *Men and women of the corporation.* New York: Basic Books.

Kauppinen-Toropainen, K., & Gruber, J. E. (1993). Antecedents and outcomes of woman-unfriendly experiences: A study of Scandinavian, former Soviet, and American women. *Psychology of Women Quarterly, 17,* 431-456.

Kenig, S., & Ryan, J. (1986). Sex differences in levels of tolerance and attribution of blame for sexual harassment on a university campus. *Sex Roles, 15,* 535-549.

Kipnis, D. (1990). *Technology and power.* New York: Springer-Verlag.

Koss, M. P. (1990). Changed lives: The psychological impact of sexual harassment. In M. Paludi (Ed.), *Ivory power: Sexual harassment on campus.* Albany: SUNY Press.

Koss, M. P., & Dinero, T. E. (1988). Predictors of sexual aggression among a national sample of male college students. In R. A. Prentky & V. L. Quinsey (Eds.), *Annals of the New York Academy of Science, 528,* 133-147.

Koss, M. P., Leonard, K. E., Beezley, D. A., & Oros, C. J. (1985). Nonstranger sexual aggression: A discriminant analysis of psychological characteristics of undetected offenders. *Sex Roles, 12,* 981-992.

Lips, H. (1991). *Women, men, and power.* Mountain View, CA: Mayfield.

MacKinnon, C. A. (1979). *Sexual harassment of working women.* New Haven, CT: Yale University Press.

Malamuth, N. M. (1986). Predictors of naturalistic sexual aggression. *Journal of Personality and Social Psychology, 50,* 953-962.

Martindale, M. (1990). *Sexual harassment in the military: 1988* (Report). Arlington, VA: Defense Manpower Data Center.

McKenzie-Mohr, D., & Zanna, M. P. (1990). Treating women as sexual objects: Look to the (gender schematic) male who has viewed pornography. *Personality and Social Psychology Bulletin, 16,* 296-308.

Meritor Savings Bank FSB v. Vinson et al., 477 U.S. 57 (1986).

Muchinsky, P. M. (1993). *Psychology applied to work: An introduction to industrial/organizational psychology* (4th ed.). Pacific Grove, CA: Brooks/Cole.

Padgitt, S., & Padgitt, J. S. (1986). Cognitive structure of sexual harassment: Implications for university policy. *Journal of College Student Personnel, 27,* 34-39.

Popovich, P. M., Licata, B. J., Nokovich, D., Martelli, T., & Zoloty, S. (1986). Assessing the incidence and perceptions of sexual harassment behaviors among American undergraduates. *Journal of Psychology, 120,* 387-396.

Powell, G. N. (1983). Definition of sexual harassment and sexual attention experienced. *Journal of Psychology, 113,* 113-117.

Pryor, J. B. (1985). The lay person's understanding of sexual harassment. *Sex Roles, 13,* 273-286.

Pryor, J. B. (1987). Sexual harassment proclivities in men. *Sex Roles, 17,* 269-290.

Pryor, J. B., & Day, J. D. (1988). Interpretations of sexual harassment: An attributional analysis. *Sex Roles, 18,* 405-417.

Pryor, J. B., LaVite, C. M., & Stoller, L. M. (1993). A social psychological analysis of sexual harassment: The person/situation interaction. *Journal of Vocational Behavior, 42,* 68-83.

Ragins, B. R., & Scandura, T. A. (1992, April/May). *Antecedents and consequences of sexual harassment.* Paper presented at the Society for Industrial/Organizational Psychology conference, Montreal, Canada.

Rapaport, K., & Burkhart, B. R. (1984). Personality and attitudinal characteristics of sexually coercive college males. *Journal of Abnormal Psychology, 93,* 216-221.

Reilly, T., Carpenter, S., Dull, V., & Bartlett, K. (1982). The factorial survey technique: An approach to defining sexual harassment on campus. *Journal of Social Issues, 38,* 75-98.

Riger, S. (1991). Gender dilemmas in sexual harassment policies and procedures. *American Psychologist, 46,* 497-507.

Ryan, J., & Kenig, S. (1991). Risk and ideology in sexual harassment. *Sociological Inquiry, 61,* 231-241.

Sheffey, S., & Tindale, R. S. (1992). Perceptions of sexual harassment in the workplace. *Journal of Applied Social Psychology, 22,* 1502-1520.

Stockdale, M. S. (1993). The role of sexual misperceptions of women's friendliness in an emerging theory of sexual harassment. *Journal of Vocational Behavior, 42,* 84-101.

Stockdale, M. S., Cashin, J. R., & Tardino, V. S. (1995). *The direct and moderating influences of sexual harassment severity, coping styles, and gender on emotional and work/school-related consequences.* Unpublished manuscript, Southern Illinois University, Carbondale, Department of Psychology.

Stockdale, M. S., & Vaux, A. (1993). What sexual harassment experiences lead respondents to acknowledge being sexually harassed? A secondary analysis of a university study. *Journal of Vocational Behavior, 43,* 221-234.

Stockdale, M. S., Vaux, A., & Cashin, J. (1995). Acknowledging sexual harassment: A test of alternative models. *Basic and Applied Social Psychology, 17,* 469-496.

Tangri, S., Burt, M., & Johnson, L. (1982). Sexual harassment at work: Three explanatory models. *Journal of Social Issues, 38,* 33-54.

Tinsley, H. E. A., & Stockdale, M. S. (1993). Sexual harassment in the workplace. *Journal of Vocational Behavior, 42,* 1-4.

U.S. Merit Systems Protection Board. (1981). *Sexual harassment in the federal workplace: Is it a problem?* Washington, DC: Office of Merit Systems Review and Studies/Government Printing Office.

U.S. Merit Systems Protection Board. (1988). *Sexual harassment in the federal government: An update.* Washington, DC: Office of Merit Systems Review and Studies/ Government Printing Office.

Valentine-French, S., & Radtke, H. L. (1989). Attributions of responsibility for an incident of sexual harassment in a university setting. *Sex Roles, 21,* 545-555.

Vroom, V. (1964). *Work and motivation.* New York: John Wiley.

Yount, K. R. (1991). Ladies, flirts, and tomboys: Strategies for managing sexual harassment in an underground coal mine. *Journal of Contemporary Ethnography, 19,* 396-422.

SECTION II

Perspectives on Sexual Harassment in the Workplace

2

Sexual Harassment in the Academy: The Case of Women Professors

ELIZABETH GRAUERHOLZ

This chapter explores the sexual harassment of women professors. Survey data from 210 women faculty at Purdue University suggest that sexual harassment is relatively widespread. Approximately one in four women professors claimed that they have been sexually harassed while at the university, and many more claimed to have experienced a variety of behaviors, ranging from sexist comments to sexual assault. The data further indicate that women experience these behaviors from all sources—superiors, peers, and students. The academic environment is then considered in terms of how it may both foster and inhibit the sexual harassment of women faculty.

For centuries, the academy has been idealized as a liberal, democratic institution that fosters equality and enlightenment. Recently, however, critics have exposed some of the problems inherent in its organization and processes. Among the most vocal expressions of concern has surrounded the issue of women—how they are treated and, especially, their vulnerability to sexual harassment (Dzeich & Weiner, 1990; Hall & Sandler, 1984).

During the past decade, numerous studies on the incidence and prevalence of sexual harassment of university students have shed a new and disturbing light on academic life. Although few cross-institutional studies exist, taken together these studies provide information on how widespread sexual harassment of students (especially women) is across a variety of academic institutions and regions. Overall, studies estimate that approximately one out of every two or three undergraduate women students, and a slightly greater proportion of women graduate students, have experienced some type of sexual harassment or sexually inappropriate behavior (Fitzgerald & Shullman, 1993; Fitzgerald, Shullman, et al., 1988; Schneider, 1987). It is not clear how these numbers differ for women of color because few studies of sexual harassment explore this dimension, but women of color most likely experience as much, if not greater, sexual harassment than white women (Defour, 1990).

Recently, there has been interest in sexual harassment of another group on campus—faculty (Goodwin, Roscoe, Rose, & Repp, 1989; Lott, Reilly, & Howard, 1982). Studies show that approximately 14% of faculty report being harassed by colleagues (McKinney, 1990; Metha & Nigg, 1983) with rates as high as 44% of women and 17% of men reported by Carroll and Ellis (1989). In another study conducted by Leonard and colleagues (1993), it was found that less than 20% of faculty claimed to have *never* experienced sexually harassing acts such as unwanted sexist comments, unwanted sexual statements, unwanted personal attention, unwanted sexual propositions, and unwanted physical or sexual advances.

The sexual harassment of faculty by students, a form of sexual harassment referred to by Benson (1984) as "contrapower harassment" (persons with less formal power harassing persons with greater formal power), has also come to light recently. McKinney (1990) surveyed 188 faculty at two public universities and found that approximately 20% of faculty claimed to have been sexually harassed by students. A much higher percentage (closer to 30%) claimed to have experienced specific behaviors that might be considered sexual harassment (e.g., obscene phone calls believed to be from students, sexist comments, undue attention). In her study (McKinney, 1994) based upon interviews with 27 faculty members from three universities who identified themselves as either having been victimized by sexual harassment or (falsely) accused of sexual harassment, several respondents (mostly women) reported instances of contrapower harassment, including disrespect from students, obscene phone calls, and sexual or physical remarks on course evaluation forms. In another study of university students, McKinney (1992) discovered that 18% of students claimed to have engaged in specific behaviors aimed at faculty members that could be potentially harassing, although none of the students admitted that she or he had "sexually harassed" a professor. Carroll and Ellis's (1989) study of male and female faculty at a small state university found that between 6% and 30% of faculty, depending upon the behavior, had experienced uninvited sexual behaviors (e.g., sexual teasing, suggestive looks, requests for dates, or sexual favors in exchange for preferential treatment). More men than women in their sample reported these behaviors from students. Fitzgerald, Weitzman, Gold, and Ormerod (1988) found that 6% of male faculty felt they had been sexually harassed by a student, and as many as 17% said that students had attempted to stroke, caress, or touch the faculty member (but these behaviors were not necessarily labeled sexual harassment). Finally, Grauerholz (1989) found that nearly half of women professors at a large public university had experienced behavior such as sexist comments, undue attention, verbal sexual comments, body language, or obscene phone calls from students. Unfortunately, again, no information on race or sexual preference differences was given in these studies.

These studies reinforce what we already understand about sexual harassment: that all women, not just those in certain types of occupations or with certain characteristics, are vulnerable to sexual harassment; that women are probably more vulnerable to harassment than men (or at least more likely to report it); and that men are more likely than women to be the initiators of sexual harassment. But they also raise new and intriguing questions about sexual harassment in the academy. Is it really possible for a student—who possesses relatively little power—to sexually harass a faculty member who possesses considerable reward and expert power as well as legitimate authority? Are women faculty as vulnerable to sexual harassment as are women in other professions? Does the academic environment provide protection to women who are potential victims or does it, through its organization, norms, and climate, actually protect potential harassers? In what ways is it unique or similar to other organizations in these respects?

This chapter attempts to answer these questions by examining data from a group of women professors from a large public university. The experiences these women have had with sexual harassment from superiors, peers, and students will be highlighted. I then consider how the academy fosters and, in some cases, inhibits sexual harassment of women faculty.

SEXUAL HARASSMENT ON ALL FRONTS: THE EXPERIENCES OF WOMEN PROFESSORS WITH SUPERIORS, PEERS, AND STUDENTS

Sample and Measures

In 1989, I conducted a survey of all women professors employed at my university. Questionnaires were mailed to the offices of all women faculty (19% of all professors at Purdue University at this time were women; $N = 340$). Respondents were asked to return the anonymous questionnaire by campus mail. Follow-up reminders or thank yous were mailed to all respondents approximately two weeks later. Of the 340 persons surveyed, 210 (62%) returned their completed questionnaires, yielding a response rate slightly higher than those found in similar studies (the typical response rate for studies of this nature is around 40%-50%; McKinney & Maroules, 1991).

The typical respondent had been employed at the university for 8 years, was 40 years old (the range was 25 to 67), a full-time employee, and housed in a department in which the majority of faculty was male. Although all schools within the university were represented in the survey, more than half of the respondents came from Liberal Arts, Consumer and Family Sciences, or Education. Close to half were tenured. Full professors constituted 11% of the sample, 28% were associate professors, 46% were assistant professors, and 15% were instructors. These characteristics of respondents are very similar to the total population of female faculty at this university.

Respondents were asked whether the following two statements were true or false: "I know a faculty member who has experienced some form of sexual harassment while employed at Purdue" and "I personally have felt harassed sexually while employed at Purdue." The term *sexual harassment* was not defined for the respondent in these two questions, which is likely to yield a conservative estimate of sexual harassment because respondents may have experienced behaviors that legally constitute sexual harassment, but not perceived them as such (Fitzgerald, Weitzman, et al., 1988; McKinney, 1990; McKinney & Crittenden,

1992). Respondents were then provided with a list of behaviors similar to those used in sexual harassment studies of students (see Adams, Kottke, & Padgett, 1983) and asked to state whether they had experienced such behavior from a superior (defined as anyone of higher rank), a peer (anyone of the same rank), or a student (graduate or undergraduate). Behaviors range from sexist comments to sexual assault (see Appendix 2.A) and correspond to categories developed by Fitzgerald (1990). Of course, not all of these behaviors are likely to be labeled as sexual harassment by respondents, so these measures are likely to inflate the reports of sexual harassment.

Findings

Of the respondents, 36% claimed to know a faculty member at the university who had experienced some form of sexual harassment, and when asked if they had ever been sexually harassed while employed at the university, about one in four women professors answered yes. These experiences were not clearly linked to any particular group of women professors (unfortunately, it was not possible from these data to determine how sexual harassment experiences differ for women of color or by sexual preference; the numbers of women of color or lesbians were too few to make meaningful comparisons). For instance, the age range of women who claimed to have been sexually harassed was virtually the same as that of women who claimed that they had not personally been sexually harassed (25-61 years and 26-67 years, respectively), and the mean age difference for these two groups was not significant ($t = -1.85$; $p = .07$). Over 50% of those who had been sexually harassed had been at the university no more than four years, which might suggest that relatively junior women are more vulnerable; however, 50% of those who had not been sexually harassed had been employed at the university no more than five years. Again, a t-test revealed that the average number of years employed at the university did not differ significantly for those claiming to have experienced sexual harassment and those who had not ($t = -.47$; $p = .63$). Furthermore, there was no significant difference in tenure status for women who claimed to have been sexually harassed and those who did not report being sexually harassed (35.2% and 48%, respectively, were tenured; chi-square = 2.66; $p > .10$).

There was some indication that full professors were less likely to be subjected to sexual harassment or to report it. Although only 3.7% of those respondents who claimed to have been sexually harassed were full professors, 13.2% of those who had not been sexually harassed were full professors (chi-square = 3.73; $p < .10$). One important finding was that women who were sexually harassed were less likely to be in a department in which the majority was female (19.2%) compared with women who claimed that they had not been sexually harassed (34.5%) (chi-square = 4.32; $p < .05$).

Overall, the women in this sample—those who claimed to have been sexually harassed and those who did not—reported experiencing a wide range of behaviors that would generally be considered, if not sexual harassment, at least sexually inappropriate behaviors, from persons at each of the three ranks—superior, peer, and subordinate (student). All of the 10 behaviors these women were asked about in terms of their experiences were reported to have occurred with persons from each group. Table 2.1 provides a breakdown of frequencies for each act. The most widespread acts, such as sexist comments, undue attention, verbal sexual comments, and body language, are those that constitute "everyday harassment" (Schneider, 1987). Examples of such behaviors given by women in my sample included the following:

> Because I am female and small, tall male students tend to feel comfortable about putting their arm around me, or attempting to rub my neck. They would never do that to a 6′ man.

> One student took photographs of me in class without my knowing it.

> I had a student who made a habit of coming to see me about problems with his paper at very inconvenient times—10 minutes before I had class. He just wouldn't get the point that I couldn't talk to him then. When he asked if I "had a minute," his reaction to my negative answer was to sit down and talk anyway.

> People react to each other sexually because they're human. Still, this kind of behavior is somewhat unsettling to me because male superiors . . . never show friendliness to male colleagues in this way and when these kinds of things happen I always feel that the other person is acting as if he had the right to take control of my body.

It is important to note also that even the most obvious cases, such as those involving explicit sexual propositioning, sexual bribery, or sexual assault, were experienced by several women in this sample.

Table 2.1. Percentage of Women Professors Experiencing a Particular Behavior by Relationship to Perpetrator

	Position of Perpetrator		
Perpetrator Behavior	*Superior*	*Peer*	*Student*
Sexist comment	54.0	50.0	32.0
Undue attention	24.0	19.0	18.0
Verbal sexual comments	30.0	24.0	14.0
Body language	18.0	16.0	12.0
Written sexual comments	2.0	3.0	8.0
Physical advances	6.0	7.0	2.0
Explicit sexual propositions	4.0	5.0	3.0
Sexual bribery	0.5	0.5	1.0
Sexual assault	0.5	0.5	0.5
Other	8.0	3.0	3.0

There were only a few significant differences in the frequencies of acts by status of offender. Respondents reported that superiors initiated more verbal sexual comments than did peers ($t = 2.08$, $p < .05$) and superiors and peers were more likely than students to engage in behaviors such as sexist comments ($t = 5.37$, $p < .001$; $t = 3.59$, $p < .001$, respectively), verbal sexual comments ($t = 4.58$, $p < .001$; $t = 2.53$, $p < .01$, respectively), and physical advances ($t = 2.16$, $p < .05$; $t = 2.71$, $p < .01$, respectively). The one behavior that students engaged in more often than superiors or peers was writing sexual comments ($t = -2.73$, $p < .01$; $t = -2.38$, $p < .05$, respectively). These comments usually appeared on anonymous student evaluation forms, which in many ways protects the "harasser" from punishment (Benson, 1984; Grauerholz, 1989).

Regardless of the status of the offender, these individuals were reported to be male in almost all cases (93% for superiors, 90% for peers, and 82% for students). All of the cases involving female perpetrators were of a less serious nature (e.g., sexist comments, undue attention, or verbal sexual comments).

When women who claimed to have been sexually harassed ($N = 54$) were compared with those who did not, the results indicated that, in almost all cases, the former were more likely than the latter to have experienced each specific behavior. The only exceptions occurred for body language by peers, sexual bribery by peers, sexual bribery by students, and sexual assault by students (i.e., women who had claimed that they had not been sexually harassed were more likely to report body language and sexual bribery from peers, and so on). These differences are negligible, however. Of interest, the women who reported experiencing sexual bribery by a peer, and bribery and assault by a student (all different respondents), do not consider themselves to have been sexually harassed!

Perhaps these women believe that sexual harassment can only be committed by someone with greater authority or power. This perception was certainly not shared by most women in this sample, however. In fact, data on the differences in perceptions (whether an act constituted sexual harassment or not) did not vary tremendously by status of the offender. In general, behaviors from peers were perceived as less harassing than those from superiors, but there was a strong consensus that most of the behaviors would constitute sexual harassment if performed by a superior, peer, *or* student (only in cases of sexist comments, for instance, did a majority state that this behavior would not constitute sexual harassment). At least two-thirds of these women thought all but sexist comments and undue attention were sexual harassment. The more physically intrusive and less ambiguous the behavior, the more likely respondents were to state that it was sexual harassment.

Implications of Data

In this study, women reported numerous incidents of unwanted sexual behavior from persons of each status—superiors, peers, and students—although reports of sexual harassment were somewhat more likely to implicate persons of higher status (superiors) than lower status (peers or students). Caution must be applied in comparing across these groups, however. On the one hand, there are many more students than colleagues that the woman professor encounters in her work role, which may make it more likely that sexual harassment experiences from students will be overrepresented. Perhaps, too, inappropriate behavior from students is more likely to be perceived as sexual harassment because it is perceived as out of role (Pryor, 1985). One professor in my study said, "I realize I am using a different standard here for my peers and superiors as opposed to students with respect to undue attention. . . . I cannot imagine situations where students could touch me and it would be appropriate." On the other hand, the time spent with students may be restricted to classroom situations and occasional office visits. Interactions with colleagues, however, may involve more socializing both in the office and outside, and there may be more pressure to be "friendly" with colleagues. This suggests that the opportunity and tendency for sexual harassment to occur among colleagues is as great, if not greater, than for students and their professors.

The sexual harassment by students is especially intriguing because, as some have argued, "harassment suggests misuse of power, and students simply do not have enough power to harass" (Dzeich & Weiner, 1990, p. 24). Yet the current study and others have produced convincing evidence that students can and do sometimes sexually harass their instructors. If we are to assume that sexual harassment involves the imposition of unwanted sexual requirements by persons in power toward those less powerful, as MacKinnon (1979) suggests, where does students' power come from? Benson (1984) argues that power inequality stemming from gender serves as the basis for sexual harassment. Indeed, almost all of the acts reported in this study were initiated by men. Thus it would appear that both gender and occupational status interact to shape women's experiences with sexual harassment in the academy.

It is highly significant that women professors experience sexual harassment from men of all statuses, including those who have equal or less achieved/formal power than themselves. Cleveland and Kerst (1993) note that an individual's formal position within an organization is a poor indicator of his or her actual power. Because women often lack legitimate power—are given less decision-making responsibility and less latitude to exercise authority than men—women may indeed lack more power than their male coworkers who share the same job title. This argument has important implications for understanding the causes and prevention of sexual harassment because it assumes that simply having women in positions of power within organizations will not prevent these women from experiencing sexual harassment, as illustrated by the case of women professors who report experiencing unwanted sexual interactions from persons of equal power and even lesser power.

In this study, approximately one in four faculty women claimed to have been sexually harassed while employed at the university. Despite this seemingly high proportion, it appears that women faculty are not as likely to be victimized by sexual harassment as are women students or women in many other professions. For instance, when female federal employees were asked about their sexual harassment experiences within the preceding two-year period, nearly half (42%) claimed to have been sexually harassed (U.S. Merit Systems Protection Board, 1981)—a considerably higher percentage despite the shorter time frame employed (two years versus an average of eight years). Among women in traditional male professions such as engineering or management, approximately three out of four have been sexually harassed in their jobs (Lafontaine & Tredeau, 1986).

It is possible that certain factors—some unique to the academic institution, others characteristic of many workplaces—may foster sexual harassment, while other factors operating in the academy inhibit such behaviors. In the following section, I explore more closely the academic environment, considering ways in which sexual harassment of women professors is both inhibited and fostered within it.

THE ACADEMY RECONSIDERED

Dzeich and Weiner (1990) argue that the academic institution, "by its own biases and organizational structure and cultures, contributes to sexual harassment" (p. 58) of students. They discuss nine factors that they believe result in this outcome. First, they claim that the ambiguous nature of professors' mission (e.g., to foster students' moral, social, spiritual, and intellectual development) makes it possible for some to abuse their role and intrude in students' personal lives. Second, the tradition of autonomy and self-regulation protects harassers' actions from being easily detected. Third, the diffused institutional authority of the academy makes governance (of harassers) difficult. Fourth, the myth of collegiality leads some professors to deny or diminish complaints about colleagues. Fifth, the academy tolerates eccentric behavior and this can serve as an excuse for some professors to abuse students. Sixth, students are perceived to be on campus temporarily and to lack a strong voice; consequently, their concerns are taken more lightly than those expressed by persons whose positions are more stable (faculty). Seventh, the pastoral self-image of colleges and universities pervades and makes it difficult to accept the ugly reality of sexual harassment. Eighth, academics are conservative in their reaction to problems and search for resolutions, having been trained to carefully evaluate, analyze, test, and retest ideas. Finally, there is a paucity of women faculty and those in the academy are clustered in lower (and more powerless) positions. These women are understandably hesitant to advocate for victims of sexual harassment for fear of alienating their male colleagues and endangering their own careers. Added to this, there is a general perception that colleges and universities are safe environments, making women who act accordingly—by letting down their guard—more vulnerable to assaults.

Do these same factors create a vulnerable climate for professional women in the academy? Are faculty women, by virtue of being female, subjected to similar behaviors, or are faculty women, by virtue of their status within the organization, protected from such actions? Is the academy a relatively safe environment in which women can work, or is it worse than other workplaces?

Factors Contributing to the Sexual Harassment of Faculty Women

Some of the above factors suggested by Dzeich and Weiner (1990) such as inequality between the sexes are also likely contribute to sexual harassment of women faculty. The academy is structured along strict hierarchical lines, and individuals in the highest ranks tend to be male. Thus, not only do men have power over women by virtue of being male and living in a male-dominated society, these men possess greater power by virtue of their occupational roles (Kelly, 1988). If these men also are of privileged race and ethnicity, they are afforded greater power than men of less privileged groups and considerably more power over women of color who occupy subordinate positions. Thus the hierarchical nature of the academy in which men possess considerable power and authority makes women—especially those in lower positions—vulnerable to sexual harassment. Stimpson (1989) argues too that this hierarchical structure sends harassers a supportive message—the higher he climbs, the more he "deserves."

Other factors, including diffused institutional authority, the myth of collegiality, tolerance of eccentricity, and academic conservatism, are also likely to contribute to faculty women's vulnerability as well as to students'. And the fact that most academic women are in untenured (unsecured, possibly temporary) positions suggests that, like students, they may be perceived as temporary and powerless—not forces with which to be reckoned.

Dzeich and Weiner's (1990) discussion of faculty women provides further insights into the dilemmas they face:

> She must succeed as a professional against tradition, against prejudice, against overwhelming odds, but she must also find a way to defuse, define, or deny her own gender, to discover a type of femaleness that will not diminish her chances for professional success. These challenges alone could occupy a lifetime. (p. 148)

When sexual harassment issues arise, faculty women are in a bind. To support a victim of sexual harassment or to come forward with their own grievances threatens their already tenuous status: "The woman professor depends on men for her continued survival in the institution, the same men she would have to confront about sexual harassment. This dependence can create enormous confusion and ambiguity when the harassment issue arises" (Dzeich & Weiner, 1990, pp. 148-149).

A factor that has been linked to sexual harassment in past research is sex role spillover (in which sex role expectations often carry over into work settings even though these gender-based roles are irrelevant or inappropriate to work; Gutek & Morasch, 1982), and this applies to the university as well. Although some fields are equally distributed by sex, most are not, and sex role spillover is possible. A male colleague, for instance, may not be able to "get beyond" the fact that his coworker is a woman, and may steer conversation back to sexual or gender topics. In my own work setting, my women colleagues and I have found that if three or more women are talking in the hallway, we receive numerous comments from some male colleagues such as "watch out, the women are organizing against the men now." Some men's discomfort with dealing with women professionals *as professionals* may lead them to rely on more familiar forms of interactions—treating women *as women,* for instance. The effect of this sex role spillover is that sexual harassment is more likely.

This tendency to rely on more familiar types of interactions was observed by Kanter (1977). In her classic study of men and women in corporations, she found that women often were cast into one of four roles—mother, seductress, pet, or iron maiden. Similarly, women academics (especially junior women) are sometimes stereotyped into specific and limited roles.

The role of seductress is especially relevant for understanding sexual harassment. Although academic women may be less sexualized than other women (a point to which I return later), there is no reason to believe that women professors' behaviors are not interpreted in this manner. Gutek and others (Gutek, 1985, 1989; Gutek, Cohen, & Konrad, 1990) have found that sexuality is pervasive in organizations and that sexuality and sexual discourse pervade male-dominated workplaces (Collinson & Collinson, 1989; Gutek, 1985). This, combined with male authority within the workplace, "enable[s] the sexualization of the workplace and make[s] it possible for men to exploit women sexually for their own benefit" (DiTomaso, 1989, p. 73).

Although no woman in my sample commented specifically about being perceived as a "seductress," conversations with my women colleagues suggest that this occurs (e.g., a male student suggested that his female instructor shave her legs more and wear shorter skirts; another commented on a student evaluation form that the best thing about the course was looking at the instructor's "large breasts"; also see Sandler, 1993). The fact that many women experienced various forms of sexual behaviors from colleagues and students reinforces further this interpretation that some women academics are cast into the seductress role. Sandler (1993) suggests that students

> uncomfortable with the strange apparition of a female faculty member . . . may fall back on the ways they behave in social situations with women, ways which often use sexuality as a means to demonstrate power. Thus they may call a woman faculty member "honey," or "dearie," or even by her first name without asking her permission to do so. She may be viewed primarily in terms of sexuality, so that male students may flirt with her and engage in sexual teasing. (p. 7)

Women may also be viewed as seductresses in part because men tend to sexualize interactions more than women do. Abbey (1982) found that men are likely to interpret women's friendliness as seductive or sexually inviting. Stockdale, Dewey, and Saal (1992, cited in Stockdale, 1993) also found that men more than women rated a female's professional and friendly behavior as sexual. In another study (Johnson, Stockdale, & Saal, 1991), male subjects viewing exchanges between instructors and students (in which the sex of actors, level of harassing behavior, and responses to behaviors were manipulated) rated actors as more sexual than female subjects did, except in the most harassing case involving a male professor. This sexualization process may occur more often for young, unmarried, minority women. Defour (1990) argues that women of color are likely to be eroticized and therefore subjected to more sexualization. For a lesbian woman, there may also be a focus by some men on her sexuality and greater efforts to (re)define her sexuality than for heterosexual women. Schneider (1987) did find that lesbians reported a higher incidence of sexual joking about their bodies or appearances at work than did heterosexual women.

If female faculty (and students) are sometimes cast into the "seductress" role, it is easy to see how sexual harassment can occur. When men interpret a situation as a *sexual* situation, a sexual script is likely to be called into play, which will then guide the interaction. In our society, sexual scripts specify that men should be active initiators and pursuers in sexual situations and that women be the sexual gatekeepers (MacCorquodale, 1989). Thus, if a man perceives a situation to be sexual, he is likely to act accordingly by initiating sexual contact (perhaps touching, making sexual comments, staring, propositioning, and so on). If the woman in this situation perceives the situation in the same manner, that is, as a sexual one, there is likely to be no problem; however, if she has a different interpretation (as the research suggests is somewhat likely), his interactions will be perceived as inappropriate, possibly harassing. To make matters worse, the man—who has been socialized to believe that women say no but mean yes and that it is legitimate to try to overcome women's initial resistance—is not likely to back off when the woman resists his advances or attempts to redefine the situation as a nonsexual one. Also, men may misperceive women's use of silence or avoidance to deal with sexual harassment by men (Gutek, 1985) as assent or encouragement (Dziech & Weiner, 1990), because they are taught to pursue contact unless (or even if) they receive a forceful no.

Even more than being seen as seductresses, women academics are probably more likely to be cast in the role of mother, given that a major part of their responsibility is teaching, a traditional role that places value on certain feminine, maternal qualities (nurturing, mentoring, counseling). As a result, women professors may be seen as caretakers or substitute mothers and have expectations placed upon them by others (students and colleagues) that demand these qualities. England (1988) found that college students expect women to behave in a maternal way (i.e., to be sensitive to emotional and psychological aspects of relationships), regardless of their role or position. On the one hand, being perceived as a "mother" may protect some women from being sexually harassed due to the cultural ideology of mothers as nonsexual beings. Kanter (1977) claimed, for instance, that the mother role was relatively safe and not vulnerable to sexual pursuits. However, it is easy to see how such expectations may lead to certain types of behaviors that may be viewed as inappropriate or harassing by faculty women. For instance, a woman professor in my study wrote:

> Male and female students seem to think I should be at their beck and call, be friendly and nurturing to them, and generally motherly. I think kids have these expectations from women faculty and react negatively when these inappropriate expectations aren't met.

Another wrote:

> I think . . . [that teaching] evaluation forms encourage students to evaluate women professors for their interpersonal behavior (i.e., "nurturing" qualities) rather than their teaching qualifications. Why should "concern for students" be evaluated at all? Such questions invite students to consider women professors as "mother figures." . . . What student actually expects a male professor to show "concern"? What student doesn't expect such from a female professor?

Again, if the woman adopts this role and is comfortable with it, there is not likely to be a problem. If, however, she does not act according to the role, she is likely to evoke anger and hostility from others (Sandler, 1993). She is also more likely to view others' expectations and behaviors negatively.

Several women in my sample also made reference to status leveling, another phenomenon observed by Kanter (1977) in which women in nontraditional occupations were often mistakenly identified as occupying traditional roles, and even after the mistaken identity was corrected, there was a tendency to treat the person as if she did indeed occupy the more typical (and subordinate) role. Respondents in my study stated: "Certain individuals like to call me by my first name rather than 'Dr. ________ ' [T]his bugs me." "Students overtly challenge my expertise in the classroom." "I teach a technical/construction-oriented course. Some students double-check my instructions with other (male) professors in our field, although my experience is greater than that of the other professors."

This type of behavior may be seen as "gender harassment" (Till, 1980) and appears to be fairly common in academic settings. Although such behaviors may not necessarily be viewed as *sexual* harassment, when combined with other qualities of male-female relationships, especially the tendency of men to sexualize interactions, they become more questionable and problematic.

Academia also emphasizes intellectual debate. Ramazanoglu (1987) suggests that "academics are verbally skilled and can use verbiage to confuse and intimidate others; they are also powerful users of the voice to convey sarcasm, to interrupt, to prevent interruption and to override counterarguments" (p. 64). The atmosphere in which academics work may contribute to sexual harassment because harassers may be especially skilled at disguising sexist or sexual comments or be convincing in their ability to pass off acts as innocent gestures. Victims also may feel that they should be able to verbally compete, and blame themselves when they are made to feel uncomfortable with interactions. Given that men tend to dominate and control social interactions, especially through language (Hoffman, Tsuneyoshi, Ebina, & Fite, 1984; Metts & Cupach, 1989), it is not surprising that women feel uneasy in such conversations, even if they are not explicitly sexual in nature. Yet, when conversations do take on a sexual tone, women are likely to feel sexually harassed. Two cases in which men used obscenities were mentioned by women in my study: "[A student] spray-paint[ed] obscenities on [my] automobile; yelled insults while [I was] both walking and driving." "A student once came into my office while I was working and began shouting obscenities."

Arliss (1991) has discussed the role of language in sexual harassment. She observes that

> compared to men, women are called by their first names more often (as are subordinates), are called by pet names more often (as are children), are metaphorized more often as cuddly animals and edible objects, and are more often the object of sexual jokes. Arguably, none of these communicative trends alone causes sexual harassment of women in any setting, but the combination of these communicative habits certainly establishes women as probable victims of unwelcome sexual innuendo. (p. 174)

Of interest, the most frequent acts mentioned by women in this study involved sexist comments and verbal sexual comments.

There may be other factors that foster sexual harassment of women professors. One, related to the occupation itself, is that the job requires overtime, business trips, and convention attendance, which places women in vulnerable positions (Conrad & Taylor, 1994). Fuehrer and Schilling (1985) also suggest that for women who are committed to the academic enterprise (which theoretically values fairness, objectivity, and impartiality), it may be difficult to recognize gender bias (also see Alpert, 1989). Finally, institutions such as the academy may be so entrenched in tradition—a tradition based on male power and thought—that altering the organizational structures, norms, and patterns of interaction may be particularly difficult. Knowing this, victims may feel disempowered to stop sexual harassment. As Kelly (1988) points out, "As individuals, women may resist such behaviour but having minimal access to power resources we are seldom able to change institutional ideologies and structures which legitimize, or fail to challenge, routine exercises of power by men" (p. 27).

Lest this sound like the woman faculty member is subjected to more sexual harassment than other women, given these conditions, it should be stressed that many of these factors apply to other professional workplaces and women therein. Indeed, Dzeich and Weiner (1990) suggest that the dilemmas challenging faculty women mirror those women face in other professions, especially women who chose historically male professions. This suggests that academic women are not necessarily more vulnerable to sexual harassment than are women in other workplaces. In fact, there are a number of factors that may reduce their vulnerability.

Factors Inhibiting the Sexual Harassment of Faculty Women

One factor that may reduce sexual harassment of faculty women is the autonomy of women academics (although this may contribute to sexual harassment of students; Conrad & Taylor, 1994; Dzeich & Weiner, 1990). Women professors usually do not work one-on-one with a superior. As a result, there is less dependency built into the work relationship. This is not to say that administrators or persons of higher rank do not exert power over these women, but it may be possible for them to avoid harassers more easily than someone in a one-on-one work situation (e.g., as with a secretary and boss). Of course, untenured women faculty are encouraged to find mentors (usually male, given the paucity of senior women), and these relationships may be especially prone to exploitation (Haring-Hidore & Paludi, 1987).

Another important difference between the academy and many other institutions is that it is not likely to be as highly sexualized. Sexuality is not a salient aspect of the professor's role so that sexual harassment may be curtailed somewhat. As Kelly (1988) notes,

> What men consider acceptable treatment of strippers would not be acceptable treatment of barmaids, and what is considered acceptable in the latter case would not be routinely acceptable in the office. What men are able to get away with in male-dominated environments has to be moderated in mixed sex and women-dominated work situations. (pp. 105-106)

Dzeich and Weiner (1990) also insist that faculty women often learn to survive in their workplaces by "disguising their femininity" (p. 151). As a result, they may be viewed as more androgynous than sexual, thereby reducing the amount of inappropriate sexual attention they receive. Also, in the academy, sexual harassment may be inhibited because the institution is not strongly based on "macho" values (as is, say, the military) but on ideals of democracy and liberalism. Sexism is not explicitly built into the academic fabric as it is in some other occupations. These norms can reduce incidents of sexual harassment, even when other factors are present (Pryor, LaVite, & Stoller, 1993).

We also cannot discount the impact that two decades of scholarly work on sexual harassment—much of it on academic sexual harassment—has had on the awareness of academics. Despite the fact that the university climate is still a "chilly" one for many women, there is no doubt more awareness of gender issues (thanks in part to the rise in women's studies programs on campuses), including sexual harassment. And faculty women may be fairly progressive in their attitudes toward sexual harassment. Stimpson (1989) also argues that the university has made progress in combating sexual harassment by doing such things as "naming the problem *as a problem*" (p. 3), conducting workshops, and creating grievance procedures; many other organizations still are lagging in this respect.

CONCLUSIONS

Although there are several factors that may contribute to the sexual harassment of faculty women, it is important to acknowledge that women faculty may actually be subjected to less sexual harassment than women in other professions, given the nature of their jobs and the structure and norms of the academy. (The extent to which this is true still needs to be empirically studied.) To suggest that academic women may not experience as much sexual harassment as women in other professions is not to diminish the fact that many faculty women are sexually harassed—some very egregiously. Nor can it be denied that sexual harassment can occur within every aspect of a woman professor's role—researcher, teacher, counselor—and this can come from peers, superiors, or students.

What effects do these experiences have? Numerous studies have shown that victims suffer a variety of negative job-related outcomes, including changing jobs, but few studies have looked at this specifically for academic women (for an exception, see McKinney, 1994). Are victims' academic progress and advancement through the ranks impeded? The number of women who have left professorships due to sexual harassment is unknown, but the relatively low rate of retention of women faculty suggests that the environment is not supportive for many (Aisenberg & Harrington, 1988). What part does sexual harassment play in promoting a "chilly atmosphere" for women within the academy and forcing some women to exit the environment rather than endure or constantly challenge the sexual harassment they face? The exact toll of sexual harassment on countless women in academia is unknown, but as with the sexual harassment of all working women, the losses are felt not only at the individual level but at the institutional and societal levels as well.

APPENDIX 2.A: ITEMS IN THE SURVEY INSTRUMENT

1. Sexist Comments (e.g., jokes or remarks that are stereotypical or derogatory to members of your sex)
2. Undue Attention (e.g., flirtation, touching, being overly friendly)
3. Verbal Sexual Comments (e.g., inquiries on sexual values, remarks about dress or body, but not a proposition)
4. Written Sexual Comments (e.g., comments about sexual behavior, body, dress, or sexual values on written communications to you) (When this element was asked about in terms of students' behavior, "written communications to you" was replaced with "student evaluations of you.")
5. Body Language (e.g., leering, standing too close)
6. Physical Advances (e.g., kissing, hugging, pinching, fondling)
7. Explicit Sexual Propositions (e.g., clear invitations for sexual encounter but no threat stated)
8. Sexual Bribery (e.g., explicit sexual propositions that include or strongly imply promises of rewards for complying or punishment for refusing)

9. Sexual Assault (e.g., rape or attempted rape)
10. Have you experienced any other behavior from a superior (peer/student) that you consider to be sexual harassment? If so, please describe.

REFERENCES

Abbey, A. (1982). Sex differences in attributions for friendly behavior? Do males misperceive females' friendliness? *Journal of Personality and Social Psychology, 42,* 830-838.

Adams, J. W., Kottke, J. L., & Padgett, J. S. (1983). Sexual harassment of college students. *Journal of College Student Personnel, 24,* 484-490.

Aisenberg, N., & Harrington, M. (1988). *Women of academe: Outsiders in the sacred grove.* Amherst: University of Massachusetts Press.

Alpert, D. (1989). Gender inequity in academia: An empirical analysis. *Initiatives, 52,* 9-14.

Arliss, L. P. (1991). *Gender communication.* Englewood Cliffs, NJ: Prentice-Hall.

Benson, K. (1984). Comment on Crocker's "An analysis of university definitions of sexual harassment." *Signs, 9,* 516-519.

Carroll, L., & Ellis, K. L. (1989). Faculty attitudes toward sexual harassment: Survey results, survey process. *Initiatives, 52,* 35-41.

Cleveland, J. N., & Kerst, M. E. (1993). Sexual harassment and perceptions of power: An under-articulated relationship. *Journal of Vocational Behavior, 42,* 49-67.

Collinson, D. L., & Collinson, M. (1989). Sexuality in the workplace: The domination of men's sexuality. In J. Hearn, D. L. Sheppard, P. Tancred-Sheriff, & G. Burrell (Eds.), *The sexuality of organization.* London: Sage Ltd.

Conrad, C., & Taylor, B. (1994). The context(s) of sexual harassment: Power, silences and academe. In S. Bingham (Ed.), *Conceptualizing sexual harassment as discursive practice.* Westport, CT: Greenwood.

Defour, D. C. (1990). The interface of racism and sexism on college campuses. In M. Paludi (Ed.), *Ivory power: Sexual harassment on campus.* Albany: SUNY Press.

DiTomaso, N. (1989). Sexuality in the workplace: Discrimination and harassment. In J. Hearn, D. L. Sheppard, P. Tancred-Sheriff, & G. Burrell (Eds.), *The sexuality of organization.* London: Sage Ltd.

Dzeich, B. W., & Weiner, L. (1990). *The lecherous professor* (2nd ed.). Urbana: University of Illinois Press.

England, E. M. (1988). College student stereotypes of female behavior: Maternal professional women and assertive housewives. *Sex Roles, 19,* 365-385.

Fitzgerald, L. F. (1990). Sexual harassment: The definition and measurement of a construct. In M. A. Paludi (Ed.), *Ivory power: Sexual harassment on campus.* Albany: SUNY Press.

Fitzgerald, L. F., & Shullman, S. L. (1993). Sexual harassment: A research analysis and agenda for the 1990s. *Journal of Vocational Behavior, 42,* 5-27.

Fitzgerald, L. F., Shullman, S. L., Bailey, N., Richards, M., Swecker, J., Gold, Y., Ormerod, M., & Weitzman, L. (1988). The incidence and dimensions of sexual

harassment in academia and the workplace. *Journal of Vocational Behavior, 32,* 152-175.
Fitzgerald, L. F., Weitzman, L. M., Gold, Y., & Ormerod, M. (1988). Academic harassment: Sex and denial in scholarly garb. *Psychology of Women Quarterly, 12,* 329-340.
Fuehrer, A., & Schilling, K. M. (1985). The values of academe: Sexism as a natural consequence. *Journal of Social Issues, 41,* 29-42.
Goodwin, M. P., Roscoe, B., Rose, M., & Repp, S. E. (1989). Sexual harassment: Experiences of university employees. *Initiatives, 52,* 25-33.
Grauerholz, E. (1989). Sexual harassment of women professors by students: Exploring the dynamics of power, authority, and gender in a university setting. *Sex Roles, 21,* 789-801.
Gutek, B. A. (1985). *Sex and the workplace.* San Francisco: Jossey-Bass.
Gutek, B. A. (1989). Sexuality in the workplace: Key issues in social research and organizational practice. In J. Hearn, D. L. Sheppard, P. Tancred-Sheriff, & G. Burrell (Eds.), *The sexuality of organization.* London: Sage Ltd.
Gutek, B. A., Cohen, A. G., & Konrad, A. M. (1990). Predicting social-sexual behavior at work: A contact hypothesis. *Academy of Management Journal, 33,* 560-577.
Gutek, B. A., & Morasch, B. (1982). Sex-ratios, sex-role spillover, and sexual harassment of women at work. *Journal of Social Issues, 38,* 55-74.
Hall, R., & Sandler, B. R. (1984). *The classroom climate: A chilly one for women?* Washington, DC: Project on the Status of Women.
Haring-Hidore, M., & Paludi, M. A. (1987). Sexuality and sex in mentoring and tutoring: Implications for women's opportunities and achievement. *Peabody Journal of Education, 64,* 164-172.
Hoffman, C. D., Tsuneyoshi, S. E., Ebina, M., & Fite, H. (1984). A comparison of adult males' and females' interactions with girls and boys. *Sex Roles, 11,* 799-811.
Johnson, C. B., Stockdale, M. S., & Saal, F. E. (1991). Persistence of men's misperceptions of friendly cues across a variety of interpersonal encounters. *Psychology of Women Quarterly, 15,* 463-475.
Kanter, R. M. (1977). *Men and women of the corporation.* New York: Basic Books.
Kelly, L. (1988). *Surviving sexual violence.* Minneapolis: University of Minnesota Press.
Lafontaine, E., & Tredeau, L. (1986). The frequency, sources, and correlates of sexual harassment among women in traditional male occupations. *Sex Roles, 1*(5), 433-442.
Leonard, R., Ling, L. C., Hankins, G. A., Maidon, C. H., Potorti, P. F., & Rogers, J. M. (1993). Sexual harassment at North Carolina State University. In G. Kreps (Ed.), *Sexual harassment: Communication implications.* Cresskill, NJ: Hampton.
Lott, B., Reilly, M. E., & Howard, D. (1982). Sexual assault and harassment: A campus community case study. *Signs, 8,* 296-319.
MacCorquodale, P. (1989). Gender and sexual behavior. In K. McKinney & S. Sprecher (Eds.), *Human sexuality.* Norwood, NJ: Ablex.
MacKinnon, C. (1979). *Sexual harassment of working women.* New Haven, CT: Yale University Press.
McKinney, K. (1990). Sexual harassment of university faculty by colleagues and students. *Sex Roles, 23,* 421-470.
McKinney, K. (1992). Contrapower sexual harassment: The effects of student sex and type of behavior on faculty perceptions. *Sex Roles, 27,* 1-17.
McKinney, K. (1994). Sexual harassment and college faculty members. *Deviant Behavior, 15,* 171-191.

McKinney, K., & Crittenden, K. (1992). Contrapower sexual harassment: The offender's viewpoint. *Free Inquiry Into Creative Sociology, 20,* 3-10.

McKinney, K., & Maroules, N. (1991). Sexual harassment. In E. Grauerholz & M. Koralewski (Eds.), *Sexual coercion: A sourcebook on its nature, causes and prevention.* Lexington, MA: Lexington.

Metha, A., & Nigg, J. (1983). Sexual harassment on campus: An institutional response. *Journal of the National Association of Women Deans, Administrators and Counselors, 46,* 23-29.

Metts, S., & Cupach, W. R. (1989). The role of communication in human sexuality. In E. McKinney & S. Sprecher (Eds.), *Human sexuality.* Norwood, NJ: Ablex.

Pryor, J. B. (1985). The lay person's understanding of sexual harassment. *Sex Roles, 13,* 273-286.

Pryor, J. B., LaVite, C. M., & Stoller, L. M. (1993). A social psychological analysis of sexual harassment: The person/situation interaction. *Journal of Vocational Behavior, 42,* 68-83.

Ramazanoglu, C. (1987). Sex and violence in academic life or you can keep a good woman down. In J. Hanmer & M. Maynard (Eds.), *Women, violence and social control.* Atlantic Highlands, NJ: Humanities Press International.

Sandler, B. (1993). *Women faculty at work in the classroom, or, why it still hurts to be a woman in labor.* Washington, DC: Center for Women Policy Studies.

Schneider, B. E. (1987). Graduate women, sexual harassment and university policy. *Journal of Higher Education, 58,* 46-65.

Stimpson, C. R. (1989). Over-reaching: Sexual harassment and education. *Initiatives, 52,* 1-5.

Stockdale, M. S. (1993). The role of sexual misperceptions of women's friendliness in an emerging theory of sexual harassment. *Journal of Vocational Behavior, 42,* 84-101.

Till, F. J. (1980). *Sexual harassment: A report on the sexual harassment of students.* Washington, DC: Government Printing Office.

U.S. Merit Systems Protection Board. (1981). *Sexual harassment in the federal workplace: Is it a problem?* Washington, DC: Office of Merit Systems Review and Studies/ Government Printing Office.

3

Sexual Harassment and Women of Color: Issues, Challenges, and Future Directions

AUDREY J. MURRELL

The issue of sexual harassment as it affects women of color within the workplace is the focus of this chapter. After reviewing the empirical and theoretical literature on experiences, definitions, and consequences of sexual harassment for women of color, issues and recommendations concerning the future direction of this research are offered. Only a scant amount of existing empirical evidence focuses on women of color and sexual harassment; most studies do not explicitly examine race/ethnic differences or report the racial composition of the sample. Thus it is suggested that future models of sexual harassment for women of color should conceptualize sexual harassment for women of color not only as a form of sex discrimination but also as a form of race discrimination in the workplace. The implications of this conceptualization for defining a hostile work environment, structuring organizational policies, and clarifying legal standards are discussed.

In this chapter, I focus on the issue of sexual harassment as it affects women of color within the workplace. A number of the major cases that define our understanding of the issue of sexual harassment involve the direct experiences of women of color (e.g., Michelle Vinson in *Meritor*

Savings Bank v. Vinson, 1986, or Anita Hill in the Hill-Thomas controversy). The experiences of these women should provide a critical foundation for our understanding of the issue of sexual harassment and thus permeate both empirical and theoretical work in this area. Ironically, however, only a scant amount of empirical literature is available that either specifically examines women of color and sexual harassment or merely includes information on the racial/ethnic composition of the sample. Theoretical writings on this issue frequently promote the idea that sexual harassment for women of color is rarely a matter of sex-based discrimination alone but is a consequence of sexual racism. However, little previous work has advanced beyond this point to explore some of the implications of viewing sexual harassment for women of color as a form of sexual racism for the range of issues currently being addressed in this area of research.

Before exploring the implications of expanding current thinking on sexual harassment to be more inclusive, the existing empirical and theoretical literatures on sexual harassment for women of color are reviewed within three broad categories: overall experiences with sexual harassment, definitions of sexual harassment, and consequences of exposure to sexual harassment. A number of issues for future research in each of these three areas are outlined. Then, the implications of including women of color in models for research on sexual harassment are discussed. Three issues will be highlighted: defining a hostile work environment, structuring organizational policies, and clarifying the "reasonable woman" standard in legal cases of sexual harassment.

In beginning this chapter on the issue of sexual harassment as it affects women of color, I struggled with two initial questions. First, to whom does the term *women of color* apply? I fully acknowledge that including a variety of different ethnic groups of women under one label should not carry with it the assumption of uniformity in culture, in general, or experiences with sexual harassment, in particular. Solely for the purpose of this discussion, *women of color* will refer to those individuals who, as Bell, Denton, and Nkomo (1993) describe them, "are simultaneously racial and ethnic minorities . . . collectively . . . black, Latina, Native American and Asian American women" (p. 125, n. 1). Thus the term *women of color* is used here to highlight the need for research that focuses on a diverse collection of women who, while differing in their ethnic and cultural experiences, may share both a common vulnerability to sexual harassment and a common exclusion from research aimed at understanding this phenomenon.

The second question that I asked at the outset of constructing this text is this: Why include a separate chapter on sexual harassment for women of color? After all, the broad definition established by the Equal Employment Opportunity Commission (EEOC) in 1980 states that sexual harassment is "unwelcome sexual advances, requests for sexual favors, and other verbal physical conduct of a sexual nature." It does not contain either an implicit or an explicit reference to the impact that race and ethnicity have on the defining features of sexual harassment. In other words, why should sexual harassment for women of color be looked at differently than sexual harassment for white women?

There are three contexts in which issues of sexual harassment for women of color may need to be separated from previous work on sexual harassment that focuses exclusively on sexual harassment among white women. First, it may be the case that sexual harassment occurs with different frequency for women of color; that is, women of color are somewhat more likely to be victims of sexual harassment than white women. Second, the definition or meaning of sexual harassment may differ between women of color and their white counterparts. For example, is sexual harassment a form of sexual racism, or an act of sex discrimination that simply involves race? And, third, are the effects or consequences of sexual harassment different when the victim is a woman of color, that is, in strength, direction, or type of consequences on things such as career outcomes or psychological well-being? If the answer to any of these questions is yes, then the issue of sexual harassment for women of color should and must be examined separately from the sexual harassment experiences of white women.

After examining these three domains to determine whether there are empirical and theoretical explanations for a unique focus on women of color when examining the issue of sexual harassment, several important implications of this focus can be explored. First, however, I must examine previous research on sexual harassment to determine the amount and nature of existing knowledge on this issue as it affects women of color. Although the previous literature on sexual harassment is extensive, three areas that are most central to harassment for women of color are examined here: experiences with sexual harassment, defining harassment, and the consequences of sexual harassment experiences.

REVIEW OF THE LITERATURE

Experiences With Sexual Harassment

There has been a great deal of speculation that race or ethnicity may increase one's risk of being sexually harassed. Unfortunately, carefully designed studies using diverse samples simply have not been done. A few studies that examine different ethnic groups of women either report finding no differences or report that women of color, in some instances, have more frequent experiences with sexual harassment than white women. Gutek (1985) reported that women of color were no more likely to be harassed than other women. Data reported in the original U.S. Merit Systems Protection Board (MSPB) (1987) study indicated no connection between race or ethnicity and the frequency of sexual harassment among African American women. There has been some disagreement about the interpretation of the U.S. MSPB findings, however (e.g., Fain & Anderton, 1987; Lach & Gwartney-Gibbs, 1993), and, unfortunately, the follow-up study did not include race of the victim as a variable.

Gruber and Bjorn (1982, 1986) found in two studies that not only do black women autoworkers receive more sexual harassment than whites, but black women also are harassed more severely than white women. Interviews conducted by Essed (1992) found frequent references to sexual harassment of black women by white men, although no specific gender comparison data were collected. Segura (1992) examined Chicanos in white-collar jobs and found evidence for frequent incidences of sexual harassment, but, again, no comparative data were presented. Unfortunately, studies of other groups of ethnic women, particularly Asian and Native American women, have not been done.

The lack of large-scale representative empirical data leads me to use primarily theoretical arguments to address the question of whether women of color are more vulnerable to sexual harassment than white women. Here, two types of theoretical arguments have been proposed: direct and indirect. Direct arguments contend that exposure to sexual harassment for women of color is an explicit result of their ethnic group membership (i.e., being black or Asian). The majority of these arguments focus on the nature of social stereotypes and how they affect a likely perpetrator's view of a woman of color in such a way that these perceptions place her at risk of being harassed. Indirect arguments focus on the overlap between ethnic group membership and other factors that increase the likelihood of sexual harassment. A great many of these indirect arguments center on factors such as power and minority status or marginality as the driving forces in determining risk of being sexually harassed. These perspectives suggest that it is not ethnicity, per se, but lack of power or marginality that makes women of color vulnerable to sexual harassment.

Early on, MacKinnon (1979) argued that race may be an important factor in determining risk of being sexually harassed. She suggested that blacks, for example, may be the targets of harassment more often than whites because of cultural and economic marginality or vulnerability that accrues to women with minority group status. Defour (1990) and later, Karsten (1994) also argued that minority group status (i.e., minority group membership) increases the risk of being sexually harassed because this status denotes marginality and lack of power within the workplace. There is some evidence to support the view that low-status characteristics or low-power positions within the workplace are often accompanied by frequent experiences with sexual harassment. Younger women are more often the targets of harassment than older women (Gutek, 1985; Lafontaine & Tredeau, 1986). Unmarried women are also reported as somewhat more likely than married women to be victims of harassment (Benson & Thomson, 1982). Women who represent a numerical minority within the organization are at risk of being victims of sexual harassment (Gutek, Cohen, & Konrad, 1990). Thus, based on some ancillary evidence, there appears to be an overlap between marginality within the workplace and race/ethnic group membership that places women of color in greater jeopardy of sexual harassment than white women.

It is difficult to say, however, whether women of color's increased vulnerability to sexual harassment is because racial/ethnic minority status is actually a proxy for lack of power or marginality, or whether ethnic/racial group membership itself increases vulnerability to sexual harassment and marginality simply intensifies this vulnerability. Put another way, does marginality moderate or mediate the impact of race/ethnicity on the likelihood of sexual harassment? Using this analogy, a mediational model would predict that the presence of marginality or the lack of power reduces or eliminates the impact that race has on the likelihood of sexual harassment. Ethnicity or race is only a surrogate for the effect that power has on the likelihood of being sexually harassed. If, however, race itself exerts a direct effect on the likelihood of sexual harassment that cannot be eliminated or reduced by the presence of marginality (or the absence of power), then a moderational relationship may exist. Here, both race/ethnicity and minority group status can exert their own unique and direct effects on the likelihood of being sexually harassed. In addition, the combination or interaction of race/ethnic and marginality would increase vulnerability to sexual harassment.

The distinction between a hypothesized moderational or mediational relationship between race/ethnic group status and marginality or power is of critical importance. If I assert that marginality or power is actually the underlying dimension that increases vulnerability to sexual harassment (the mediational view), then establishing equality within the workplace that is not directed exclusively at, but does include, women of color would be the most effective strategy for decreasing the incidence of sexual harassment for women of color. If, however, I were to argue that racial or ethnic group status has a direct impact that is intensified by the presence of marginality (the moderational view), then establishing equality within the workplace will be only partially effective at reducing the likelihood that women of color will be sexually harassed. What is needed in this second scenario is an understanding of the direct contribution that race or ethnicity itself plays in making women of color frequent victims of sexual harassment. To understand this latter case, it seems necessary to examine the different meanings or definitions of harassment that are associated with racial or ethnic group membership and how these definitions may be connected to sexual harassment experiences.

Defining Harassment

Some theorists have argued that in the case of sexual harassment, it is necessary to make a distinction between sexism and sexual racism (e.g., Collins, 1990; Essed, 1992; hooks, 1984). Sexual racism affects women of different ethnic/racial groups and, as Essed (1992) asserts, is a "hybrid form of control" (p. 211). Black feminists have widely discussed how rape and other forms of sexual aggression are embedded in a system of interlocking race, gender, ethnicity, and class oppression (Collins, 1990; Davis, 1978, 1981; Hall, 1983; hooks, 1984). As Collins (1990) states, "African-American women inhabit a sex/gender hierarchy in which the inequalities of race and social class have been sexualized" (p. 165). One implication of this idea is that because women of color have been sexually exploited historically, sexism for women of color is actually a form of sexual racism. In other words, for women of color, the threat of racial/ethnic intimidation and violence carries with it the additional fear of sexual aggression and harassment.

For example, an early study of domestic workers found that mothers, aunts, and community women warned young black women about the threat of sexual violence by white men (Lewis, 1985). Davis (1978) suggests that sexual violence against black women has been central to the economic and political subordination of African Americans overall, that is, the basis for racial discrimination in this country. Black women often experience a parallel form of race- and gender-specific sexual violence. Treating African American women as pornographic objects and portraying them as sexualized animals, and as prostitutes, created the stereotype of black women as the "hypersexual Jezebel" (Collins, 1990). Rape and other acts of sexual aggression were justified by the myth of black female hypersexuality and served to continue the oppression of these women that had its historical roots in slavery. Therefore, sexual aggression, violence, and sexual harassment should be defined as the outgrowth of racial exploitation and discrimination.

Similar arguments can be made for other ethnic groups of women. The image of Asian women in pornography is one of being submissive and tortured (Bell, 1993). Latina women are depicted as "hot-blooded" and passionate, yet submissive to Latino men who are often portrayed as dominating and macho. As Collins (1990) states, "The relationships among black women and white men have long been constrained by the legacy of black women's sexual abuse by white men and the unresolved tensions this creates" (p. 191). These images serve a dual function of perpetuating a system of gender and racial oppression. This suggests that for women of color, sexual harassment should be defined as sexual racism rather than sex discrimination that involves race. Thus, for women of color, sexual harassment should be defined as a form of both sex discrimination and race discrimination because they are historically and experientially tied to one another. There is some limited empirical evidence that incidents of racial and sexual harassment are related. Mansfield, Koch, Henderson, and Vicary (1991) found that black tradeswomen were likely to experience sexual harassment along with race discrimination and to interpret them as interrelated incidents. McClelland and Hunt (1992) examined the perceived seriousness of racial harassment behaviors and found that perceptions of racial harassment varied in a manner similar to behaviors that constitute sexual harassment.

The view of sexual harassment of women of color as a form of racial discrimination may be necessary for three reasons. First, sex and race discrimination may covary, especially in situations involving a white male supervisor and a woman of color as subordinate. Some argue that whenever cross-racial or ethnic harassment occurs, it is by definition a form of sexual racism (Essed, 1992) and thus a form of race discrimination. Second, the behaviors of perpetrators who sexually harass women of color may be based on stereotypes of these women as hypersexual, hot-blooded, and submissive. Thus sexual harassment that is fueled by race-based stereotypes is, by definition, a form of racial discrimination. And, third, victims of sexual harassment may perceive sexual advances, especially by white men, as due primarily to their race and also their gender. Women of color will rarely perceive their treatment as solely based on sex (Collins, 1990; King, 1988; Williams, 1988). Thus the cognitive explanations by women of color who are sexually harassed may be quite complex (in terms of category associations) by focusing on the presence of racial or ethnic group bias and hostility rather than sexism or sexual aggression.

Adding a dimension to definitions of sexual harassment targeted at women of color suggests the potential for a dual impact of harassment for these women. Defining harassment as both race and sex discrimination may enhance both the perceived and the experienced severity of sexual harassment incidents for women of color. This leads to a need to examine some of the range and severity of consequences of harassment experiences for women of color.

Consequences of Harassment

Gutek and Koss (1993) categorized the outcomes of sexual harassment into three domains: somatic health, psychological health, and work outcomes. However, only a scant amount of evidence exists that examines these three sets of outcomes for women of color. In addition, there has been little systematic research investigating the factors that predict whether women of color will report incidents of sexual harassment and no research examining individual responses to or the impact of sexual harassment on work outcomes for these women. Again, the majority of evidence is either theoretical or secondary in nature. For example, some ancillary evidence can be found in studies of black women and rape. Black women are less likely to report rape, less likely to have their cases come to trial, less likely to have their trials result in convictions, and less likely to seek counseling and other support services (Collins, 1990). Some evidence suggests that African American women are aware of this "lack of protection" and may resist, but not report, rape more than other groups (Bart & O'Brien, 1985).

Direct evidence on responses to harassment finds that, in general, one of the frequent responses to harassment is to quit one's job (e.g., Sandroff, 1992; U.S. MSPB, 1988). Women who do complain are often fired (Coles, 1986) or are not able to work in their field because of bad references (Hamilton, Alagna, King, & Lloyd, 1987). Gutek (1985) found, however, that minority women who experienced sexual harassment within her sample were less likely to report quitting a job because of this harassment. This finding is similar to that reported in other studies of minority women and incidents of sexual violence and aggression. Although this finding may have a number of implications, there has been no subsequent research that replicates Gutek's original findings and extends this work to other groups of ethnic women.

A number of women who experience harassment remain in their jobs and do not report the incidents. For women who remain in their jobs, sexual harassment affects their overall satisfaction with their jobs and the way they think about their organizations (see Gutek & Koss, 1993). Women who experience sexual harassment may be particularly prone to experiencing negative career outcomes in terms of career development, sponsorship within the organization, work attitudes, and career mobility as well as job stress and withdrawal as a result of negative experiences at work (Fitzgerald & Shullman, 1993). If, as Gutek (1985) found, women of color are less likely to leave their jobs following threat of or exposure to sexual harassment, these women may suffer a range of consequences that have negative implications for their future career development. For example, women of color, because of the threat of sexual harassment, may limit the nature of their interpersonal contacts at work, which may include career-enhancing relationships.

Thomas (1989, 1990, 1993) and Thomas and Clayton (1989) find that black women are wary of developing and maintaining career-enhancing relationships with white male supervisors. These women are often fearful of either being exposed to harassing behaviors or being labeled as a "white man's slut" (Thomas, 1989, p. 282). Thomas (1989) argues that a pervasive stereotype operating within the workplace is that black women can be appropriated by white males and, to avoid stigmatization because of this perception, black women often avoid contact with individuals who can enhance their career mobility.

This suggests that a potential impact of sexual harassment for women of color (similar to their white counterparts) is a range of negative effects on career outcomes such as turnover, lack of promotion, and negative career mobility. Although minority women may be less likely to quit their jobs because of harassment than white women, harassment can still derail their careers by providing few opportunities for advancement because of the deterioration of interpersonal relationships at work. Because women of color, particularly black and Latina women, are often in subordinate positions within organizations, there are a number of implications for stigmatized interpersonal relationships with white males in the workplace. For example, do women of color adopt different strategies for career development in the absence of traditional social support systems within organizations? Do these stigmatized interpersonal relationships extend to relations with white male coworkers? These issues as well as their implications should be addressed in future research.

Summary

Based on the scant amount of previous research that focuses on sexual harassment for women of color, I have examined three areas of research and suggested some issues and challenges within each of these three areas. These issues and challenges raise a number of questions for future research, three of which seem particularly critical. First, future research should examine whether women of color are differentially exposed to and affected by sexual harassment in the workplace compared with their white counterparts. This research must control for related factors such as individual attitudes (e.g., sex role ideology, gender group identity), economic vulnerability (e.g., social class), and organizational power (e.g., level or tenure within the organization).

Second, future research must examine whether sexual harassment for women of color is, indeed, inextricably tied to experiences with racial discrimination. Examining this question would most likely involve a series of longitudinal studies that identify women of color among different racial and ethnic groups who experience sexual harassment. Then, this research could determine whether these women are more prone to also experience racial harassment within their work environments.

Third, subsequent research needs to explore whether sexual harassment has a different range or severity of consequences for women of color compared with white women. Exploring the consequences of sexual harassment experiences is an essential step in developing adequate coping strategies for the psychological impact of sexual harassment. In addition, understanding how both actual harassment experiences and the fear of harassment may block access to resources and opportunities for women of color would be invaluable to help correct and direct career paths for these women.

Documenting this connection also would be invaluable for directing organizations as to whether separate or interconnected policies on sexual and racial harassment and discrimination are needed. One of the primary bases of the need for separate legal standards or organizational policies rests on the ability to demonstrate that a gap exists between experiences, perceptions, or consequences of sexual harassment between women of color and their white counterparts. Although I do not mean to advocate for a fragmented view of sexual harassment (in a sense, cutting the pie into smaller pieces) for each individual group of ethnic women that are present within a given work environment, the potential difference in perceptions, experiences, and consequences of sexual harassment for women of color must be acknowledged and incorporated into our legal, empirical, theoretical, and organizational strategies for addressing the issues of sexual harassment.

CHALLENGES AND FUTURE DIRECTIONS

It is reasonable to suggest that more research should be conducted in this area that includes women of color. The majority of existing research excludes women of color and a number of issues concerning sexual harassment continue to be shaped in the absence of a more inclusive perspective. Thus there are a number of ways in which our current thinking in the area of sexual harassment would be challenged by a greater infusion of research and theory that is more inclusive of women of color. I will briefly highlight three: defining a hostile work environment, outlining organizational policies, and clarifying legal standards in cases of sexual harassment.

Defining a Hostile Work Environment

One current issue that will be affected by a more inclusive perspective is the definition of the features of a hostile work environment. Karsten

(1994) speculated that women of color are more likely to be harassed than their white counterparts because stereotypes about these women may lead to conclusions that they would be less upset about being harassed, thus making them likely targets. These stereotypes include, for example, a view of African Americans, in general, as sexually driven and mentally deficient and of black women, in particular, as being permissive, hot-blooded, and hypersexual. Latina women are seen as passive and easily dominated by their men (Horowitz, 1983) and also as hypersexual (Williams, 1988). Asian women are also seen as passive and submissive (Osajima, 1988; Woo, 1985) and anxious to please their male partner sexually. Thus the content of racial stereotypes itself may exert a direct effect on the likelihood of being sexually harassed.

The dual contribution of sex-based stereotypes and race-based stereotypes can make women of color conspicuous within the workplace and thus make these women readily available targets for sexual harassment and both sex and race discrimination. Thus stereotypical thinking concerning women of color can change the meaning of a hostile work environment to include not only harassment based on sex but also harassment that is based on race. Thus the criteria for both legal and psychological definitions of a hostile work environment must acknowledge sexual harassment of women of color as a form of race discrimination as well as a form of sex discrimination in the workplace.

Environments that are skewed in terms of race or ethnicity may have the potential for being highly "racialized" work environments. Harassment can occur for women of color when skewed ethnic ratios enhance the salience of racial stereotypes for women of color, which often have a highly sexualized content. This suggests that perhaps, for women of color, the defining features of a hostile work environment should include factors that are both sexualized and racialized in nature, because each of these factors contributes to increasing their exposure to sexual harassment and discrimination.

Clarifying Legal Standards

Another implication of incorporating the notion of a "racialized" work environment into definitions of sexual harassment concerns the problem recently faced by the legal system in how best to determine what constitutes a "hostile work environment." To address this problem, a legal precedent was established in the case of *Ellison v. Brady* (1991) in the creation of a "reasonable woman" standard. This standard requires that in sexual harassment claims that involve a hostile environment, the objective standard should be what a "reasonable woman" defines as hostile. There is a great deal of debate over the implications of employing a sex-based standard in cases of sexual harassment (see O'Connor & Gutek, in press, for a discussion of these issues).

The significance of the reasonable woman standard for a more inclusive perspective concerns the use of other group-based standards in cases of harassment and discrimination. As O'Connor and Gutek (in press) suggest, the presence of a reasonable woman standard opens speculation on the need for a "reasonable black person" standard or a "reasonable standard for women of color" (see also the discussion by Chamallas, 1992). Although I am not advocating a further fragmentation of this legal standard, the implications of this index used in legal cases must be explored.

One such implication is that a single community standard to determine what constitutes a hostile environment treats women as one large, relatively homogeneous group and therefore is insufficient for explaining the perceptions and experiences for women of color. In addition, using one standard to determine what a "reasonable woman" would consider to be sexual harassment necessitates applying standards that were based on research focused exclusively on samples of white women to discuss the experiences of an ethnically diverse group of women.

Outlining Organizational Policies

A third area that would be altered by the inclusion of more research focusing on women of color is how organizational policies addressing sexual harassment are outlined and executed. Fitzgerald and Shullman (1993) identified a set of criteria for an effective prevention program for sexual harassment. Some of the elements included in their analysis are the presence of a strong policy statement that defines sexual harassment and indicates that sexual harassment will not be tolerated, an effective grievance procedure designed for reporting and investigating allegations of sexual misconduct, and an effective means of communicating and disseminating information.

One way in which this issue should be reshaped to include women of color would require evaluating the effectiveness of organizational policies that separate racial and sexual harassment compared with policies that incorporate these incidents into a single, global workplace policy statement. In a survey by the *Equal Opportunities Review* ("Racial

Harassment," 1993), 75 out of 166 organizations reported having explicit racial harassment policies, but only 17 companies indicated they have policies that distinguish racial and sexual harassment. However, of these 166 companies, 58 have general workplace policies that include both racial and sexual harassment. The basic question here is how to structure workplace policies that effectively address the issue of sexual harassment to include the experiences of women of color. Thus organizations must establish a sexual harassment policy that explicitly acknowledges the link between sexual and racial harassment when the victim is a woman of color. In addition, organizations should acknowledge the costs of ignoring a highly sexualized workplace and the connection between a sexualized and a racialized workplace for women of color, a growing segment of the future workforce.

CONCLUDING COMMENTS

This chapter began by asking one basic question: Why include a separate chapter on sexual harassment for women of color? After highlighting some of these issues and challenges, the case is clear that a complete understanding of the issue of sexual harassment must include some attention, both separate and equal, to the issue of sexual harassment for women of color. Unfortunately, given the scant amount of empirical evidence focused on women of color and sexual harassment, I have raised more questions for future research than I was able to resolve based on existing literature. Thus this area of research carries with it a great many opportunities as well as challenges. Given that the number of women of color in the workforce will increase substantially in the future, it seems clear that we can no longer afford to ignore the experiences of this important group. Further exclusion of this group from theory and research runs the risk of continuing with models and perspectives that, while triggered by the experiences of women of color, fail to explore, understand, and address these experiences.

REFERENCES

Bart, P. B., and O'Brien, P. H. (1984). Stopping rape: Effective avoidance strategies. *Signs, 10*(1), 83-101.

Bell, E. L. (1993). Myths, stereotypes, and realities of black women: A personal reflection. *Journal of Behavioral Applied Behavioral Science, 28,* 363-376.

Bell, E. L., Denton, C., & Nkomo, S. M. (1993). Women of color in management: Toward an inclusive analysis. In L. Larwood & B. Gutek (Eds.), *Women in management: Trends, issues and challenges* (Women and work, Vol. 4). Newbury Park, CA: Sage.

Benson, D. J., & Thomson, G. E. (1982). Sexual harassment on a university campus: The confluence of authority relations, sexual interest, and gender stratification. *Social Problems, 29,* 236-251.

Chamallas, M. (1992). Feminist constructions of objectivity: Multiple perspectives in sexual and racial harassment litigation. *Texas Journal of Women and the Law, 1,* 95-142.

Coles, F. S. (1986). Forced to quit: Sexual harassment complaints and agency response. *Sex Roles, 14,* 81-95.

Collins, P. H. (1990). *Black feminist thought: Knowledge, consciousness, and the politics of empowerment.* Boston: Irwin Hyman.

Davis, A. Y. (1978). Rape, racism and the capitalist setting. *Black Scholar, 9*(7), 24-30.

Davis, A. Y. (1981). *Women, race and class.* New York: Random House.

Defour, D. C. (1990). The interface of racism and sexism on college campuses. In M. A. Paludi (Ed.), *Ivory power: Sexual harassment on campus.* Albany: SUNY Press.

Ellison v. Brady, 924 F.2d 872 (9th Cir. 1991).

Equal Employment Opportunity Commission (1980). Guidelines on discrimination on the basis of sex (29 CFR Part 1604). *Federal Register, 45*(219).

Essed, P. (1992). Alternative knowledge sources in explanations for racist events. In M. L. McLaughlin, M. L. Cody, & S. J. Read (Eds.), *Explaining one's self to others: Reason-giving in a social context.* Hillsdale, NJ: Lawrence Erlbaum.

Fain, T. C., & Anderton, D. L. (1987). Organizational context and diffuse status. *Sex Roles, 17,* 291-311.

Fitzgerald, L. F., & Shullman, S. L. (1993). Sexual harassment: A research analysis and agenda for the 1990s. *Journal of Vocational Behavior, 42,* 5-27.

Gruber, J. E., & Bjorn, L. (1982). Blue-collar blues: The sexual harassment of women autoworkers. *Work and Occupations, 9,* 271-298.

Gruber, J. E., & Bjorn, L. (1986). Women's responses to sexual harassment: An analysis of sociocultural, organizational, and personal resource models. *Social Science Quarterly, 67,* 814-826.

Gutek, B. A. (1985). *Sex and the workplace: Impact of sexual behavior and harassment on women, men and organizations.* San Francisco: Jossey-Bass.

Gutek, B. A., Cohen, A. G., & Konrad, A. M. (1990). Predicting social-sexual behavior at work: A contact hypothesis. *Academy of Management Journal, 33,* 560-577.

Gutek, B. A., & Koss, M. P. (1993). Changed women and changed organizations: Consequences of and coping with sexual harassment. *Journal of Vocational Behavior, 42,* 28-48.

Hall, J. D. (1983). The mind that burns in each body: Women, rape and racial violence. In A. Snitow, C. Stansell, & S. Thompson (Eds.), *Powers of desire: The politics of sexuality* (pp. 329-349), New York: Monthly Review Press.

Hamilton, J. A., Alagna, S. W., King, L. S., & Lloyd, C. (1987). The emotional consequences of gender-based abuse in the workplace: New counseling programs for sex discrimination. *Women and Therapy, 6,* 155-182.

hooks, b. (1984). *Feminist theory: From margin to center.* Boston: South End.

Horowitz, R. (1983). *Honor and the American dream.* New Brunswick, NJ: Rutgers University Press.

Karsten, M. F. (1994). *Management and gender: Issues and attitudes.* Westport, CT: Praeger.

King, D. K. (1988). Multiple jeopardy, multiple consciousness: The context of black feminist ideology. *Signs, 14*(1), 42-72.

Lach, D. H., & Gwartney-Gibbs, P. A. (1993). Sociological perspectives on sexual harassment and workplace resolution. *Journal of Vocational Behavior, 42,* 102-115.

Lafontaine, E., & Tredeau, L. (1986). The frequency, sources, and correlates of sexual harassment among women in traditional male occupations. *Sex Roles, 15,* 433-443.

Lewis, D. K. (1975). The black family: Socialization and sex roles. *Phylon, 36*(3), 221-237.

MacKinnon, C. (1979). *The sexual harassment of working women.* New Haven, CT: Yale University Press.

Mansfield, P. K., Koch, P. B., Henderson, J., & Vicary, J. R. (1991). The job climate for women in traditionally male blue-collar occupations. *Sex Roles, 25,* 63-79.

McClelland, K., & Hunt, C. (1992). The perceived seriousness of racial harassment. *Social Problems, 39,* 92-107.

Meritor Savings Bank v. Vinson, 477 U.S. 57 (1986).

O'Connor, M., & Gutek, B. A. (in press). A psycholegal analysis of the reasonable woman standard. *Journal of Social Issues.*

Osajima, K. (1988). Asian Americans as the model minority: An analysis of the popular press in the 1960s and 1980s. In G. Y. Okihire, S. Hume, A. Hansen, & J. Liu (Eds.), *Reflections on shattered windows: Promises and prospects for Asian American studies.* Pullman: Washington State University Press.

Racial harassment at work. (1993). *Equal Opportunities Review, 49,* 17-23.

Sandroff, R. (1992, June). Sexual harassment: The inside story. *Working Woman,* pp. 47-51.

Segura, D. A. (1992). Chicanos in white color jobs: "You have to prove yourself more." *Sociological Perspectives, 35,* 163-182.

Thomas, D. A. (1989). Mentoring and irrationality: The role of racial taboos. *Human Resource Management, 28,* 279-290.

Thomas, D. A. (1990). The impact of race on managers' experiences of developmental relationships. *Journal of Organizational Behavior, 11,* 479-492.

Thomas, D. A. (1993). Racial dynamics in cross-race developmental relationships. *Administrative Science Quarterly, 38,* 169-194.

Thomas, D. A., & Clayton, P. A. (1989). The influence of race on career dynamics: Research and theory in minority career experiences. In M. Arthur, B. Hall, & B. Lawrence (Eds.), *Handbook on career theory* (pp. 133-157). Cambridge, MA: Cambridge University Press.

U.S. Merit Systems Protection Board. (1981). *Sexual harassment in the federal workplace: Is it a problem?* Washington, DC: Office of Merit Systems Review and Studies/Government Printing Office.

U.S. Merit Systems Protection Board (1988). *Sexual harassment in the federal government: An update.* Washington, DC: Office of Merit Systems Review and Studies/ Government Printing Office.

Williams, N. (1988). Role making among married Mexican American women: Issues of class and ethnicity. *Journal of Applied Behavioral Science, 24*(2), 203-217.

Woo, D. (1985). The socioeconomic status of Asian American women in the labor force: An alternative view. *Sociological Perspectives, 28,* 307-338.

4

Men's Misperceptions of Women's Interpersonal Behaviors and Sexual Harassment

FRANK E. SAAL

This chapter describes a series of studies designed to investigate the hypothesis that men who tend to misperceive women's friendly, outgoing behavior as a sign of sexual interest or availability are more likely to endorse and ultimately engage in sexual harassment of women. With minor exceptions, the data reported do *not* support this hypothesis. Whether male subjects responded to statements that reflect callous attitudes and sexually aggressive behavior toward women, or reacted to videotaped or written portrayals of other men engaging in behaviors that might be construed as sexual harassment, the men in these studies who were more prone to misperceiving women's friendly behaviors as "sexy" were generally *not* more likely to respond or react in ways that reflected tolerance for or endorsement of men who sexually harass women. Theoretical and practical implications of these findings for advancing our understanding and facilitating the elimination of sexual harassment are discussed.

Recent research supplemented by stories in the popular mass media indicate that sexual harassment of women by men is a pandemic problem that transcends geographic boundaries and organizational types, and that it is extremely costly at both individual and organizational levels. Unfortunately, we know a lot less about the individual, interpersonal, and situational factors that facilitate or precipitate men's sexual harassment of women in organizational settings. This relative dearth of information about the causes of sexual harassment becomes apparent when we take a look at the models or theories currently available to help us explain these behaviors.

A review of the theoretical literature reveals three rather different kinds of explanations, one of which has commanded very little respect and stimulated even less empirical research support. This is the so-called Biological or Natural Model of Sexual Harassment, which stipulates that men are naturally attracted to women and have a stronger sex drive than women. Sexual harassment ostensibly occurs when men lose or abdicate control over their stronger sex drive in an organizational setting (Tangri, Burt, & Johnson, 1982). Fortunately, two other explanatory approaches have generated a great deal more interest as well as more encouraging research data.

One of these focuses on the unequal distribution of power among women and men. Tangri et al. (1982) described two variations of this approach: the Organizational Model and the Sociocultural Model, which focus, respectively, on the organizational and sociocultural contexts in which men and women work and live. The Organizational Model attributes sexual harassment to differential levels of power typically associated with traditionally "male" (e.g., manager) and traditionally "female" (e.g., secretary) positions in organizational hierarchies, and to the social norms and climates that permeate organizations. Somewhat broader in scope, the Sociocultural Model suggests that sexual harassment of women by men is best understood as a mechanism by which existing disparities in these two groups' access to social and economic power and status are maintained throughout a society. Each of these models views sexual harassment primarily as an expression of men's power and dominance over women, and each received some support when Tangri et al. reanalyzed data collected during the U.S. Merit Systems Protection Board (1981) study.

The third perspective bears some resemblance to the Organizational Model in that it highlights the numerical ratios of women to men in particular jobs, occupations, and organizational settings. Known as the Sex Role Spillover Model (Gutek, 1985; Gutek & Morasch, 1982), its basic premise is that gender-based expectations about behavior carry over into the workplace, which is deemed far more likely to occur whenever the ratio of women to men in a specific context is seriously skewed in either direction. When women drastically outnumber men (e.g., nurses, clerical workers), the job itself assumes feminine sex role characteristics (e.g., helpful, nurturing) and men tend to treat all female incumbents as women rather than as employees. When women constitute a very small minority (e.g., construction workers, upper-level managers), their sex is such a salient characteristic that, once again, their male colleagues tend to see them as women rather than as fellow workers. These unbalanced ratios are thought to facilitate sexual harassment because one very important component of the traditional female sex role is to be sexually attractive and at least potentially available to men. Gutek's (1985) telephone survey of Los Angeles County residents provided encouraging support for the Sex Role Spillover Model.

Of interest, and somewhat surprising, none of these models addresses the possibility that at least some instances of sexual harassment may result from men's misperceptions of women's behaviors and intentions. I suspect that very few heterosexual men have been spared the embarrassment of misreading a woman's behavior in a social setting and responding to her based on that misperception, only to learn that she hadn't the slightest interest in exploring or pursuing a more intimate personal relationship. Similarly, many women relate anecdotes suggesting that they too have experienced awkward situations when their expressions of interest and friendliness were misconstrued by men as signs of sexual interest or availability. When these embarrassing and awkward encounters take place in organizational settings, might not the men's misguided responses be interpreted as examples of sexual harassment? Data collected during the past decade leave little doubt that when men and women observe interpersonal exchanges between other men and women, they don't always see the same things. Men tend to report observing greater levels of sexuality in women's (and, to a lesser extent, other men's) everyday, social behaviors than do women, who are more likely to see friendliness and sincerity in other women's (as well as their own) behaviors. These sex differences emerge when social encounters are viewed firsthand, or when interpersonal interactions are portrayed on videotape, and they tend to generalize across a variety of social and organizational settings including the workplace, academia, and purely social settings (Abbey, 1982, 1987; Abbey & Melby, 1986; Johnson, Stockdale, & Saal, 1991; Saal, Johnson, & Weber, 1989; Shotland & Craig, 1988).

Despite these reliable group differences, all men are *not* alike. Variance in the measures of interpersonal perceptions reported in the studies listed above indicates that some men are more inclined than others to see sexiness instead of friendliness in women's social behaviors. Based on these indices of dispersion, Saal et al. (1989) and Johnson et al. (1991) hypothesized that those men who are more inclined to misperceive women's friendly, outgoing behaviors as signals of sexual interest or availability might be more apt to respond in ways that women could construe as sexual harassment. Such responses might include persistent invitations to socialize outside the workplace, suggestive remarks about clothing or other aspects of physical appearance, intimate questions, or sexual propositions (Stockdale, 1993). Empirical support for this rather intuitive chain of hypothetical events would add a new dimension to available theories and models of sexual harassment based on power differences and skewed ratios of women and men in jobs, occupations, and work/school settings. On the other hand, failure to generate such empirical support would undermine the arguments of those who claim that many (and perhaps most) instances of so-called sexual harassment represent nothing more than honest, innocent misunderstandings between men and women.

This chapter describes a series of studies designed to address the hypothesis that men who sexually harass women often do so in response to their misperceptions of the women's behavior and intentions. Because direct assessment of actual sexual harassment behaviors entails profound ethical, pragmatic, and psychometric problems, we were content to examine surrogate measures of these behaviors. Some of this research therefore explored relationships between men's misperceptions of women's friendliness as sexiness and samples of self-reported behaviors or characteristics that might render those men more likely to tolerate or even endorse sexually harassing behaviors. Other studies examined men's reactions to videotaped or written scenarios that depicted various forms of sexual harassment. In each case, we inferred men's proclivities to engage in sexually harassing behaviors themselves from these surrogate measures. The validity of our conclusions therefore depends on the extent to which those inferences are warranted.

MEN'S MISPERCEPTIONS

The same basic methodology for assessing men's misperceptions of women's friendly behaviors as sexy was used in each of the studies described in this chapter. Following procedures developed by Abbey

(1982) and modified by Saal et al. (1989), male subjects viewed one of three alternate videotapes. Two of these portrayed a female college student meeting with a male professor, asking him for an extension of his deadline for turning in term papers. These two videos were identical except for the final few moments of the conversation. At this time, the professor in one of the videos (hereafter referred to as the "nonsuggestive" tape) offers to lend a book to the student that might help her with the term paper project. The professor in the other video (hereafter referred to as the "suggestive" tape) concludes the interview by inviting the student to return to his office later that evening so that they might discuss her term paper in more detail in quieter surroundings. A third videotape used to gauge men's misperceptions of women's behaviors (hereafter referred to as the "department store" tape) portrayed a male assistant manager orienting a recently hired female cashier in a discount department store. Each of these three videotapes depicted more or less normal, pedestrian exchanges between a man and a woman in either an academic or an employment setting. The actors portrayed friendly, outgoing people. Except for the final seconds of the "suggestive" student-professor exchange, they said or did nothing that could be construed as sexually suggestive or inappropriate. Each videotape ran for approximately 10 minutes.

The actual purpose of these studies was disguised to make it less likely that the men would respond in socially desirable ways. Subjects who viewed either the suggestive or the nonsuggestive term paper video were (mis)informed that the study was intended to investigate the effects of nonverbal behaviors such as smiles and gestures on face-to-face communication. Those who viewed the department store tape were led to believe that their reactions to it would be considered by actual retailers who were contemplating use of the video for training purposes. Of course, all subjects in each study were thoroughly debriefed immediately following data collection.

After viewing one of the three videotapes, subjects in each study responded to a short questionnaire that included one page of distractor items addressing the alleged purpose of the research (i.e., effects of nonverbal forms of communication or suitability of a training device) and 14 semantic-differential scales tapping their perceptions of how the female (and male) actors in the video were trying to behave: cheerful, friendly, assertive, flirtatious, considerate, warm, enthusiastic, likable, seductive, intelligent, attractive, sexy, sincere, and promiscuous. Each of the following studies, of course, then asked subjects to provide one or more indices of personal characteristics or reactions to verbal or visual stimuli. The crucial analyses in each study examined the relationships between these characteristics or reactions and subjects' tendencies to describe either the female student or the female cashier as flirtatious, seductive, promiscuous, or sexy.

MISPERCEPTIONS AND SEXUAL HARASSMENT

Hypermasculinity and Sexually Aggressive Behavior

Parkinson (1989) investigated the hypothesis that men who misperceive women's friendliness as sexiness might be more likely to reveal somewhat callous attitudes and report engaging in sexually aggressive behaviors toward women. She obtained misperception data from 130 male and 144 female undergraduate students who viewed either the "nonsuggestive" or the "suggestive" student-professor (term paper) videotape and then responded to the 14 semantic-differential items. She then asked the male subjects to respond to Mosher and Sirkin's (1984) Hypermasculinity Scale and to a modified version of Mosher and Anderson's (1986) Aggressive Sexual Behavior Inventory. Men with high scores on the Hypermasculinity Scale display a lack of sexual sensitivity toward women, associate violence with "manly" qualities, and view danger as exciting. Men with high scores on the Aggressive Sexual Behavior Inventory claim to have engaged more frequently in various forms of sexual aggression such as getting a woman drunk or being verbally or physically abusive so as to have sex. (Measuring instruments, scales, and the results of data analyses for all studies reported in this chapter are available from the author.) Parkinson's study was based on the assumption that hypermasculine, sexually aggressive men are more likely to engage in sexually harassing behaviors. Because the possibility exists that some men may bias their responses on these two questionnaires in socially desirable directions (e.g., underreporting frequencies of socially unacceptable behaviors), male subjects were also asked to complete the Marlowe-Crowne Social Desirability Scale (Crowne & Marlowe, 1964).

Multivariate comparisons of male and female subjects' perceptions of how the female student was trying to behave when requesting a term paper deadline extension from her professor revealed the expected sex-of-subject effect. Men saw the female student in either the suggestive or the nonsuggestive videotape as trying to be more flirtatious, more promiscuous, more seductive, and more sexy (as well as more attractive) than did women.

Pearson product-moment correlation coefficients describing linear relationships between male subjects' misperceptions of the female student's friendly behavior toward her professor as sexy and their responses on the Hypermasculinity Scale and the Aggressive Sexual Behavior Inventory were almost uniformly nonsignificant. That is, men who saw the female student as trying to be more flirtatious, more seductive, and more sexy described themselves neither as particularly hypermasculine nor as more inclined to engage in sexually aggressive behaviors. Because her subjects showed no apparent tendencies to distort their responses in socially acceptable ways (Crowne & Marlowe, 1964; O'Grady, 1988; Tanaka-Matsumi & Kameoka, 1986), Parkinson (1989) concluded that men who misperceive women's friendliness as sexiness are not more likely to see violence and danger as manly or exciting, or to be insensitive or sexually aggressive toward women. If these latter characteristics do, in fact, render men more likely to engage in sexual harassment behaviors, these data suggest that misperceiving women's friendliness as a sign of sexual interest or availability is not associated with sexual harassment.

Reactions to Sexual Harassment

Halvorson (1993) took a more direct approach by investigating the hypothesis that men who misperceive women's friendliness as sexiness might be more likely to tolerate or even endorse sexually harassing behavior on the part of other men. His study relied on the assumption that men who tolerate or endorse other men who sexually harass women are more likely to engage in sexually harassing behaviors themselves. He obtained misperception data from 83 men and 73 women who were employed either at a community college or at a computer software company in the Pacific Northwest. Under the guise of investigating nonverbal communication processes during emotional interpersonal exchanges, he asked them to view one of two videotapes that portrayed interactions between women and men that might be construed as sexual harassment. One of these portrayed a scene in a hotel room in which a male employee shares some personal family problems with a female colleague prior to their departure for a business dinner. He responds to her verbal expression of sympathy by throwing his arms around her in an apparent search for additional emotional support. She is clearly not comfortable with his response. The second tape depicted a far less ambiguous, more egregious situation in which a male foreman repeatedly subjects a female member of his work crew to blatant sexual comments and physical gestures. After viewing one of these tapes (selected randomly), male subjects responded to an 18-item questionnaire that assessed their reactions to the observed sexual harassment (and addressed the alleged purpose of the study, that is, nonverbal communication during emotional social exchanges).

To facilitate interpretation of subsequent analyses, the 14-item semantic-differential measure of misperceptions and the 11 items from the questionnaire that tapped subjects' reactions to observed sexual harassment were subjected to separate principal components analyses. The 14-item index of misperceptions yielded two interpretable components that explained 26.5% and 22.1% of the total variance of that measure (prior to a VARIMAX rotation that further improved their interpretability). Based on the specific items with relatively large loadings on each component, these were labeled Personal Attractiveness (high loadings on perceived likableness, sincerity, friendliness, warmth, considerateness, and so on) and Sexual Attractiveness (high loadings on perceived sexiness, seductiveness, flirtatiousness, promiscuity, and attractiveness), respectively. The 11 items that tapped subjects' reactions to sexual harassment yielded three interpretable components that explained 30.6%, 15.3%, and 11.1% of the total variance of those items (prior to a VARIMAX rotation that further improved their interpretability). Again, based on the specific items with relatively large loadings on each component, these were labeled Acceptability of Harassment (e.g., large loading on "His behavior is acceptable"), Impact of Harassment (e.g., large loading on "His behavior decreased morale"), and Pervasiveness of Harassment (e.g., large loading on "His behavior is common in organizations"), respectively.

Comparisons of male and female subjects' perceptions of how the recently hired female cashier was trying to behave during her male supervisor's orientation presentation (in the "department store" videotape) revealed the expected sex-of-subject effect on Sexual Attractiveness component scores but not on Personal Attractiveness component scores. Thus, although there was no disagreement regarding the female cashier's efforts to be warm, likable, sincere, and friendly, male subjects saw her trying to be significantly more sexy, seductive, flirtatious, promiscuous, and attractive than did female subjects.

Pearson product-moment correlation coefficients describing linear relationships between male subjects' misperceptions of the female cashier's friendly behavior toward her male supervisor as sexy and their reactions to observed sexual harassment revealed one "reaction" item that was significantly related (albeit modestly, $.20 < r < .35$) to perceived sexiness, flirtatiousness, seductiveness, and promiscuity ("His behavior decreased morale"). Only 15 of the remaining 51 correlations were sufficiently large to be statistically significant at $p < .05$ ($.19 < r < .35$), and only 7 of these reached significance at $p < .01$ ($.24 < r < .30$). Given the modest sizes and relative rarity of statistically significant correlations, these data offer (at best) only weak support for Halvorson's (1993) hypothesis. Men who saw more sexuality in the female cashier's behaviors were only occasionally and marginally more likely to tolerate or endorse another man's sexual harassment of a woman.

Nevertheless, to further explore empirical relationships that might support his basic hypothesis, Halvorson (1993) generated three multiple-regression equations using subjects' ages, genders, and scores on the Personal and Sexual Attractiveness components described above to predict the three components of their reactions to sexual harassment: Acceptability, Impact, and Pervasiveness. None of these predictors (i.e., age, gender, and so on), either individually or in linear combination, explained statistically significant proportions of variance in any of the three dependent variables (i.e., Acceptability of Harassment and so on). Because consistent differences between men's and women's perceptions of and reactions to sexual harassment have been reported in the empirical literature, the nonsignificance of gender as a predictor in these equations came as something of a surprise. Nevertheless, these findings further undermine the hypothesis that men's misperceptions of women's friendly behaviors as signs of sexual interest or availability are associated with tolerance or endorsement of other men's sexual harassment behaviors (or, by implication, the likelihood that they will engage in sexually harassing behaviors themselves).

Saal's (1990) study was similar to Halvorson's (1993) in its more direct approach to the hypothesis that men who misperceive women's friendliness as sexiness might be more likely to tolerate or endorse other men's sexually harassing behaviors toward women (and therefore might be more likely to engage in sexual harassment themselves). Misperception data were obtained from 108 male undergraduate students using the "nonsuggestive" student-professor (term paper) videotape. Rather than asking them to view additional videotapes (as in the Halvorson study), however, Saal then asked them to read 29 one- or two-sentence vignettes that described a variety of exchanges between women and men, each of which could be construed as sexual harassment. Three examples are listed here:

- A male supervisor asks a female employee personal questions about her sex life.
- A male executive and his female associate are planning a business trip, and he reserves only one hotel room.
- A manager tells his female secretary that she must sleep with him because it is his right—he pays her salary.

After reading each vignette, subjects used 7-point scales to respond to six questions designed to tap their reactions to the portrayed examples of sexual harassment. The following are examples of these questions: (a) How appropriate/inappropriate is this man's behavior? (b) How would you respond if you overheard/observed a male colleague behaving in this manner? (c) How likely is it that you might one day behave in a manner similar to the man in this scenario? Subjects were (mis)informed that this part of the research was designed to examine some of the implications of the dramatic influx of women into various work roles.

Pearson product-moment correlation coefficients describing linear relationships between these 108 male subjects' misperceptions of the female student's friendly behavior toward her male professor as sexy and their reactions to the 29 written descriptions of sexual harassment were calculated and examined. Of those 696 correlations (29 scenarios × 6 reaction questions per scenario × 4 perceptions: flirtatious, promiscuous, seductive, and sexy), only 133 (19%) were statistically significant at $p < .05$, and only 35 (5%) were statistically significant at $p < .01$. Given the danger of inflated experiment-wise alpha error rates when testing the significance of large numbers of correlation coefficients, these are not impressive numbers of statistically significant relationships. Further, most of these significant correlations were quite small ($.20 < r < .30$).

Nevertheless, two patterns within these statistically significant correlation coefficients suggest that dismissing them as Type I errors might be unwise. First, the algebraic signs of all 133 significant ($p < .05$) correlations were consistent with the hypothesis that men who perceive more sexuality in women's normal, everyday social interactions are more likely to tolerate or endorse other men's sexual harassment of women. That is, male subjects who saw more sexuality in the female student's behavior in the presence of her professor were (a) less likely to judge the behavior of the men portrayed in the written scenarios as inappropriate, (b) less likely to criticize those men, (c) less likely to be willing to testify in the women's defense, (d) more likely to be willing to testify in the men's defense, (e) less likely to be dissuaded from accepting a job offer from the company in which the harassment took place, and (f) more likely to indicate that they might engage in similar behaviors themselves. If these significant correlations were Type I errors, we would not expect them all to have algebraic signs consistent with the hypothesis of the study.

A second noteworthy pattern is that the 133 statistically significant ($p < .05$) correlations were not uniformly distributed across the four sexual (mis)perceptions of the female student's behaviors or across the six responses to each written scenario. For example, each of the four sexual (mis)perceptions contributed to 174 correlation coefficients (29 vignettes × 6 questions per vignette). Male subjects' perceptions of how "sexy" the student's behavior was yielded 39 significant correlations (22%), and their perceptions of how "promiscuous" her behavior was generated only 27 significant correlations (15%). More impressive differences emerged across subjects' responses to the six questions that followed each scenario, each of which contributed to 116 correlation coefficients (29 scenarios × 4 perceptions of sexuality). Subjects' opinions concerning the appropriateness of the men's behaviors described in the vignettes resulted in 43 statistically significant correlations (37%), but their beliefs that they would be dissuaded from accepting job offers after witnessing or hearing about such behaviors led to only 3 significant correlations (3%). Finally, if most or all of the 133 significant correlations were attributable to Type I errors, they should be distributed more or less evenly across the 29 vignettes, each of which generated 24 correlations (6 questions per vignette × 4 perceptions of sexuality). They were not. Vignettes that yielded higher percentages (in parentheses) of significant correlations included the following:

- An editor informs a female reporter that it is her job to make sure that he has a cup of coffee every morning. (42%)
- A manager tells his secretary that she should wear a dress, because if her legs are like the rest of her, she has nothing to hide. (38%)

- While at work, a woman is violently raped by her employer, who tells her not to tell anyone or she will be fired. (37%)
- A woman is employed in an office. Her boss threatens to fire her if she does not engage in sexual intercourse with him. (37%)
- A male manager asks a female worker what she plans to do during her vacation. She replies, "Spend time with my husband celebrating our first wedding anniversary." The manager replies, "Well, that won't take more than a few minutes!" (37%)

At the other extreme, several scenarios failed to generate any statistically significant correlations:

- A male employee compliments his female supervisor on how nicely she fills out her blouse.
- A manager calls his secretary "honey" in front of a group of people.
- A male manager says to a female sales clerk, "You look sexy today—where are we going tonight?"
- At a company picnic planned by a female employee, her male boss walks by and pats her on the back to "thank her for her help." In the process, he purposely "snaps" her bra.
- A female management trainee in an advertising firm is given an assignment to make a speech about her most exciting sexual experience.

Thus, although far from overwhelming, Saal's (1990) data are a bit more supportive of the basic hypothesis than Parkinson's (1989) or Halvorson's (1993). Men who (mis)perceived the female student's normal, outgoing behavior in the presence of her professor did respond to written sexual harassment vignettes in ways suggesting greater willingness to tolerate, endorse, and perhaps even engage in those forms of harassment than men who saw less sexuality in the female student's request for a term paper extension from her male professor. Saal's data are not, however, sufficiently compelling to negate Parkinson's and Halvorson's results. At best, these patterns of small but statistically significant correlations suggested that it might have been premature to abandon the central hypothesis that guided all these studies. With this thought in mind, we designed and conducted a final study that afforded an even more direct look at the empirical relationship between men's (mis)perceptions of women's everyday social exchanges and the likelihood that those men might engage in behaviors that constitute sexual harassment.

Likelihood to Sexually Harass

Perhaps the most direct approach to examining the hypothesis that men who misperceive women's friendly behaviors as sexual are more likely to engage in sexually harassing behaviors themselves was taken by Saal, Smalley, and Gruver (1993). They obtained misperception data from 88 male and 125 female undergraduate students after the students had viewed the same "department store" videotape used by Halvorson (1993). Male subjects then read each of the 10 scenarios included in Pryor's (1987) Likelihood to Sexually Harass Scale, and responded to the three questions that followed each scenario. Each of the 10 scenarios asks respondents to imagine themselves in a position where they could offer a very desirable work- or school-related outcome to a woman in return for sexual favors, with absolutely no danger of being discovered or punished. Although the specific content and wording of the three questions that followed each scenario varied with the content of the scenario, the generic gists of those questions are as follows:

1. Would you provide a special favor to an attractive woman?
2. Would you ask her for sexual favors in exchange for such a favor?
3. Would you invite her to join you for dinner so that you might discuss the favor?

Pryor (1987) generated evidence of his scale's validity for making inferences about men's tendencies to sexually harass women by comparing their scores on the Likelihood to Sexually Harass Scale with the extent to which they took advantage of a situation where some physical contact with a woman was appropriate (e.g., teaching her how to grip and swing a golf club). He found that men who scored high on his scale also tended to engage in physical contact during the golf lessons that was rated as more sexual in nature.

Unlike the results of other studies, comparisons of male and female subjects' mean perceptions of how sexually the recently hired female cashier in the "department store" videotape was trying to behave in the presence of her male supervisor revealed no statistically significant sex-of-subject differences when each perception was examined individually (i.e., flirtatious? seductive? promiscuous? sexy?). Comparisons of composites (i.e., sums) of these four individual perceptions, however, did yield the typical significant ($p = .03$) sex-of-subject difference. Male subjects saw the female cashier as trying to be more sexual than did female subjects.

Pearson product-moment correlation coefficients describing linear relationships between these 88 male subjects' misperceptions of the female cashier's friendly behavior toward her male supervisor as sexy and their responses to the Likelihood to Sexually Harass items were calculated and examined. Of those 150 correlations (10 scenarios × 3 questions per scenario × 5 perceptions: flirtatious, seductive, promiscuous, sexy, and a composite of these), only 22 (15%) were statistically significant ($p < .05$). This is an even smaller percentage than the 19% reported by Saal (1990), and, like Saal's correlations, all of these are quite small ($.12 < r < .30$).

Other similarities between these data and those reported by Saal (1990) deserve a brief comment, however. Like Saal's, these statistically significant correlations did not appear to be randomly or uniformly distributed across the four (mis)perceptions of the female cashier's behavior during the conversation with her male supervisor, across the 10 Likelihood to Sexually Harass Scale scenarios, or across the three questions that followed each scenario. Of interest, the most provocative of the three types of questions (Would you ask a woman for sexual favors in return for a special work- or school-related outcome?) generated as many statistically significant correlations as the other two types of questions combined. Unlike the data described by Saal, however, the algebraic signs associated with these 22 significant correlations were not all in the predicted direction. In fact, 5 of the 6 correlations associated with the first type of question (Would you provide a special favor to an attractive woman?) and 9 of the 11 correlations associated with the second, most provocative question (see above) had algebraic signs opposite to those predicted by the basic hypothesis of the study. That is, male subjects who saw more sexuality in the female cashier's everyday behavior were less inclined to say that they would provide a special favor to an attractive woman or that they would ask a woman for sexual favors in return for such a special outcome. Only the third type of question (Would you ask a woman to dinner so that you might discuss such a favor?) consistently yielded correlations (5 out of 5) with the predicted algebraic sign. Thus, because most of our 22 statistically significant correlations contradict the central hypothesis that guided the study, our assertion that they should not be dismissed as Type I errors is not particularly gratifying.

GENERAL DISCUSSION AND CONCLUSIONS

The series of studies described in this chapter addressed the intuitively appealing hypothesis that some of the less egregious examples of sexual harassment of women in organizational environments are attributable to men's misperceptions of women's friendly, outgoing behaviors as signals of sexual interest or availability, and to those males' subsequent responses (e.g., intimate questions or invitations, suggestive looks, physical contact) based on their misperceptions. Considered all together, these studies failed to yield any notable support for this very plausible hypothesis. Although there still exists a possibility that the hypothesis has merit, and that these studies simply failed to test it adequately, my interpretation of the data leads me to believe that it just isn't true. What are the implications of "accepting the null hypothesis" that there is no viable relationship between men's misperceptions and the likelihood that they will tolerate, endorse, or ultimately engage in sexual harassment behaviors themselves?

From one perspective, especially that of many men, these are disappointing results. After all, if we could appeal to honest misperceptions to explain our unacceptable social-sexual behaviors in organizational settings ("Everyone makes mistakes!"), we might thereby render sexual harassment less premeditated and therefore less deserving of criticism and punishment. In a sense, such an explanation would let many of us "off the hook" both in our own minds and in the eyes of our organizations. But the series of studies described above suggest that this is a specious argument. Is there any "good news"? I think there is.

If we acknowledge that there is, in fact, nothing "sexy" about sexual harassment (just as we now accept the fact that there is nothing sexual about rape—that rape is a crime of violence rather than an expression of sexuality), then men can rest a bit more easily about the possibility that they might misperceive a female colleague's expressions of friendship as signs of sexual interest. After all, there is no convincing evidence that such misperceptions lead to sexual harassment. Similarly, women who are victimized by sexual harassment can at least take some solace in the realization that they are not to blame for their plight, that there is no justifiable reason for them to feel guilty in the belief that men's sexually harassing behaviors are nothing more than "honest mistakes" prompted by their (the women's) friendly, outgoing behaviors. Further, women who are victimized by sexual harassment can feel free to confront their tormentors and demand that the offensive behaviors stop, without fear that they (the women) will be offending well-intentioned (albeit misperceiving) men.

Other pragmatic and theoretical advantages accrue to dispelling the notion that sexual harassment is attributable to men's misperceptions of women's friendly behaviors as signs of sexual interest or availability. For example, although the reliable sex difference between men's and women's perceptions of the friendly versus "sexy" intentions of others cannot be denied and should not be ignored, there is no apparent reason to predicate organizational training seminars or orientation sessions intended to reduce or eliminate sexual harassment on the premise that men's misperceptions contribute to such harassment. Further, dismissal of a "misperception model" of sexual harassment tends to increase the scientific value and importance of the two types of models that have survived empirical investigation—power-based models such as the Organizational and Sociocultural Models (Tangri et al., 1982) and Gutek's Sex Role Spillover Model (Gutek, 1985; Gutek & Morasch, 1982). Future empirical efforts might best be directed at further clarifying and elaborating these models.

In the process of refuting a misperception-based explanation of sexual harassment, these studies represent a small step in the direction of such clarification and elaboration. Recall that Gutek's Sex Role Spillover model suggests that men tend to treat female employees more as women than as coworkers, either because their token status in male-dominated occupations highlights their femininity, or because their female-dominated occupation itself becomes "feminized." If we accept the idea that sexual harassment is not associated with men's perceptions of "sexiness" in women's behavior, the data reported in this chapter suggest that the increased frequencies of sexual harassment associated with greater levels of perceived femininity (prompted by skewed sex ratios, according to Gutek's model) are probably not mediated by increases in men's perceptions of their female coworkers' sexuality. We should, therefore, turn instead to other possible components of "femininity" as we search for a mediating mechanism. Given the current state of the empirical literature, the most likely candidate would seem to be powerlessness. Thus the studies reported here suggest that men who sexually harass women when sex ratios are skewed do so not because they see the women as more "sexy" but because they perceive women in either male- or female-dominated occupations to be less powerful

This hypothesis should be relatively easy to investigate. If substantiated, it would go a long way toward integrating the two remaining viable explanations of men's sexual harassment of women in organizations: unequal distributions of power and sex role spillover.

REFERENCES

Abbey, A. (1982). Sex differences in attributions for friendly behavior: Do males misperceive females' friendliness? *Journal of Personality and Social Psychology, 32,* 830-838.

Abbey, A. (1987). Misperceptions of friendly behavior as sexual interest: A survey of naturally occurring incidents. *Psychology of Women Quarterly, 11,* 173-194.

Abbey, A., & Melby, C. (1986). The effects of nonverbal cues on gender differences in perceptions of sexual intent. *Sex Roles, 15,* 283-298.

Crowne, D., & Marlowe, D. (1964). *The approval motive.* New York: John Wiley.

Gutek, B. A. (1985). *Sex and the workplace.* San Francisco: Jossey-Bass.

Gutek, B. A., & Morasch, B. (1982). Sex ratios, sex role spillover, and sexual harassment of women at work. *Journal of Social Issues, 38,* 55-74.

Halvorson, J. V. (1993). *Men's perceptions of women's behavior and endorsement of sexual harassment.* Unpublished master's thesis, Kansas State University, Manhattan, KS.

Johnson, C. B., Stockdale, M. S., & Saal, F. E. (1991). Persistence of men's misperceptions of friendly cues across a variety of interpersonal encounters. *Psychology of Women Quarterly, 15,* 463-475.

Mosher, D. L., & Anderson, R. D. (1986). Macho personality, sexual aggression, and reactions to guided imagery of realistic rape. *Journal of Research in Personality, 20,* 77-94.

Mosher, D. L., & Sirkin, M. (1984). Measuring a macho personality constellation. *Journal of Research in Personality, 18,* 150-163.

O'Grady, K. E. (1988). The Marlowe-Crowne & Edwards Social Desirability Scales: A psychometric perspective. *Multivariate Behavioral Research, 23,* 87-101.

Parkinson, A. E. (1989). *The relationship between sexual aggressiveness, hypermasculinity, and misperceptions of women's friendliness.* Unpublished master's thesis, Kansas State University, Manhattan, KS.

Pryor, J. B. (1987). Sexual harassment proclivities in men. *Sex Roles, 17,* 269-290.

Saal, F. E. (1990). Sexual harassment in organizations. In K. R. Murphy & F. E. Saal (Eds.), *Psychology in organizations: Integrating science and practice* (pp. 217-239). Hillsdale, NJ: Lawrence Erlbaum.

Saal, F. E., Johnson, C. B., & Weber, N. (1989). Friendly or sexy? It may depend on whom you ask. *Psychology of Women Quarterly, 13,* 263-276.

Saal, F. E., Smalley, K., & Gruver, A. (1993). *An attempt to predict sexually harassing behavior.* Unpublished manuscript.

Shotland, R. L., & Craig, J. M. (1988). Can men and women differentiate between friendly and sexually interested behavior? *Social Psychology Quarterly, 51,* 66-73.

Stockdale, M. S. (1993). The role of sexual misperceptions of women's friendliness in an emerging theory of sexual harassment. *Journal of Vocational Behavior, 42,* 84-101.

Tanaka-Matsumi, J., & Kameoka, V. A. (1986). Reliabilities and concurrent validities of popular self-report measures of depression, anxiety, and social desirability. *Journal of Consulting and Clinical Psychology, 54,* 328-333.

Tangri, S. S., Burt, M. R., & Johnson, L. B. (1982). Sexual harassment at work: Three explanatory models. *Journal of Social Issues, 38,* 33-53.

U.S. Merit Systems Protection Board. (1981). *Sexual harassment in the federal workplace: Is it a problem?* Washington, DC: Office of Merit Systems Review and Studies/Government Printing Office.

5

The Implications of U.S. Supreme Court and Circuit Court Decisions for Hostile Environment Sexual Harassment Cases

RAMONA L. PAETZOLD
ANNE M. O'LEARY-KELLY

This chapter explores current legal theory regarding hostile environment sexual harassment. We begin with a discussion of the first hostile environment case heard by the U.S. Supreme Court (*Meritor Savings Bank v. Vinson*). Following this, we discuss both legal theory and factual information (types of conduct, harassers, and plaintiffs) on cases that have been heard by U.S. federal appeals courts since *Vinson*. Finally, we discuss the second, recent Supreme Court case, *Harris v. Forklift Systems, Inc.*, and its potential implications for future hostile environment sexual harassment cases.

The sexual harassment of employees in the workplace is a phenomenon that currently is receiving a great deal of attention in various spheres of American society. The general public has become focused on this issue because of recent and highly publicized allegations of harassment against prominent government figures (Paetzold & O'Leary-Kelly,

1994). For example, in recent years, a Supreme Court justice candidate, several prominent politicians, and multiple U.S. Navy officers involved in the Tailhook incident have been named as harassers. Perhaps driven by the public discussions that followed these allegations, there also appears to be increased research attention to this issue by social scientists. In addition, it is clear that the legal system is increasingly attending to the issue of sexual harassment, as evidenced by an increase in the number of sexual harassment complaints (for example, sexual harassment charges filed with the EEOC increased by 112% from 1989 to 1993; "Study Finds," 1994).

In their consideration of sexual harassment, the courts have clearly identified two types: quid pro quo harassment and hostile environment harassment. The former requires sexual compliance in exchange for the retention of some current job opportunity or the possibility of some future opportunity. The latter involves a situation in which sexual conduct has the purpose or effect of unreasonably interfering with an individual's work performance or creating an intimidating, hostile, or offensive working environment. The courts have adopted different legal frameworks for dealing with each of these types of harassment. The purpose of this chapter is to summarize and discuss implications of the legal theory that has evolved around hostile environment sexual harassment. An understanding of the legal rationale used in these cases is critical to both employers and potential plaintiffs, particularly as damage awards continue to increase (total awards to plaintiffs increased by 98% from 1992 to 1993; "Study Finds," 1994). We discuss hostile environment rather than quid pro quo harassment because the former tends to be more ambiguous and difficult for a plaintiff to establish. For example, although quid pro quo harassment involves a harasser with organizational power over the target of harassment, hostile environment cases may involve either harassers with greater organizational power (e.g., a supervisor), harassers with relatively equal power (e.g., coworkers, customers, clients), or even harassers who have less organizational power than the plaintiff (e.g., a subordinate). Therefore, hostile environment cases require fact finders (judges and juries) to recognize that sexual harassment can occur in the absence of apparent organizational power differentials that favor the harasser. Similarly, hostile environment cases do not involve strict liability for the employer, as do quid pro quo cases, making the establishment of employer liability a more difficult issue for plaintiffs. That is, not only must plaintiffs establish that they were harassed, they must establish that their employer should be held liable for the harassment they suffered. In addition, although most fact finders easily recognize forced sexual compliance (i.e., quid pro quo cases) as harassing conduct, hostile environment cases may involve conduct that is considered offensive by some individuals but not by others. Because hostile environment cases involve this additional ambiguity, a consideration of the legal definition of hostile environment sexual harassment is especially important.

This is a particularly useful time to review legal issues related to hostile environment harassment because the legal framework necessary to establish this type of harassment has become quite clear in recent years. The first Supreme Court case addressing this issue, *Meritor Savings Bank v. Vinson* (1986), sanctioned the legal theory of hostile environment harassment that previously had been emerging in the U.S. Court of Appeals. Since that case, the appellate courts have further refined and interpreted this theory. Recently, the Supreme Court heard a second case addressing hostile environment harassment, *Harris v. Forklift Systems, Inc.* (1993). Although this case did not change the framework for establishing hostile environment harassment, it did alter the conceptualization of two of the elements of this framework (unwelcomeness and severity/pervasiveness, as discussed below).

Our discussion of legal issues related to hostile environment harassment tracks this historical progression. We begin with a description of the *Meritor Savings Bank v. Vinson* case. We then discuss hostile environment harassment cases brought under Title VII that have been heard by the federal courts of appeal since the *Meritor Savings Bank* case and prior to *Harris*. Specifically, we focus on providing both factual and legal information regarding these cases. It should be noted that only appellate- and not trial-level cases are discussed.[1] An understanding of legal theory is best obtained by a consideration of federal appeals court decisions because it is in them that issues of law (versus issues of fact) are determined. Following our discussion of *Meritor Savings Bank* and the appellate cases, we will discuss the recent Supreme Court case *Harris v. Forklift Systems, Inc.* Facts related to the case itself, as well as the implications of the Court's decision for future hostile environment sexual harassment cases, will be discussed.

MERITOR SAVINGS BANK V. VINSON (1986)

Michelle Vinson was hired by Sidney Taylor, a vice president for Meritor Savings Bank, in 1974. She worked her way up from teller to assistant branch manager, a pattern of advancement that the court recognized as indisputably due to merit. During the four years of her employment, Vinson alleged, Taylor frequently requested sexual relations with her. Although at first refusing, she stated that she eventually agreed out of fear of losing her job. Vinson suggested that Taylor's behavior during this time period included fondling her in front of other employees, following her into the women's rest room, exposing himself to her, having intercourse with her on 40-50 occasions, and raping her several times. Because of her reported fear of Taylor, Vinson did not use the bank's complaint procedure to make her employer aware of his conduct. In its decision in this case, the U.S. Supreme Court held that hostile environment sexual harassment represents sex discrimination and is actionable under Title VII of the Civil Rights Act.

Meritor Savings Bank argued against Vinson on several counts. It suggested that because the losses suffered by Vinson were psychological, not tangible and of "an economic character" (p. 2404), they were not covered by Title VII. The Supreme Court rejected this argument, stating that an economic loss is not required to establish hostile environment sexual harassment under Title VII.

The Court also rejected "voluntariness" as a defense against Vinson's sexual harassment charges. Specifically, it suggested that the central issue in a hostile environment case involves determining whether the sexual conduct was unwelcome, not whether the target voluntarily participated. The Court clearly established that the gravamen, or substance, of any sexual harassment claim is that the alleged behavior was unwelcome.

In *Meritor Savings Bank*, the Court also addressed the issue of employer liability. Prior to this case, varying standards for employer liability in hostile environment cases were being used by the courts of appeal (Paetzold & O'Leary-Kelly, 1994). Because quid pro quo sexual harassment cases involve strict liability for the employer (i.e., the employer is automatically liable for the harassment), some circuit courts extended strict liability to hostile environment cases, but other courts did not. Although the Supreme Court did not issue a definitive ruling on liability in *Meritor Savings Bank*, it did suggest that the plaintiff's failure to use an existing grievance policy did not insulate the employer from liability.

U.S. COURTS OF APPEAL CASES

This section reviews hostile environment sexual harassment cases brought under Title VII and heard by the federal appellate courts since

Meritor Savings Bank and through 1993. These cases were identified via a LEXIS search, with the following types of cases eliminated from further consideration: cases that addressed harassment issues based on a protected class other than sex, procedural cases (i.e., those that did not address substantive sexual harassment issues), and cases that involved the wrongful discharge claims of sexual harassers. This search resulted in 60 usable and published cases.

Two types of information about these cases are presented in the following sections. First, factual information is reviewed to provide context regarding the types of conduct, harassers, and plaintiffs involved in the cases. Second, the hostile environment legal theory that has evolved in the appeals courts is described. This section explains the elements necessary for a plaintiff to establish a case of hostile environment harassment.

Factual Information

Information on conduct. There was considerable variety in the sexually harassing conduct alleged by plaintiffs across the cases. Various schemes for classifying harassing conduct have been used in previous research; however, we found the framework of Terpstra and Cook (1985) to be the most concise. This classification system was used as a model, with additional categories added where needed (for example, an added category describing conduct that involved the use of pornography and/or obscene graffiti).

Specific information on the conduct alleged by the plaintiff was unavailable in five cases. Table 5.1 outlines the most frequent types of conduct alleged in the remaining 55 cases. The two most common types of harassment reported by plaintiffs were unwelcome, nonviolent physical contact (e.g., touching the plaintiff's hips, stroking the plaintiff's hair, leaning up against the plaintiff) and offensive language directed at the plaintiff (e.g., sexual comments regarding parts of the plaintiff's body, an offensive joke told to the plaintiff), both of which were alleged in over half of the cases. Many plaintiffs also reported that harassers sexually propositioned them (44% of the cases) or used language that was offensive but not specifically addressed to them (e.g., language derogatory to women in general; 29% of cases). Allegations regarding more violent behavior were also relatively common. In 22% of the cases, allegations of various degrees of sexual assault (e.g., fondling of breasts, rape) were involved. In addition, violent physical contact (contact that could cause physical harm such as being shoved, being dangled from a stairwell) was alleged in 18% of these cases. The use of plaintiff-specific graffiti or pornography (e.g., obscene graffiti naming the plaintiff or pornography shown specifically to the plaintiff) was also common (reported in 18% of cases). Allegations of repeated date requests (13%) and of nonspecific graffiti or pornography (e.g., generally obscene graffiti, pornography hanging in the workplace; 11% of cases) were somewhat less common.

Information on harassers. The harassing conduct was further examined in light of the position of the alleged harasser. In 73% of the cases, a harasser was the plaintiff's supervisor; in 42%, a harasser was a coworker. In 9% of the cases, the harasser was unknown (e.g., pornographic material left in the plaintiff's mailbox by an unknown person). These percentages do not sum to 100% because some cases involved more than one alleged harasser.

Table 5.1 also outlines the type of conduct reported when the alleged harasser is a supervisor and when the alleged harasser is a coworker. As this table shows, there are some differences between cases involving supervisors and coworkers. In these allegations, coworkers were clearly more likely than supervisors to use plaintiff-specific offensive language. In addition, coworkers were named in allegations of nonspecific graffiti/pornography and violent physical contact more frequently than were supervisors. Supervisors, on the other hand, were more likely to be involved in allegations of sexual propositioning, nonviolent physical contact, and sexual assault. There were also some interesting similarities in the conduct alleged in these cases. Supervisors and coworkers appeared to be relatively equally named in reports of nonspecific offensive language and plaintiff-specific graffiti/pornography.

Information on plaintiffs. In all but one of the cases reviewed here, the plaintiff was female. Because women were overwhelmingly the targets of harassment, the plaintiff will hereafter be referred to as female.

Based upon information provided in the cases, plaintiffs were placed into one of the following occupational categories: (a) professional (e.g., attorney, nurse, manager, police officer), (b) nonprofessional (e.g., factory worker, security guard, hotel maid, retail clerk), and (c) clerical (e.g., secretary, receptionist). Five of the cases provided insufficient information for classifying occupational status. Of the plaintiffs who

Table 5.1. Types of Conduct Alleged in Court Cases

Conduct	*Overall*[a] *(N = 55)*	*Supervisor Is Harasser (N = 40)*	*Coworker Is Harasser (N = 23)*
Date request	13% (7)[b]	15% (6)	9% (2)
Offensive language			
plaintiff specific	56% (31)	48% (19)	70% (16)
nonspecific	29% (16)	23% (9)	22% (5)
Graffiti/pornography			
plaintiff specific	18% (10)	10% (4)	13% (3)
nonspecific	11% (6)	3% (1)	13% (3)
Sexual propositions	44% (24)	50% (20)	17% (4)
Physical contact			
nonviolent	58% (32)	53% (21)	26% (6)
violent	18% (10)	10% (4)	22% (5)
Sexual assault	22% (12)	25% (10)	9% (2)

a. Percentages do not sum to 100% because of allegations of multiple types of behavior within cases.
b. Number in parentheses indicates the number of cases in the category.

could be classified, the largest percentage (46%) worked in nonprofessional positions, followed by professional (35%) and clerical (19%).

It is informative to consider plaintiff occupation in conjunction with the type of harassing conduct that was alleged (Table 5.2 outlines the types of conduct reported within each of the three occupational categories). The most common types of sexually harassing conduct reported by both nonprofessional and professional women were plaintiff-specific offensive language and nonviolent physical contact. On the other hand, plaintiffs holding clerical positions most frequently complained of nonviolent physical contact and sexual assault. It is interesting to note that the vast majority of sexual assault allegations were brought by women in clerical positions.

Because the factual information reported above is based upon sexual harassment incidents that have proceeded through the court system, it is unclear whether this information is representative of all sexual harassment incidents. To gauge the degree of similarity between cases that

Table 5.2. Alleged Conduct by Plaintiff Occupational Status

Conduct	*Nonprofessional*[a] *(N = 25.5)*[b]	*Professional N = 19)*	*Clerical (N = 10.5)*
Date request	8% (2)[c]	11% (2)	19% (2)
Offensive language			
plaintiff specific	61% (15.5)	47% (9)	43% (4.5)
nonspecific	29% (7.5)	32% (6)	24% (2.5)
Graffiti/pornography			
plaintiff specific	16% (4)	16% (3)	0% (0)
nonspecific	8% (2)	21% (4)	0% (0)
Sexual propositions	37% (9.5)	32% (6)	43% (4.5)
Physical contact			
nonviolent	59% (15)	42% (8)	67% (7)
violent	24% (6)	16% (3)	10% (1)
Sexual assault	8% (2)	11% (2)	57% (6)

a. Percentages do not sum to 100% because of allegations of multiple types of behavior within cases.
b. *N*s that are not whole numbers reflect situations in which a case involves multiple plaintiffs of different occupational status.
c. Number in parentheses indicates the number of cases in the category.

progress through the court system and those that do not, we compared factual information from the cases with information available from a large-scale survey (U.S. Merit Systems Protection Board, 1988). In the Merit Systems Protection Board survey, more than 8,000 federal employees were asked to self-report information on their experiences with sexual harassment.

As might be expected for lawsuits surviving through trial and appeal, alleged conduct was more severe than conduct reported by female subjects in the survey. The most extreme example of this involved allegations of sexual assault. In the court cases, 22% of plaintiffs alleged sexual assault, whereas only .8% of the survey subjects reported sexual assault. In fact, the court cases showed higher percentages than the survey for all reported types of conduct except repeated date requests. In addition, the court cases reflected a higher percentage of supervisor as harasser allegations (73%) than did the self-report survey (31%).

Elements of a Prima Facie Case

Since the *Meritor Savings Bank* decision, U.S. Courts of Appeal have continued to develop the framework of hostile environment legal theory. Although different circuits may vary in their specific wordings, the general elements required are relatively well defined. To establish a case of hostile environment sexual harassment under Title VII, the plaintiff must prove five elements. First, she must be a member of a protected class. Second, she must show that unwelcome sexually harassing conduct occurred. Next, the plaintiff must show that this harassment occurred because of her sex, and that the conduct was severe or pervasive enough to affect a term, condition, or privilege of her employment. Finally, the plaintiff must establish that there is an employer who should be held liable for this harassment. Each of these elements will be described in detail.

Member of a protected class. In most cases, it is not difficult for a plaintiff to establish that he or she is a member of a protected class. Title VII extends protection to both men and women and, therefore, this element simply requires a plaintiff to establish his or her gender.

Subject to unwelcome harassment. As mentioned earlier, the Supreme Court clearly established in *Meritor Savings Bank* that the central issue in hostile environment sexual harassment cases is the unwelcomeness of the conduct. The Court also made clear that evidence regarding the plaintiff is relevant to determining unwelcomeness. Since *Meritor Savings Bank*, the circuit courts have continued to consider the plaintiff's personality and behavior when deciding whether allegedly harassing conduct was, in fact, unwelcome. For example, in *Rabidue v. Osceola Refining Company* (1986), the Sixth Circuit suggested that "the presence of actionable sexual harassment would be different depending upon the personality of the plaintiff" (p. 620). Specifically, the courts have held that a plaintiff cannot successfully establish this element if she invited or incited the conduct of which she is complaining.

In determining whether the plaintiff invited or incited the allegedly harassing conduct, the courts have considered evidence regarding the plaintiff's response to the conduct, her manner of dress, personality, and previous sexual conduct. For example, in *Reed v. Shepard* (1991), the court suggested that a plaintiff might fail on this element if she herself has used offensive language or engaged in sexual joking in the workplace, or even if she chooses not to wear a bra. In *Jones v. Wesco Investments, Inc.* (1988), the circuit court stated that it would consider provocative speech or dress on the part of the plaintiff when determining unwelcomeness. Similarly, in *Staton v. Maries County* (1989), the court held that the plaintiff had invited the harassing conduct she experienced because she sometimes flirted with the men in her office.

Based on sex. To establish this element, the plaintiff must establish that the allegedly harassing conduct occurred because of her sex; that is, had she been a man, she would not have been subjected to the conduct. This element establishes that the complained of behavior was sex-conscious and, therefore, intentional discrimination.

If the conduct that the plaintiff alleges is sexual, the courts typically have little trouble recognizing that it is "based upon sex." For example, if a heterosexual male coworker sexually propositions a female employee, it is not difficult for fact finders to recognize that this behavior was based upon sex; if the employee had been a man, the coworker would not have engaged in this sexual behavior. The same holds true for other explicitly sexual behavior such as sexual language and innuendo, pornography, and sexual graffiti.

Some courts have also recognized behavior that is not sexual, but that is gender related, to be "based upon sex." For example, in *Burns v. McGregor Electronics Industries, Inc.* (1993), the court recognized that "sexual harassment can take place in many different ways. A female worker need not be propositioned, touched offensively, or harassed by sexual innuendo" (p. 964). Similarly, in *Hall v. Gus Construction Co.* (1988), the court held that "intimidation and hostility toward women because they are women can obviously result from conduct other than explicit sexual advances" (p. 1014). In this case, the court found nonsexual behavior (e.g., coworker urinating into plaintiffs' water bottles, vandalism to plaintiffs' cars) that was directed at three female employees on an otherwise all-male road construction crew to be "based upon sex" because this conduct was directed only to the female members of the crew.

Severe or pervasive. This element requires the plaintiff to show, through the totality of circumstances, that the harassment affected a term, condition, or privilege of her employment. As mentioned earlier, the Supreme Court's decision in *Meritor Savings Bank* established that the plaintiff is not required to show an economic loss, that a psychological detriment is sufficient.

Most courts use a two-prong test in determining whether the harassment affected a term, condition, or privilege of the plaintiff's employment. Under this test, the plaintiff is required to establish both a subjective and an objective element. The subjective element involves showing that the plaintiff herself was adversely affected by the alleged harassment. The objective element, on the other hand, involves showing that a *reasonable person* who had experienced the allegedly harassing conduct would be adversely affected. This second element is considered in addition to the first to guard against what the courts have called "hypersensitive" plaintiffs.

In the establishment of the objective element, the *reasonable person* standard has been replaced in some circuits (for example, the third circuit in *Andrews v. City of Philadelphia*, 1990; the ninth circuit in *Ellison v. Brady*, 1991) by the *reasonable woman* standard. The latter standard is based upon the premise that women and men view harassing conduct differently (i.e., that what is perceived as offensive by some women may not be viewed as offensive by some men). Because the reasonable woman standard involves adopting the perspective of the target of harassment, it is sometimes generically referred to as the *reasonable victim* standard. (The term *target* is often preferred in the social sciences; however, legal terminology uses the term *victim*.) Although some legal scholars have argued that the "reasonable woman" standard (or any objective prong) may not, in fact, prove beneficial to female plaintiffs (Paetzold & Shaw, 1994), there is a trend toward this standard in several circuits.

There is considerable difference across courts as to how pervasive the alleged harassment must be to meet this element. All courts consider the nature and severity of the harassment, as well as the frequency with which it occurred, when determining pervasiveness. Different circuits appear to use different standards, however, when defining terms such as *severity* and *frequency*. One explanation for the differences across circuits relates to the extent to which the court is willing to consider a broad versus narrow range of incidents as relevant. In determining pervasiveness, some courts will consider occurrences that are not specifically linked to the workplace (e.g., in *Andrews*, the appeals courts stated that vandalism of the plaintiffs' automobiles and anonymous phone calls to the plaintiffs' homes were relevant) in conjunction with the harassing conduct that does occur on the job. In addition, some courts are willing to consider the harassing conduct directed at other female employees of which the plaintiff is aware (e.g., *Hall v. Gus Construction Co.*, 1988; *Hicks v. Gates Rubber Company*, 1987; *Jones v. Flagship International*, 1986). Similarly, some decisions (*Hicks v. Gates Rubber Company*, 1987) have considered both sexual and racial harassment together. Clearly, whenever the court is willing to "aggregate" events in these ways, it is easier for the plaintiff to establish the "severe or pervasive" element of her prima facie case.

Employer liability. As discussed earlier, in the *Meritor Savings Bank* case, the Supreme Court did not clearly define when an employer is liable for the harassing conduct of its employees. Since then, the circuit courts have frequently addressed this issue, and the "employer liability" element has taken shape.

In general, the circuit courts have suggested that an employer is liable for the hostile work environment created by its employees when "management-level employees had actual or constructive knowledge about the existence of a sexually hostile environment and failed to take prompt remedial action" (*Andrews v. City of Philadelphia*, 1990, p. 1486). To prove this element, therefore, plaintiffs must establish both employer knowledge and employer lack of action.

Establishment of actual knowledge involves showing that the employer was informed of the harassment (e.g., the plaintiff reported her experiences to the Human Resources Department). Constructive knowledge, on the other hand, involves showing that although the plaintiff may not have directly informed the employer, the employer should have been aware of it (perhaps due to the nature of the harassment, or changes in the plaintiff's behavior).

Once the plaintiff shows that the employer had actual or constructive knowledge of the harassment, she must also establish that the employer failed to take appropriate action. Again, different circuits appear to use somewhat different standards in defining "appropriate action," but several conclusions do seem warranted. First, although the courts look favorably upon the existence of a grievance procedure and policy against discrimination, employers cannot wait for employees to access this procedure before taking action. Second, the employer should thoroughly investigate all charges of sexual harassment, making certain that the individual leading the investigation has sufficient authority. Third, the action taken by the employer must be sufficiently severe to deter this harasser (or others) from further harassment. It should be noted that the courts do not require the employer to fire all harassers but, instead, to ensure that the harassing conduct ends. In addition, employers should ensure that any actions taken do not have detrimental consequences for the target of harassment (e.g., transferring the plaintiff to a less desirable work location). Similarly, if the harasser is not fired, the employer should ensure that the target is not required to interact with him or her, as such interaction has been viewed as additional harassment by the courts (*Ellison v. Brady*, 1991).

Although the elements that a plaintiff must prove to establish hostile environment harassment are relatively well established, the most recent Supreme Court decision, in *Harris v. Forklift Systems, Inc.* (1993), involved significant changes in several of these elements. The next section outlines this case and its implications.

HARRIS V. FORKLIFT SYSTEMS, INC. (1993)

In *Harris*, Ms. Teresa Harris was employed as a rental manager, under direct supervision of Mr. Charles Hardy, the company's president. At trial, the magistrate found that Mr. Hardy subjected Ms. Harris to a barrage of inappropriate sex-based comments. Evidence indicated that Mr. Hardy demeaned her in front of other employees by stating, "You're a woman, what do you know?" "You're a dumb-ass woman," and "We need a man as a rental manager." Other male employees apparently also joined in this commentary. Some of Mr. Hardy's comments were more sexual in nature and were also made in front of other employees and/or customers. He once told Ms. Harris, "Let's go to the Holiday Inn to negotiate your raise." He frequently threw objects on the ground in front of her and other female employees, asking them to retrieve them, and then commented on how they should dress to expose their breasts. He would ask Ms. Harris and other women to retrieve coins from his front pants pocket. He frequently made sexual innuendos about the clothing and breast size of female employees, and at one point suggested that Ms. Harris and he should start "screwing around" (Petitioner's Brief, 1993, pp. 2-3).

As a result of Mr. Hardy's behavior, Ms. Harris became extremely anxious, embarrassed, and would sometimes shake uncontrollably. She indicated that she did not want to go to work, that she could not sleep, that she cried and drank frequently, and that her relationships with her family had become strained. Her physician prescribed tranquilizers and sleeping pills for her, noting her high level of anxiety. Despite this, and despite the fact that the magistrate found that Mr. Hardy's behavior was offensive and would have offended a reasonable woman in Ms. Harris's position, the magistrate ruled that the offensive behavior did not interfere with Ms. Harris's work performance nor did it seriously affect her psychological well-being. The Sixth Circuit, consistent with its holdings in a string of hostile environment cases, summarily affirmed the district court's decision.

On appeal to the Supreme Court, the plaintiff argued that proof of psychological harm was not required under Title VII. However, she additionally argued that offensive conduct should be viewed from the perspective of a reasonable person *in the position of the plaintiff* (i.e., a "reasonable victim" perspective). At the time, three courts of appeal and the EEOC had rejected the ordinary "reasonable person" standard in favor of the "reasonable victim" perspective, on the grounds that the "reasonable person" standard would tend to systematically ignore the experience of women. The plaintiff argued that adoption of a reasonable victim standard would guarantee that courts would not "sustain ingrained notions of reasonable behavior fashioned by the offender" (Petitioner's Brief, 1993, p. 37). Finally, in the alternative, the plaintiff argued that a reasonableness standard was not required at all—that proof of the plaintiff's working conditions being altered would be sufficient to establish a Title VII violation.

The Supreme Court rejected the "psychological harm" requirement, indicating that proof of psychological harm was but one type of evidence that the alleged harassment was sufficiently severe or pervasive so as to alter the plaintiff's conditions of employment. Although some circuits (including the Sixth Circuit) had adopted the "psychological harm" requirement, others had established that an abusive or hostile work environment alone—one that overwhelmingly subjected the plaintiff to "discriminatory intimidation, ridicule, and insult"—would satisfy the severity/pervasiveness element (relying on *Meritor Savings Bank*, 1986, p. 65). In rejecting the requirement of psychological harm, the Supreme Court indicated that it was reaffirming the *Meritor Savings Bank* standard that Title VII is violated when the workplace is permeated with discriminatory abuse that is "sufficiently severe or pervasive to alter the conditions of the victim's employment and create an abusive working environment" (*Harris*, 1993, p. 370).

However, the Supreme Court rejected the plaintiff's argument that a reasonableness standard was not required under the severity/pervasiveness element of the plaintiff's case, noting that "so long as the environment would *reasonably* be perceived, and is perceived, as hostile or abusive, there is no need for it also to be psychologically injurious" (*Harris*, 1993, p. 371; emphasis added). In other words, harm must be proven both subjectively and objectively. Additionally, the Court held that "conduct that is not severe or pervasive enough to create an objectively hostile or abusive work environment—an environment that a reasonable person would find hostile or abusive—is beyond Title VII's purview" (*Harris*, 1993, p. 370). Without explicitly rejecting the "reasonable woman" standard, the Court's reliance on the "reasonable person" standard suggests that the "reasonable woman" standard may be inappropriate.[2] Ambiguity remains, however. The Supreme Court noted that it "need not answer . . . all the potential questions" raised by the case (*Harris*, 1993, p. 371).

Because of its ruling on the "reasonableness" issue, the *Harris* decision has particularly important implications regarding two elements of the plaintiff's hostile environment case: unwelcomeness and severity/pervasiveness. These implications are discussed below.

Unwelcomeness

As previously discussed, courts of appeal have construed unwelcomeness to mean that the plaintiff cannot have invited or incited the conduct of which she complains. These earlier holdings reflect judicial determination that it is not reasonable to consider behavior unwelcome when the plaintiff behaves "provocatively." Additionally, the plaintiff's conduct may look unreasonable if she attempts to minimize the harassing behavior in an attempt to preserve her employment relationship. For example, a plaintiff who does not sufficiently complain about conduct she believes to be harassment because she wants to avoid making "a big stink about it" may signal to a court that the behavior must not have been unwelcome to her (*Highlander v. K.F.C. National Management Co.*, 1986, p. 650).

Thus courts often imply a reasonableness element in a determination of unwelcomeness. How reasonableness is to be interpreted can have important consequences for the plaintiff. A "reasonable person" perspective may represent a failure to understand the multiplicity of ways in which women respond to sexual harassment. For example, women may respond by joking or other similar strategies so as to maintain harmonious relationships in the workplace (Bingham, 1991). Relatedly, courts have sometimes failed to see sexual harassment as a long-term pattern of behavior, involving plaintiff responses over time and shifting context (Paetzold & O'Leary-Kelly, 1993). Additionally, the concept of "provocative" has been viewed from a gendered perspective. Women who do not dress or behave according to specific sex role (or gender role) stereotypes may fail to establish unwelcomeness of conduct that they find harassing. The "reasonable person" perspective may account for the court's view of what is appropriate in response to harassing behavior, which in turn influences the court's determination of whether the behavior was unwelcome.

Although not specifically addressing these issues, *Harris* has implications for the unwelcomeness element of the plaintiff's case. Harris had argued that adoption of the "reasonable person" standard would allow sex-based stereotypes to predominate in the assessment of the plaintiff's working conditions (i.e., severity/pervasiveness). Similarly, however, a "reasonable person" perspective may not exclude stereotypes in the determination of what is unwelcome (as evidenced above).

A "reasonable woman/victim" perspective can provide very different outcomes for plaintiffs on the unwelcomeness issue. For example, consider *Burns v. McGregor Electronic Industries, Inc.* (1993), in which the plaintiff had posed nude in a national magazine. Subsequently, she was sexually harassed by her supervisor and coworkers. The employer argued that the type of person who would "appear nude in a national magazine could not be offended by the behavior which took place at the McGregor plant" (p. 963). The Eighth Circuit rejected this logic, stating that

> the plaintiff's choice to pose for a nude magazine outside work hours is not material to the issue of whether plaintiff found her employer's work-related conduct offensive. This is not a case where Burns posed in provocative and suggestive ways at work. Her private life, regardless how reprehensible the trier of fact might find it to be, did not provide lawful acquiescence to unwanted sexual advances at her work place by her employer. (p. 963)

Most important, the Eighth Circuit rejected the "reasonable person" standard, noting that men's view of "reasonableness" was irrelevant in determining the severity or pervasiveness of the harassment. Although explicitly incorporating the reasonableness test as part of the severity/pervasive element, the willingness to adopt the "reasonable woman" standard may have influenced the court's view of unwelcomeness as well. Although men may view posing in a nude magazine while away from the workplace as opening the door to sexual commentary, a reasonable woman may view such posing as unconnected to the plaintiff's ordinary work environment.

Severity/Pervasiveness

Courts of appeal have generally noted that severity or pervasiveness is to be determined from the totality of the circumstances, taking into account such factors as the nature and gravity of the conduct, the frequency with which it occurred, and whether it was physically threatening or humiliating. *Harris* endorsed the totality of the circumstances approach, noting that psychological harm is but one factor to be considered. Contrary to the respondent's argument, *Harris* also noted that unreasonable interference with her job performance is not an essential part of the plaintiff's case but is simply one factor to be considered. The Court pointed out that hostile environments can "discourage employees from remaining on the job, or keep them from advancing in their careers," even though job performance is not affected and psychological harm does not result (p. 371). In this regard, *Harris* has articulated a broad view of actionable harms under the hostile environment model of discrimination.

However, because *Harris* may have rejected the "reasonable woman" standard, it signals that a generic, all-purpose standard provides an appropriate filter through which to view the plaintiff's response to harassing conduct. Although it is not entirely clear how the federal courts of appeal will react to the *Harris* language, endorsement of the "reasonable woman" standard may be diminished. The *EEOC Proposed Guidelines* (1993) continue the EEOC's earlier position that the "reasonable person" standard should include consideration of the perspective of the plaintiff's race, gender, and other protected characteristics. If endorsed by courts, the reasonable person standard *may* become sufficiently diverse to encompass the "reasonable woman" standard. The extent to which the reasonable woman and reasonable person standards overlap is not yet clear.

In a recent case relying on the *Harris* decision, we believe that a negative impact for women can already be discerned. In *Saxton v.*

American Telephone & Telegraph (1993), the Seventh Circuit dismissed Ms. Saxton's claim by noting that there was insufficient evidence that a reasonable person would have found her work environment to be hostile. Ms. Saxton presented the following incidents of offensive conduct by her supervisor. At the supervisor's request, Ms. Saxton accompanied him to a nightclub. There, he repeatedly placed his hand upon her thigh, even though she consistently removed his hand and asked him to stop. When they left the club, he kissed her until she pushed him away. The next day she told him she did not appreciate his advances, and he apologized and told her it would not happen again. Only a few weeks later, however, he invited her to lunch to discuss work-related business. On their way back from lunch, he stopped at an arboretum to take a walk. Ms. Saxton walked off on her own, but he jumped out at her from behind some bushes, as if to grab her. She ran away to avoid him, making clear that his advances were unwelcome. Later, he became sullen, refused to talk to her at work, and treated her in a condescending manner. The Seventh Circuit ruled that even accepting her version of what had happened, a "reasonable person" would not find this conduct to be sufficiently pervasive to violate Title VII.

Many hostile environment cases have involved physical touching and stroking, forceful kissing, and/or attempted grabbing. There would seem to be little doubt that many women would find such behaviors from a supervisor to be abusive and offensive. Additionally, it is a woman's fear that her direct responses will result in changes in a professional relationship. Many women have "gone along" to avoid the negative consequences of having their supervisor shun them or otherwise treat them differently on the job (U.S. Merit Systems Protection Board, 1988). The use of the "reasonable person" standard allowed the Seventh Circuit to view the supervisor's conduct as somewhat offensive but insufficient to alter the conditions of Ms. Saxton's employment. And, despite the fact that the court noted in a nonbinding remark that the outcome would be the same even if a "reasonable woman" standard had been used, we believe circuits that have used the "reasonable woman" standard have taken a much more sensitive view of the workplace risks that women face. In particular, such courts have noted the particular fears of sexual assault that women face in society, which are particularly relevant when a male's conduct involves forceful kissing, stopping the car on the way back to work to "take a walk," and jumping from behind a bush to lunge at the plaintiff.

CONCLUSION

The recent *Harris* decision, applauded in some circles for its more lenient definition of what constitutes actionable hostile environment sexual harassment, in reality sent mixed signals throughout the legal and business communities. Although the types of harms recognizable at law have been broadened, so that no one type of harm is necessary to a showing of hostile environment sexual harassment, the fuzziness surrounding the reasonable person/reasonable woman standard may limit *Harris*'s apparent leniency.

The difference between "reasonable person" and "reasonable woman" or "reasonable victim" is arguably much more than semantic. Although the position of the Supreme Court on the appropriate standard is not entirely clear, there is the possibility that courts of appeal and trial courts will maintain or revert to the "reasonable person" standard. As we have indicated, this standard has the potential to adversely affect plaintiffs in two elements of the hostile environment claim, thereby ultimately making it more difficult for women to prove unlawful sexual harassment.

NOTES

1. Sexual harassment cases pursued in the federal courts are first heard at trial in U.S. District Court. First appeal is made to the appropriate federal court of appeals; eventually, an appeal may be made to the U.S. Supreme Court. It is primarily the job of the courts of appeal to assist in "fleshing out" and interpreting the law articulated by the Supreme Court.

2. At a 1994 course on employment discrimination given by the American Law Institute-American Bar Association, lawyers and federal judges debated whether the reasonable woman standard survived the Supreme Court's *Harris* decision. Although no clear consensus was reached, some participants strongly felt that the standard should be the "reasonable person." For example, Judge Manuel Real of the U.S. District Court for the Central District of California concluded that *Harris* is "very clear" that the standard should be the "reasonable person" ("Court's *Harris* Opinion," 1994).

REFERENCES

Andrews v. City of Philadelphia, 895 F.2d 1469 (3d Cir. 1990).

Bingham, S. (1991, June). Communication strategies for managing sexual harassment in organizations: Understanding message options and their effects. *Journal of Applied Communication Research*, pp. 88-115.

Burns v. McGregor Electronics Industries, Inc., No. 92-2059 (8th Cir. 1993).

Court's *Harris* opinion provokes debate on standard for evaluating harassment. (1994, May). *Daily Labor Report* (on-line service). Washington, DC: Bureau of National Affairs.

EEOC proposed guidelines on harassment based on race, color, religion, gender, national origin, age, or disability, 29 CFR Pt. 1609 (1993).

Ellison v. Brady, 924 F.2d 872 (9th Cir. 1991).

Hall v. Gus Construction Co., 842 F.2d 1010 (8th Cir. 1988).

Harris v. Forklift Systems, Inc., 114 S. Ct. 367 (1993).

Hicks v. Gates Rubber Company, 833 F.2d 1406 (10th Cir. 1987).

Highlander v. K.F.C. National Management Co., 805 F.2d 644 (6th Cir. 1986).

Jones v. Flagship International, 793 F.2d 714 (5th Cir. 1986).

Jones v. Wesco Investments, Inc., 846 F.2d 1154 (8th Cir. 1988).

Meritor Savings Bank v. Vinson, 477 U.S. 57 (1986).

Paetzold, R. L., & O'Leary-Kelly, A. M. (1993). Continuing violations and hostile environment sexual harassment: When is enough, enough? *American Business Law Journal, 31*, 365-395.

Paetzold, R. L., & O'Leary-Kelly, A. M. (1994). Hostile environment sexual harassment in the United States: Post-*Meritor* developments and implications. *Gender, Work & Organization, 1*, 50-57.

Paetzold, R. L., & Shaw, B. (1994). A postmodern feminist view of "reasonableness" in hostile environment sexual harassment. *Journal of Business Ethics, 13*, 681-691.

Petitioner's Brief, *Harris v. Forklift Systems, Inc.*, WESTLAW 302216 (U.S. Tenn. Pet. Brief, 1993).

Rabidue v. Osceola Refining Company, 805 F.2d 611 (6th Cir. 1986).

Reed v. Shepard, 939 F.2d 484 (7th Cir. 1991).

Saxton v. American Telephone & Telegraph, No. 92-1545 (7th Cir. 1993).

Staton v. Maries County, 868 F.2d 996 (8th Cir. 1989).

Study finds sexual harassment awards from EEOC doubled from 1992 to 1993. (1994, May). *Daily Labor Report* (on-line service). Washington, DC: Bureau of National Affairs.

Terpstra, D. E., & Cook, S. E. (1985). Complainant characteristics and reported behaviors and consequences associated with formal sexual harassment charges. *Personnel Psychology, 38*, 559-574.

U.S. Merit Systems Protection Board. (1988). *Sexual harassment in the federal government: An update.* Washington, DC: Office of Merit Systems Review and Studies/ Government Printing Office.

6

Sexual Harassment as a Moral Issue: An Ethical Decision-Making Perspective

LYNN BOWES-SPERRY
GARY N. POWELL

The purpose of this chapter is to demonstrate how recent developments in the theory of ethical decision making may be applied to the phenomenon of how observers react to incidents of sexual harassment that they witness in their workplaces. We will describe how Rest's (1986) model of ethical decision making and behavior and Jones's (1991) construct of the moral intensity of an issue may be used as the basis for an ethical decision-making model of sexual harassment. We will also generate propositions consistent with an ethical perspective of sexual harassment and compare this model with other relevant theories of sexual harassment.

Sexual harassment has been examined from many different theoretical perspectives. It has hardly ever been examined from an ethical perspective, however (see Vaux, 1993, for an exception). The purpose of this chapter is to demonstrate how recent developments in the theory of ethical decision making may be usefully applied to the phenomenon of how observers react to incidents of sexual harassment.

Sexual harassment has been decried by almost every researcher who has talked about it. For example, Tinsley and Stockdale (1993) referred to sexual harassment as "morally and ethically reprehensible" (p. 1), and Terpstra and Cook (1985) regarded it as "ethically and morally unacceptable" (p. 561). Although such statements may be construed as normative, an examination of the literature on moral philosophy indicates that they are actually descriptive. According to Velasquez and Rostankowski (1985), an action falls within the domain of morality if it poses the potential for harm or benefit to others provided that the actor is acting of his or her own volition. Classification of social-sexual behavior as sexual harassment places the behavior within the domain of morality, because the definition of the term *harass* ("to disturb persistently; torment, as with troubles or cares; bother continually; pester; persecute"; Random House, 1987, p. 870) implies that the target person suffers the risk of harm. Targets of sexual harassment are often harmed in terms of their mental and physical health as well as their job-related outcomes (Gutek & Koss, 1993). Thus sexual harassment is appropriately categorized as a moral issue.

In this chapter, we will describe how Rest's (1986) model of ethical decision making and behavior and Jones's (1991) construct of the moral intensity of an issue may be used as the basis for an ethical decision-making model of sexual harassment. We will also generate propositions consistent with an ethical perspective of sexual harassment and compare this model with other relevant theories of sexual harassment. In so doing, we will focus on the cognitive and behavioral reactions of bystanders who have observed behavior that may be construed as sexual harassment but have not been directly involved in its occurrence.

Observers have an important influence on the phenomenon of sexual harassment. They may act as witnesses when organizations or courts are dealing with cases of alleged sexual harassment and influence the final outcome of investigations. They may report cases of sexual harassment they have witnessed to authorities, thereby engaging in "whistle-blowing" (Dandekar, 1990; Near & Miceli, 1987). They may influence what social-sexual behaviors actually occur in a situation by their physical presence; potential initiators may take into account the likely reactions of observers in deciding whether to direct harmful social-sexual behavior toward others (Pryor, LaVite, & Stoller, 1993). Finally, they may feel that the presence of sexual harassment directed toward others in their midst has made their work environment intimidating, hostile, or offensive and charge that they have been the victims of sexual harassment themselves. Thus it is important to understand how observers react to issues related to sexual harassment. As we shall see, viewing sexual harassment from an ethical perspective will help us to better understand their reactions.

Ethical Decision Making and Behavior

According to Rest (1986), ethical behavior is the result of a series of cognitive processes. To engage in ethical behavior, individuals must (a) recognize that an issue is a moral issue; (b) make a judgment regarding the issue that places moral concerns above all others, that is, make a moral judgment; (c) intend to behave in accordance with that moral judgment; and (d) translate intentions into moral or ethical behavior.

In terms of Rest's (1986) model, individuals who perceive a particular social-sexual behavior as potentially harmful have triggered the ethical decision-making process. Individuals who fail to perceive a moral dimension inherent in such behavior, however, will make judgments on the basis of criteria outside the domain of ethics. For example, the conclusion that sexual harassment is unacceptable because it results in lost productivity is based on economic rather than moral criteria.

Labeling an incident of social-sexual behavior as sexual harassment, however, does not in itself constitute an act of ethical behavior. Individuals must next make a judgment regarding the behavior that places moral concerns above all others and establish moral intentions. For example, if individuals witness their supervisor engaging in behavior that they perceive to be harassing (although not directed toward them), they will have made a moral judgment and established moral intentions if they decide to take some action to stop the behavior, regardless of the job-related consequences that it may hold for them. Finally, this intention must be translated into ethical behavior; that is, they must engage in some action that will help stop the behavior.

Jones (1991) argued that the *moral intensity* of an issue affects individuals' progression through Rest's (1986) stages of ethical decision making and behavior. Moral intensity is a property of the issue itself rather than of the individual who is considering it or the situational context in which it occurs. Compared with issues of low moral intensity, issues of high moral intensity (a) are recognized as moral issues more frequently, (b) elicit more sophisticated moral reasoning and judgments,

(c) lead to more frequent establishment of moral intentions, and (d) lead to more frequent occurrence of ethical behavior.

In terms of Jones's (1991) construct, individuals who see particular social-sexual behaviors as high in moral intensity employ ethical decision-making processes when evaluating them and deciding how to respond to them. Their decisions regarding the classification of behaviors as sexual harassment, the assignment of responsibility for such behaviors, and the reporting of such behaviors depend, in part, on their progression through the stages of ethical decision making and behavior.

Jones (1991) viewed moral intensity as a multidimensional construct composed of six components. The first component is *social consensus,* or the degree of social agreement that an act is evil or good (e.g., "The evil involved in discriminating against minority job candidates has greater social consensus than the evil involved in refusing to act affirmatively on behalf of minority job candidates"; Jones, 1991, p. 375). The second component is *proximity,* or the feeling of nearness (social, cultural, psychological, or physical) for beneficiaries or victims of the act in question (e.g., "Layoffs in a person's work unit have greater moral proximity [physical and psychological] than do layoffs in a remote plant"; Jones, 1991, p. 376). The third component is *magnitude of consequences,* or the sum of the harms or benefits done to beneficiaries or victims of the act in question (e.g., "An act that causes the death of a human being is of greater magnitude of consequences than an act that causes a person to suffer a minor injury"; Jones, 1991, p. 374).

The fourth component of moral intensity is *concentration of effect,* which is an inverse function of the number of people affected by an act of a given magnitude (e.g., "Cheating an individual or small group of individuals out of a given sum has a more concentrated effect than cheating an institutional entity, such as a corporation or government agency, out of the same sum"; Jones, 1991, pp. 377-378). The fifth component is *probability of effect,* which is a joint function of the probability that the act in question will actually occur and will cause the anticipated harm or benefit predicted (e.g. "Selling a gun to a known armed robber has greater probability of harm than selling a gun to a law-abiding citizen"; Jones, 1991, p. 375). The sixth component is *temporal immediacy,* or the length of time between the present and the onset of consequences of the moral act in question. For example,

> Releasing a drug that will cause one percent of the people who take it to have acute nervous reactions soon after they take it has greater temporal

immediacy than releasing a drug that will cause one percent of those who take it to develop nervous disorders after 20 years. (Jones, 1991, p. 376)

THE ETHICAL DECISION-MAKING MODEL OF SEXUAL HARASSMENT

Figure 6.1 portrays an ethical decision-making model of sexual harassment that applies Rest's (1986) stages of ethical decision making and behavior and Jones's (1991) construct of moral intensity to the phenomenon of how observers react to sexual harassment. In this section of the chapter, we will describe and present propositions pertaining to different portions of this model. First, we will discuss the influence of the moral intensity of social-sexual behavior on observers' progression through the four stages of ethical decision making and behavior. Second, we will discuss influences on observers' perceptions of the moral intensity of social-sexual behavior. Third, we will discuss moderators of the relationships between observers' moral judgments, intentions, and behavior.

The Moral Intensity of Social-Sexual Behavior

Social consensus. A higher degree of social consensus exists for actions that are legally prohibited (Jones, 1991). However, although sexual harassment is legally prohibited, the U.S. Equal Employment Opportunity Commission's (1981) definition of it is imprecise. It specifies unwelcome sexual advances and propositions as sexual harassment but categorizes all other offending behaviors as "other verbal and physical conduct of a sexual nature."

In the absence of legal precision, we must turn to how individuals define sexual harassment themselves to determine the degree of social consensus. Gutek, Nakamura, Gahart, Handschumacher, and Russell (1980) conducted one of the first studies of individuals' definitions of sexual harassment. They found that about 80% of adults thought that requests for dates or sexual activity, coupled with the understanding that denial would hurt the individual's job situation and that compliance would help, constituted sexual harassment, but only 20% considered positive comments of a sexual nature (e.g., "You look sexy today") to be harassment. About half of the sample regarded negative comments of a sexual nature (e.g., "dumb prick" or "stupid bitch") or nonverbal

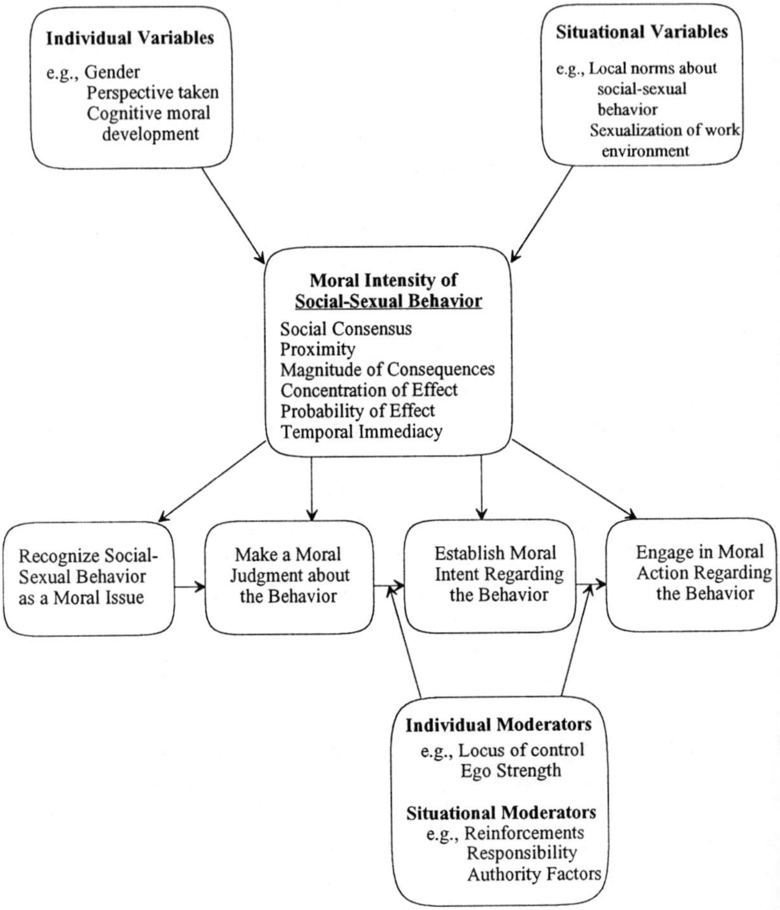

Figure 6.1. The Ethical Decision-Making Model of Sexual Harassment

NOTE: Social-sexual behavior is defined by Gutek, Cohen, and Konrad (1990) as "any non-work-related behavior having a sexual component; it includes sexual harassment, initiating dating, flirting, and the like" (p. 560).

behavior (e.g., leering, making gestures, or brushing against) as sexual harassment. Thus there was greater social consensus over the more blatant types as well as the milder types of social-sexual behavior, but little consensus over behaviors between these two extremes. In accordance with Jones (1991), the low degree of social consensus regarding negative sexually oriented comments and nonverbal behavior should result in these behaviors being recognized less frequently as moral issues than requests for sexual favors in return for job-related benefits.

- *Proposition 1:* Incidents of social-sexual behavior that result in higher social consensus that the behavior constitutes sexual harassment will be recognized more frequently as moral issues and result more often in individuals making moral judgments, establishing moral intentions, and taking action to terminate the behavior.

Proximity. Women are more likely to be the targets of sexual harassment than men. For example, when over 20,000 U.S. government employees were asked in 1980 whether they had received uninvited and unwanted sexual attention (ranging from rape to sexual remarks) on the job during the previous two years, 42% of female employees and 15% of male employees said yes (U.S. Merit Systems Protection Board [MSPB], 1981); the proportion of women who said yes was higher than the proportion of men for each type of behavior. A similar study of over 8,000 government employees in 1987 yielded virtually identical percentages (U.S. MSPB, 1988).

The higher incidence of sexual harassment experienced by women renders women as a group closer in proximity to targets of sexual harassment than men as a group. As a result of this proximity, women should be more inclined to recognize social-sexual behavior directed toward others as a moral issue. Although no research has examined perceptions of various social-sexual behaviors as moral issues, much research has investigated perceptions of such behaviors as sexual harassment. Men are consistently less likely to regard a given behavior as sexual harassment than are women (Kenig & Ryan, 1986; Powell, 1986; Roth & Fedor, 1993). In addition, men are more likely than women to perceive victims as contributing to their own harassment, either by provoking it or by not appropriately handling "proper" sexual attention (Jensen & Gutek, 1982).

Gender is not the only determinant of proximity, however. Whether the target of harassment is a member of an individual's work group may affect proximity. Also, simply asking individuals to take the perspective of the target of sexual harassment may increase psychological proximity and, in turn, attributions regarding the reason leading to harassment (Pryor & Day, 1988).

- *Proposition 2:* Individuals who feel closer in proximity to targets of sexual harassment (e.g., women, work group peers, and individuals who take the perspective of the target) will be more likely to recognize social-sexual behavior as a moral issue, make moral judgments regarding the issue, establish moral intentions regarding the issue, and take action to terminate the behavior.

Magnitude of consequences. Individuals are more likely to consider a behavior as sexual harassment as the harm done to victims increases (Powell, 1993). Positive sexually oriented comments and flirtatious behavior, which seem to be the least harmful of the possible social-sexual behaviors, are least regarded as sexual harassment. Negative sexually oriented comments and suggestive gestures, which are more likely to cause psychological harm to victims, are regarded as sexual harassment by more people than less harmful behavior. Forced sexual relations or sexual propositions accompanied by explicit job consequences, which are particularly harmful to victims because they involve physical and/or psychological coercion and violate their right to feel safe in their work environment, are most often seen as sexual harassment by individuals. In addition, actions by victims' supervisors, which are harmful because they invoke the fear of job-related retribution if the attention is rejected even if no such retribution is intended by the initiator, are more likely to be viewed as sexual harassment than the same actions by coworkers.

These distinctions suggest that individuals pay close attention to the magnitude of consequences of social-sexual behavior in weighing whether to classify it as sexual harassment. Attention to magnitude of consequences is also reflected in the outcomes of sexual harassment cases. Terpstra and Baker's (1988, 1992) analyses of sexual harassment charges filed at both the state and the federal levels indicate that the perceived seriousness of social-sexual behaviors influences the outcome (i.e., settlement or dismissal) of such cases.

- *Proposition 3:* Incidents of social-sexual behavior that are associated with a higher magnitude of consequences will be recognized more frequently as moral issues and result more often in individuals making moral judgments, establishing moral intentions, and taking action to terminate the behavior.

Concentration of effect. The U.S. Supreme Court distinguished between two types of sexual harassment in 1986 in *Meritor Savings Bank v. Vinson,* the first case of sexual harassment it considered. In *quid pro quo harassment,* sexual activity is requested as a condition for gaining a job, promotion, raise, or some other job benefit. In *hostile environment harassment,* one employee makes sexual requests, comments, looks, and so on toward another employee and thereby creates a hostile environment in which that employee must work, even when no economic benefits are lost as a result. For example, an individual may legitimately claim that hostile environment harassment exists when the work environment is abusive of one gender but not the other (Koen, 1990).

The concentration of effect component of moral intensity is relevant in distinguishing between observers' reactions to quid pro quo versus hostile environment sexual harassment. The concentration of effect is typically lower for hostile environment harassment than for quid pro quo harassment. In quid pro quo harassment, the effects are typically limited to a single individual. Furthermore, the target of the harassment is threatened with specific negative job-related outcomes such as termination or denial of promotion if he or she does not go along with the sexual attention, and/or is offered specific job-related benefits such as a raise or more favorable work assignment if he or she does go along. In hostile environment harassment, however, a whole group of employees (such as all of the women in a work setting) may be affected, especially in cases dealing with a highly sexualized work environment, thereby distributing the effects of the social-sexual behavior across a larger number of individuals. Furthermore, these effects are typically less clear-cut than the specific consequences of quid pro quo harassment, although they may have equally damaging psychological effects on their victims (Gutek & Koss, 1993).

- *Proposition 4:* Incidents of social-sexual behavior that result in a higher concentration of effect will be recognized more frequently as moral issues and result more often in individuals making moral judgments, establishing moral intentions, and taking action to terminate the behavior.

Probability of effect and temporal immediacy. According to Jones (1991), moral acts of a given magnitude will be discounted if either the probability of their occurrence or the probability that the anticipated consequences will result from their occurrence is less than 100%. The anticipated consequences of quid pro quo harassment may be perceived as more likely to occur than the consequences associated with hostile environment harassment. Such perceptions may result from the higher level of temporal immediacy that is likely to be associated with quid pro quo harassment. Although negative consequences such as involuntary termination of employment or denial of promotion are likely to follow quickly after a target refuses to participate in sexual activities, the negative consequences associated with a hostile work environment may take longer to emerge.

- *Proposition 5:* Incidents of social-sexual behavior that (a) have a higher probability of resulting in negative consequences for the target and (b) have consequences that emerge sooner after the behavior will be recognized more frequently as moral issues and result more often in individuals making moral judgments, establishing moral intentions, and taking action to terminate the behavior.

Variables That Influence Perceptions of the Moral Intensity of Social-Sexual Behavior

According to Jones (1991), moral intensity focuses on the moral issue, not the moral agent or the organizational context. It is likely, however, that both individual and situational variables influence the perceived moral intensity of an incident of social-sexual behavior.

Some of the individual variables that influence perceptions of the moral intensity of social-sexual behavior have been discussed previously. We proposed that gender, membership in the target's work group, and an individual's taking the target's perspective of sexual harassment influence the proximity component of moral intensity. In addition, an individual's level of cognitive moral development is expected to affect the strength of several of the components of moral intensity. For example, we expect that the degree of social consensus regarding the (in)appropriateness of various social-sexual behaviors will have the most pronounced effect on individuals at the conventional level of cognitive moral development. According to Trevino (1986), most managers reason at the conventional level, looking to others for cues about what is right behavior and what is wrong behavior. In contrast, principled individuals are guided by their own beliefs. Therefore, social consensus should have a stronger effect on the perceptions of individuals at the conventional level of moral development regarding the moral intensity of social-sexual behaviors than on the perceptions of individuals at the principled level of moral development.

Cognitive moral development may also influence the components of proximity, magnitude of consequences, and probability of effect. Individuals at the principled level of moral development are more likely to (a) take the perspective of the target of social-sexual behavior, thus increasing their proximity to targets; (b) have a lower threshold for judging the severity of consequences, thus increasing the perceived magnitude of consequences; and (c) foresee future consequences emanating from present behavior, thus increasing the perceived probability of effect.

- *Proposition 6:* Individuals at the principled level of cognitive moral development will perceive social-sexual behavior as higher in moral intensity than individuals at lower levels of moral development, and thus are more likely to progress through the ethical decision-making process when evaluating such behavior.

Pryor et al. (1993) argued that highly sexualized work environments (Gutek, 1985) and local norms that are permissive regarding social-sexual behavior (Haavio-Mannila, Kauppinen-Toropainen, & Kandolin, 1988) contribute to sexual harassment. We agree that these situational variables influence the incidence (and tolerance) of sexually harassing behaviors. Furthermore, we expect that this influence is indirect through the social consensus component of moral intensity: Individuals are likely to be more concerned with the consensus of members of their work environment than with the consensus of society at large. As a result, sexualized work environments and local norms regarding social-sexual behavior should influence perceptions of the moral intensity of social-sexual behavior, which in turn should influence individuals' progression through the stages of ethical decision making and behavior.

- *Proposition 7:* Individuals working (a) in more sexualized work environments and (b) in organizations with more permissive norms regarding social-sexual behavior will perceive such behavior as lower in moral intensity, and thus are less likely to progress through the ethical decision-making process when evaluating such behavior.

Moderators

As Kohlberg and Candee (1984) noted, moral judgment is a necessary but not sufficient condition for moral behavior. Trevino (1986) proposed individual and situational moderators of the relationship between moral judgments and behavior.

The ethical decision-making model of sexual harassment incorporates Trevino's (1986) individual moderators of locus of control and ego strength. Locus of control (Rotter, 1966) refers to individuals' beliefs regarding who or what controls the events in their lives. Internalizers perceive themselves as in control, whereas externalizers perceive other individuals, fate, or luck as controlling forces. We expect that observers of harmful social-sexual behavior who are internalizers will be more likely to (a) establish moral intentions once they have made a moral judgment about the behavior and (b) act on their intentions to terminate such behavior than observers who are externalizers, because they are more likely to believe that they can have an influence on events.

Ego strength, or an individual's self-regulating skills, strength of conviction, or ability to resist impulses, may also influence whether moral judgments are translated into moral intentions and behavior. Trevino (1986) proposed that individuals with high ego strength will exhibit more consistency between moral thought and action than those with low ego strength. In terms of our model, individuals with higher ego strength who observe harmful social-sexual behavior should be more likely to (a) establish moral intentions once they have made a moral judgment about the behavior and (b) act on their intentions to terminate such behavior, because they strive for consistency in their thoughts and actions.

- *Proposition 8:* The relationships between moral judgments and intentions and between moral intentions and behavior will be moderated by locus of control and ego strength, such that each relationship will be stronger for (a) individuals who are internalizers rather than externalizers and (b) individuals who are higher in ego strength.

Trevino (1986) and Jones (1991) both described situational variable that prevent individuals from acting in accordance with their judgment or beliefs. Trevino (1986) considered the variables of reinforcemen contingencies and responsibility for consequences. In terms of ou model, observers of social-sexual behavior should be less likely to (a) establish moral intentions once they have made a moral judgment about the behavior or (b) act on their intentions to terminate such behavior if they believe that they will be punished for "sticking their nose where it doesn't belong." Employers may be held liable, however, for both quid pro quo harassment and hostile environment harassment (Koen, 1990). Managers who observe sexual harassment may be regarded as legally responsible for terminating it. They may be more likely to establish intentions and take action in accordance with their moral judgments if they believe that they will be held responsible for not doing so.

From Jones's (1991) model, we incorporate the situational variable of "authority factors." Individuals who do not have formal authority may believe that it is not their responsibility to take action to terminate sexually harassing behavior that they observe. Authority factors are especially relevant when observers witness sexually harassing behavior initiated by individuals at higher levels of the organizational hierarchy. They may judge such behavior to be morally wrong, but refrain from establishing moral intentions or following up on their intentions with moral behavior because they fear the consequences of confronting their superiors.

- *Proposition 9:* The relationships between moral judgments and intentions and between moral intentions and behavior will be moderated by authority factors, reinforcement contingencies, and responsibility for consequences, such that each relationship will be weaker when (a) the initiator of social-sexual behavior is at a higher organizational level, (b) individuals fear they will be punished for taking action against such behavior, and (c) individuals do not see themselves as responsible for initiating action.

A COMPARISON TO OTHER RELEVANT THEORIES OF SEXUAL HARASSMENT

Misperception Theory

Some individuals who initiate social-sexual behavior, including behavior classified as sexual harassment, do not see it as harmful. For example, men who misperceive women's friendliness as the desire for a sexual relationship may believe that their behavior is pleasing rather than harassing or harmful to their targets (Stockdale, 1993). The ethical decision-making model of sexual harassment is consistent with Stockdale's (1993) misperception theory. Observers of social-sexual behavior directed toward a female target who believe that she desires the attention will not consider the behavior harmful or as a moral issue. Therefore, their inaction results from a failure to trigger the ethical decision-making process rather than from a failure to translate moral judgments into moral actions.

Power-Based Theories

Cleveland and Kerst (1993) noted that the statement "power is a key issue in sexual harassment" (p. 50) is widely believed but highly vague. They concluded that little is known about the nature of the relationship between power and sexual harassment.

The ethical decision-making model of sexual harassment incorporates power issues in two ways. First, it depicts actions with greater consequences as higher in moral intensity and thereby more likely to be seen as moral issues and trigger the ethical decision-making process: Actions by targets' supervisors, who hold position power over targets, typically have greater consequences than the same actions by coworkers. Second, it includes authority factors and reinforcement contingencies, which are determined by individuals in power, as moderators of the relationships between moral judgments and intentions and between moral intentions and behavior. Thus the model acknowledges the importance of power issues in understanding the phenomenon of sexual harassment. As Cleveland and Kerst (1993) also note, however, power is an insufficient explanation for sexual harassment, and other variables need to be considered.

Attribution Theory

The ethical decision-making model of sexual harassment appears to be most comparable to the attribution theory of Pryor and Day (1988), inasmuch as both focus on social cognitions. Pryor and Day (1988) found that the perspective taken when processing information in a social-sexual encounter influenced interpretations of the encounter; individuals tended to perceive social-sexual behavior as less harassing when they assumed the perspective of the initiator or actor. Pryor and Day (1988) explained this finding in terms of attribution theory: Individuals who take the actor's perspective attribute his or her behavior to situational factors (e.g., misperceptions of women's friendliness), whereas individuals who take the target's perspective attribute the actor's behavior to dispositional factors such as hostility or callousness toward the target.

The findings of Pryor and Day (1988) may also be explained in terms of an ethical perspective. For individuals to be considered moral agents, they must not only pose the potential for harm or benefit to others but also be acting of their own volition (Velasquez & Rostankowski, 1985). Observers of social-sexual behavior who make situational attributions perceive the initiator's behavior as driven by external circumstances and thereby involuntary, whereas observers who make dispositional attributions see the initiator's behavior as more a matter of choice. As a result, individuals who make situational attributions are less likely to recognize the initiator as a moral agent or the behavior as a moral issue than individuals who make dispositional attributions and therefore are less likely to trigger the ethical decision-making process.

Thus the ethical perspective of sexual harassment allows us to reframe Pryor and Day's (1988) predictions. We propose the existence of a relationship between attributions regarding the cause of a social-sexual behavior and the interpretation of such behavior as a moral issue, the formation of moral judgments, the establishment of moral intentions, and ethical behavior:

- *Proposition 10:* Individuals who attribute behavior to situational factors will be less likely to recognize social-sexual behavior as a moral issue, make moral judgments regarding the issue, establish moral intentions regarding the issue, and take action to terminate the behavior than individuals who attribute behavior to dispositional factors.

CONCLUSIONS

Social-sexual behaviors that have the potential to harm individuals in the workplace constitute moral issues. Research on sexual harassment, however, has consistently neglected to consider the domain of morality or ethics. The objective of this chapter has been to begin to fill the "black hole" regarding morality and ethics that currently characterizes research and thought about sexual harassment. Based on its review, the ethical decision-making model of sexual harassment should be added to the list of theories that are used to explain the antecedents of and responses to sexual harassment.

The ethical decision-making perspective offers unique insight into why different people consider some social-sexual behaviors but not other behaviors as sexual harassment. As we have seen, it suggests classification of different types of social-sexual behavior according to their magnitude of consequences, temporal immediacy, probability of effect, and concentration of effect. Behaviors that have greater effects, more immediate effects, more likely effects, and more concentrated effects are higher in moral intensity and thereby more likely to trigger an ethical response in individuals. This perspective also suggests that judgments regarding sexual harassment are not made in a social vacuum. Individuals' sense of how others view the acceptability of social-sexual behaviors and their sense of proximity to targets of social-sexual behaviors influence whether they classify behaviors as sexual harassment. Behaviors for which there is greater social consensus are more likely to trigger an ethical response in individuals. Also, individuals who feel closer to targets of social-sexual behavior are more likely to respond to the behavior as a moral issue.

In addition, the ethical decision-making perspective suggests that observers' possible responses to incidents of social-sexual behavior go far beyond their deciding whether to classify the behavior as sexual harassment. Doing so only takes them through the first stage of Rest's (1986) model of ethical decision making and behavior. Observers may then decide to place moral concerns above all others in reacting to the behavior (i.e., make a moral judgment that the behavior is wrong regardless of mitigating factors), establish an intention to act in accordance with their moral judgment (e.g., by acting as a witness in a formal investigation, showing their displeasure to initiators, offering support to victims, or reporting behavior they regard as sexual harassment to authorities), and then proceed to take such actions. The abundance of prior research on personal definitions of sexual harassment has only addressed the first stage of how individuals' cognitive and behavioral responses to sexual harassment may be influenced by ethical concerns. Later stages of ethical decision making and behavior pertaining to sexual harassment also warrant research attention.

Because sexual harassment is appropriately characterized as a moral issue, models of ethical decision making and behavior may provide additional insight into the processes of "naming, blaming, and claiming" in sexual harassment (Roth & Fedor, 1993). Many of the existing research findings can be explained in terms of progression through the stages of ethical decision making. More specifically, the perceived moral intensity of incidents of social-sexual behavior is likely to influence the recognition of such behaviors as sexual harassment and to prompt individuals to take some action to terminate such behaviors.

The perceived moral intensity of an incident of social-sexual behavior may, however, be influenced by situational variables such as organizational norms and individual variables such as cognitive moral development. Many individuals work in organizational cultures that suggest that social-sexual behavior occurring between other employees is none of their business. As a result, although they may feel uncomfortable with the situation and feel empathy or sympathy for the target, they may not recognize such behavior as a moral issue and instead see the target as bearing responsibility for discouraging the initiator's behavior. Individuals at the principled level of moral development, however, may disregard organizational norms when reacting to social-sexual behavior that occurs in their presence. Therefore, future studies of the role of moral intensity in influencing individuals' responses to social-sexual behavior should examine the main and interactive effects of possible antecedents of moral intensity.

Future research is also needed to determine whether the various components of moral intensity fall into some sort of hierarchy. For example, social or psychological proximity to targets of social-sexual behavior may be less important when the magnitude of consequences is great, the probability of effect is high, or the consequences are expected to occur in the very near future. In addition, research that investigates the relationship between recognizing social-sexual behavior as a moral issue and classifying it as sexual harassment may provide important insights into the "naming" process. For example, is recognizing an incident of social-sexual behavior as a moral issue a necessary condition for classifying it as sexual harassment; is it a sufficient condition; or are the two concepts unrelated? We have proposed that to classify social-sexual behavior as sexual harassment is in effect to classify it as a moral issue. However, this proposition, as well as all others in this chapter based on the ethical decision-making perspective, warrants empirical research attention.

We have limited our application of the ethical decision-making model to consideration of observers' reactions to sexual harassment. This model could also be used to trace the decision-making processes of initiators of social-sexual behavior and their targets. Initiators and targets do not necessarily follow the same cognitive processes as observers, however. For example, targets may not acknowledge abuse that observers would consider a moral issue because they are ambivalent about labeling their own experiences as sexual harassment (Stockdale & Vaux, 1993). Also, initiators may be disinclined to recognize their own behavior as a moral issue, even if it clearly has the potential of harming others, because they are concerned only with the magnitude, probability, and immediacy of consequences for themselves rather than others. Thus, although we recommend that an ethical decision-making perspective be applied to the cognitive and behavioral reactions of perpetrators of social-sexual behavior and their targets, we see such a task as falling beyond the scope of this chapter.

Finally, in focusing on sexual harassment as a moral issue, we have not examined other types of moral concerns that may also influence how far individuals proceed through the stages of ethical decision making and behavior. For example, in considering whether to report behavior that is clearly sexual harassment, observers may be concerned about the possible harmful effects of their reporting the behavior on initiators to whom they feel close. Coworkers who are found to have engaged in sexual harassment in formal hearings by their organizations are subject to punitive action. In addition, strong norms exist in many social systems against "ratting" on coworkers. Thus, individuals who observe behavior that they regard as sexual harassment may weigh which action on their part would cause the greater harm: to report the behavior (or testify as witnesses that it actually occurred) or not to report it (or testify that it didn't occur). For example, a review of the investigation of the 1991 Tailhook Association Convention, at which hundreds of incidents of sexual harassment were alleged to have occurred but none for which anyone was seriously disciplined, suggests that most witnesses of sexual harassment at the convention took the latter option (Goodman, 1994; U.S. Department of Defense, 1993). It is beyond the scope of this chapter to examine how such ethical dilemmas are resolved by observers, or whether they are even seen as ethical dilemmas. It seems likely, however, that observers are influenced by the various components of moral intensity (social consensus, proximity, and so on) associated with competing moral issues (taking action against harmful social-sexual behaviors versus taking action that harms their colleagues) in resolving their ethical dilemmas.

In conclusion, the ethical decision-making perspective represents a framework for the interpretation of reactions to social-sexual behavior in the workplace that offers considerable promise. Consideration of the moral intensity of social-sexual behaviors and its influence on the ethical decision-making process helps us to understand better why observers of sexual harassment think and act the way they do.

REFERENCES

Cleveland, J. N., & Kerst, M. E. (1993). Sexual harassment and perceptions of power: An under-articulated relationship. *Journal of Vocational Behavior, 42,* 49-67.

Dandekar, N. (1990). Contrasting consequences: Bringing charges of sexual harassment compared with other cases of whistleblowing. *Journal of Business Ethics, 9,* 151-158.

Equal Employment Opportunity Commission. (1981). Guidelines on discrimination because of sex. In U.S. Merit Systems Protection Board, *Sexual harassment in the workplace: Is it a problem?* (pp. E9-E10). Washington, DC: Office of Merit Systems Review and Studies/Government Printing Office.

Goodman, E. (1994, February 13). Who will take responsibility for Tailhook? *Hartford Courant, 156*(44), p. B4.

Gutek, B. (1985). *Sex and the workplace.* San Francisco: Jossey-Bass.

Gutek, B. A., Cohen, A. G., & Konrad, A. (1990). Predicting social-sexual behavior at work: A contact hypothesis. *Academy of Management Journal, 33,* 560-577.

Gutek, B. A., & Koss, M. P. (1993). Changed women and changed organizations: Consequences of and coping with sexual harassment. *Journal of Vocational Behavior, 42,* 28-48.

Gutek, B. A., Nakamura, C. Y., Gahart, M., Handschumacher, I., & Russell, D. (1980). Sexuality and the workplace. *Basic and Applied Social Psychology, 1,* 255-265.

Haavio-Mannila, E., Kauppinen-Toropainen, K., & Kandolin, I. (1988). The effect of sex composition of the workplace on friendship, romance, and sex at work. In B. A. Gutek, A. H. Stromberg, & L. Larwood (Eds.), *Women and work* (Vol. 3, pp. 123-137). Newbury Park, CA: Sage.

Jensen, I. W., & Gutek, B. A. (1982). Attributions and assignment of responsibility in sexual harassment. *Journal of Social Issues, 38*(4), 121-136.

Jones, T. (1991). Ethical decision making by individuals in organizations: An issue-contingent model. *Academy of Management Review, 16,* 366-395.

Kenig, S., & Ryan, J. (1986). Sex differences in levels of tolerance and attribution of blame for sexual harassment on a university campus. *Sex Roles, 15,* 535-549.

Koen, C. M., Jr. (1990). Sexual harassment claims stem from a hostile work environment. *Personnel Journal, 69*(8), 88-99.

Kohlberg, L., & Candee, D. (1984). The relationship of moral judgment to moral action. In W. M. Kurtines & J. L. Gerwitz (Eds.), *Morality, moral behavior and moral development* (pp. 52-73). New York: John Wiley.

Meritor Savings Bank v. Vinson, 477 U.S. 57 (1986).

Near, J. P., & Miceli, M. P. (1987). Whistle-blowers in organizations: Dissidents or reformers? In B. M. Staw & L. L. Cummings (Eds.), *Research in organizational behavior* (Vol. 9, pp. 321-368). Greenwich, CT: JAI.

Powell, G. N. (1986). Effects of sex role identity and sex on definitions of sexual harassment. *Sex Roles, 14,* 9-19.

Powell, G. N. (1993). *Women and men in management* (2nd ed.). Newbury Park, CA: Sage.

Pryor, J. B., & Day, J. D. (1988). Interpretations of sexual harassment: An attributional analysis. *Sex Roles, 18,* 405-417.

Pryor, J. B., LaVite, C. M., & Stoller, L. M. (1993). A social psychological analysis of sexual harassment: The person/situation interaction. *Journal of Vocational Behavior, 42,* 68-83.

Random House. (1987). *The Random House dictionary of the English language* (2nd ed.). New York: Random House.

Rest, J. R. (1986). *Moral development: Advances in theory and research.* New York: Praeger.

Roth, J., & Fedor, D. B. (1993, August). *In the eye of the beholder: Naming, blaming, and claiming in the sexual harassment process.* Paper presented at the annual meeting of the Academy of Management, Atlanta.

Rotter, J. B. (1966). Generalized expectancies for internal versus external control of reinforcement. *Psychological Monographs: General and Applied, 80,* 609.

Stockdale, M. S. (1993). The role of sexual misperceptions of women's friendliness in an emerging theory of sexual harassment. *Journal of Vocational Behavior, 42,* 84-101.

Stockdale, M. S., & Vaux, A. (1993). What sexual harassment experiences lead respondents to acknowledge being sexually harassed? A secondary analysis of a university survey. *Journal of Vocational Behavior, 43,* 221-234.

Terpstra, D. E., & Baker, D. D. (1988). Outcomes of sexual harassment charges. *Academy of Management Journal, 31,* 185-194.

Terpstra, D. E., & Baker, D. D. (1992). Outcomes of federal court decisions on sexual harassment. *Academy of Management Journal, 35,* 181-190.

Terpstra, D. E., & Cook, S. E. (1985). Complainant characteristics and reported behaviors and consequences associated with formal sexual harassment charges. *Personnel Psychology, 38,* 559-574.

Tinsley, H. E. A., & Stockdale, M. S. (1993). Sexual harassment in the workplace. *Journal of Vocational Behavior, 42,* 1-4.

Trevino, L. K. (1986). Ethical decision making in organizations: A person-situation interactionist model. *Academy of Management Review, 11,* 601-617.

U.S. Department of Defense, Inspector General. (1993). *Report of investigation: Tailhook 91—Part 2, Events at the 35th Annual Tailhook Symposium.* Washington, DC: Government Printing Office.

U.S. Merit Systems Protection Board. (1981). *Sexual harassment in the workplace: Is it a problem?* Washington, DC: Office of Merit Systems Review and Studies/Government Printing Office.

U.S. Merit Systems Protection Board. (1988). *Sexual harassment in the federal government: An update.* Washington, DC: Office of Merit Systems Review and Studies/ Government Printing Office.

Vaux, A. (1993). Paradigmatic assumptions in sexual harassment research: Being guided without being misled. *Journal of Vocational Behavior, 42,* 116-135.

Velasquez, M. G., & Rostankowski, C. (1985). *Ethics: Theory and practice.* Englewood Cliffs, NJ: Prentice-Hall.

SECTION III

Research Frontiers

7

Organizational Influences on Sexual Harassment

CHARLES L. HULIN
LOUISE F. FITZGERALD
FRITZ DRASGOW

Building on broad theories of organizational climate and culture, this chapter examines the hypothesis that an organization's climate for sexual harassment is a critical antecedent to sexually harassing behavior and may be a direct contributor to negative outcomes beyond the personal experiences of sexual harassment. Using a facet analysis approach, we describe scale development of the Organizational Tolerance for Sexual Harassment Inventory (OTSHI), which measures the extent to which respondents perceive that sexually harassing behavior will be associated with negative consequences in their organization. Data from graduate students at a midwestern university ($N = 263$) and employees at a West Coast public utility ($N = 1,156$) provide evidence of the scale's reliability and validity. Moreover, the OTSHI not only predicted occurrences of sexual harassment but was found to be a stronger predictor of negative work-related, psycho-

AUTHORS' NOTE: The conceptual developments that led to the items and scales assessing organizational culture/climate are the product of weekly research group meetings that have been conducted during the past three years. The contributions of Jennifer Berdahl, Michele Gelfand, Vicki Magley, Diane Payne, Kim Schneider, Craig Waldo, and Mike Zickar are gratefully acknowledged. The contributions of the alphabetically hindmost of this group to data analysis are also noteworthy. In addition, Kathy Hanisch has contributed to the background thinking of the causal model, patterned ways individuals behave in organizations, and to the conviction that we must study sexual harassment in organizations as it occurs within a broader organizational framework.

logical, and physical outcomes than were direct experiences of sexual harassment. Implications for the role of sexual harassment climate on general well-being of employees and for creating harassment-free workplaces are discussed.

Sexual harassment in organizations has a long past but a short history. Documented in historical accounts since the advent of the Industrial Revolution led large numbers of women to work outside the home (Bularzik, 1978), it has only lately been recognized as an important social problem. Recently, as the impact of sexual harassment has become increasingly well documented (Dansky & Kilpatrick, in press; Fitzgerald, 1993; Fitzgerald & Ormerod, 1993; Fitzgerald & Shullman, 1993; Gutek, 1985; Gutek & Koss, 1993; Koss, 1990; Pryor & McKinney, in press; U.S. Merit Systems Protection Board [MSPB], 1981, 1988), organizations have been confronted with new issues of corporate ethical responsibility, legal liability, organizational productivity, and employee well-being. Organizational networks of roles, authority, and responsibility, as well as the high degree of control often exercised by harassers over targets' jobs and careers, imply that harassment is an organizational problem of significant magnitude rather than simply one of individual deviance.

The organizational settings in which harassment occurs can be conceptualized very generally as comprising *technical systems* (which determine task characteristics and work flow) and *social systems* (which comprise individuals, work groups, and their interrelations). Such technical and social systems, and their complex interfaces, are considered by some to represent the core of an organization (Trist & Bamforth, 1951); we argue here that each is likely to influence the occurrence and impact of sexual harassment and that the scientific study of such behaviors requires that we develop theoretical frameworks that reflect these influences (Hulin & Roznowski, 1985; Perrow, 1965; Trist & Bamforth, 1951; Woodward, 1965, 1970).

Although both technical and social systems are relevant to such an undertaking, the effects of the former are relatively indirect, exerting their influence mainly via the social-technical interface; that is, technical systems determine to a large extent the particular tasks performed in an organization and influence the kinds of individuals hired to perform these tasks. Group characteristics of work teams are an emergent property of such sociotechnical systems. Manifestations of social systems, on the other hand, in particular the interrelations of individuals and their work groups, more directly affect the occurrence of sexual harassment and the systemic context in which it unfolds; it is these social systems that are the focus of this chapter.

CONCEPTUAL BACKGROUND

In a recent paper (Fitzgerald, Hulin, & Drasgow, 1995), we described a theoretical model of the antecedents and consequences of sexual harassment in work organizations. Briefly, we proposed that sexual harassment is primarily a function of a masculine job gender context and a tolerant organizational climate. By *masculine job gender context,* we mean the degree to which a work group is numerically dominated by men, and the job duties and tasks are those usually thought of as stereotypically masculine in nature. By *organizational climate,* we refer to the degree to which an organization (or its relevant proximal component) is perceived as insensitive to or tolerant of sexual harassment. Although not denying the role of individual differences in men's propensity to sexually harass (Pryor, 1987; Pryor, LaVite, & Stoller, 1993), we contend that organizational factors are generally most critical in determining whether harassment will occur. With respect to consequences, the model predicts that harassment exerts negative effects on target's job and career, psychological well-being, and physical health—consequences that are thought to be moderated by the target's personal vulnerability as well as her mode of responding to and coping with the harassment. The model appears in Figure 7.1.

The general idea that sexual harassment is to some degree a function of organizational variables is not new in this burgeoning literature. The first major study of sexual harassment found a relationship between what we refer to as a masculine job gender context and higher levels of sexual harassment (U.S. MSPB, 1981) nearly 15 years ago; not only was this replicated some years later (U.S. MSPB, 1987), but a recent reanalysis of these data demonstrated relationships between organizational context (operationalized as ratings of the presence and effectiveness of sexual harassment policies and procedures) and incidence of harassing behavior (Hesson-McInnis & Fitzgerald, 1995). Similarly, Gutek (1985) has argued that a sexualized work environment (e.g., one where

*organischa where managers took SH
seriously had less
cases of SH*

130 Organizational Influences

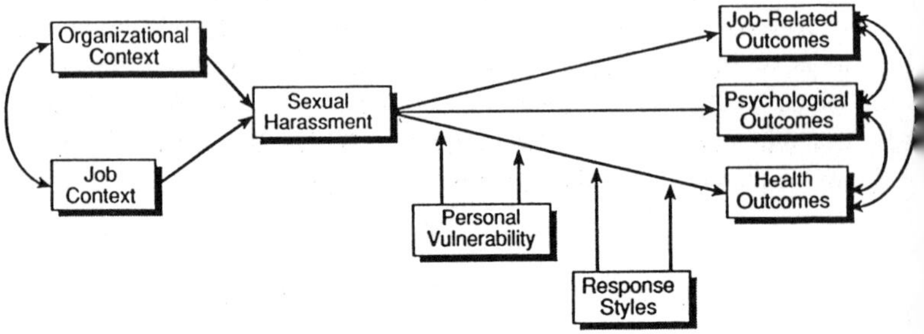

Figure 7.1. An Integrated Process Model of the Antecedents and
Consequences of Sexual Harassment in Organizations

sexual innuendo, comments, and interactions are rife) leads to greater
frequency of harassment, and Bond (1988) reported that academic
departments in which faculty-student dating was the norm were those
where female graduate students were more likely to say they had been
harassed.

The most explicit statement of the role of organizational variables has
been made by Pryor (Pryor, Giedd, & Williams, 1995; Pryor et al., 1993;
Pryor & Whalen, in press). Briefly, Pryor argues that sexual harassment
occurs when a man who is predisposed to do so finds himself in a setting
where such behavior is tolerated, modeled, or encouraged. Pryor's first
set of studies (1992; Pryor, et al., 1993) examined data from a federal
agency employing several thousand workers, geographically dispersed
in offices across the country. Employees were surveyed about their own
experiences of sexual harassment as well as their perceptions of management's stance toward this issue. Women's reports of various types
of sexually harassing experiences were significantly correlated with
their impressions of organizational tolerance of such harassment; those
who thought that management had made good-faith attempts to stop
harassment and provided good role models were less likely to have
experienced sexual harassment on the job. The reverse was true for
those who believed that management ignored the problem, discouraged
reporting, and so forth.

More recently, Pryor and Stoller (1994) found that men high in
likelihood to sexually harass tended to emulate the sexually harassing
behaviors of a high-authority role model in an experimental situation,

whereas Pryor et al. (1995) reported that such men also followed the harassing lead of peers, particularly when group cohesion was high. Thus Pryor and Whalen (in press) assert,

> Men who want to sexually exploit do so when the circumstances or local social norms permit such behavior. Such behavior seems unlikely to occur when the social situation is not ripe for sexual exploitation (Pryor et al., 1995). . . . For sexual exploitation to occur repeatedly, facilitative local norms *must* exist.

Summary. This brief review reveals a considerable literature arguing and demonstrating that organizational variables act as facilitators, inhibitors, or triggers for sexually harassing behavior. A variety of variables, both behavioral and attitudinal, have been studied and show promise for our understanding of harassment. One shortcoming of this research, however, is that it lacks any conceptual grounding in the more general literature on organizational behavior as well as any systematic method for assessing the critical variables. We address these lacunae below.

ORGANIZATIONAL CULTURE AND CLIMATE

We hypothesize that organizational climate, as reflected in an organization's tolerance of the harassment of some of its members by other members, is a critical antecedent of sexual harassment (Fitzgerald, Swan, & Fisher, 1995; Hulin, 1993; Zickar, 1994) and may be a direct and independent contributor to negative psychological and other outcomes, over and above the effects of harassment itself. We locate our argument within classic formulations of organizational culture and climate, with specific reference to the theoretical proposals of Naylor, Pritchard, and Ilgen (1980).

We begin our development by asking how organizational culture, and the specific aspects of climate related to sexual harassment, are translated into individual behavior. First, it is reasonable to propose that organizations[1] that are more tolerant of sexual harassment are likely to be the settings where greater frequency of harassment occurs; thus individuals within such organizations are not only more likely to experience harassment firsthand, but are likely to have less institutional recourse and fewer effective remedies when they do. They may be less likely to complain about their experiences and more likely to be retaliated against if they do so. In other words, a tolerant organizational climate should give rise not only to higher levels of harassment itself but also to worse outcomes for those who experience it. These manifestations are, however, only the most obvious consequences of an organizational climate tolerant of sexual harassment; we propose that the effects of climate reach beyond those experienced by victims themselves to affect female employees generally. Whether directly harassed or not, women employed in such organizations, who observe harassment occurring to their coworkers, must accommodate themselves as best they can to a working environment that is inhospitable to women. Waiting for the sexual harassment "shoe" to drop, watching their colleagues be harassed with few or no sanctions for harassers, and wondering when or if it will happen to them are only a few of the experiences that may be nearly as stressful as being a direct target. Schneider (1995) labels this phenomenon "bystander stress."

What exactly is meant by the phrase *organizational climate,* and how can a tolerant climate be identified? When we venture onto such terrain, we move into territory that is relatively unexplored conceptually and poorly charted empirically. Schein (1990) noted that anthropology, sociology, political science, social psychology, and organizational behavior all claim some part of this concept and employ it in one or more paradigms. After implying that the concept of organizational culture was a mess, Schein (1990) supported this implication by defining it as

> a pattern of basic assumptions, invented, discovered, or developed by a given group as it learns to cope with its problems of external adaptation and internal integration that has worked well enough to be considered valid and therefore is to be taught to new members as the correct way to perceive, think and feel in relation to those problems. (p. 111)

This definition does not differentiate organizational culture from the broader concepts of group norms, shared attitudes, or common beliefs. Schein goes on to argue that organizational *climate* is a surface manifestation of organizational *culture* and is the more salient concept, lending itself to direct observation and measurement. Within the framework of this terminology, our proposed construct would be conceptualized as a specific *dimension* of organizational climate, reflecting an organization's tolerance for sexual harassment of and by its members, as reflected in employee perceptions of, or beliefs about, the consequences of sexually harassing behaviors.

We build most explicitly on aspects of Naylor et al.'s (1980) approach to organizational climate. Based in the judgment and decision-making literature, their conceptualization provides a critical link between employee *perceptions* of organizational characteristics and subsequent employee *behaviors,* lending itself to operationalization of specific dimensions of climate that are likely antecedents of relevant behavioral patterns. Specifically, we define organizational climate conceptually, following Naylor, Pritchard, and Ilgen's approach, as shared perceptions, among members of a relevant group, department, or organization, of contingencies between specific behaviors and their consequences, both private and public, positive and negative.

This framework is also consistent with the definition of culture as discussed by Triandis (1972). He argues that each cultural group possesses a distinctive subjective subculture—that is, a particular way of viewing the human-made part of their environment, including values, norms, attitudes, and roles—that is shaped by that group's ecological environment. The environment comprises, inter alia, available resources, past reinforcements for specific behaviors by group members, and the group's history. Triandis operationalizes group culture by its values that frame assumptions about what is important. The degree to which negative outcomes accompany and are contingent upon certain behaviors reflects the values of at least some influential organizational members. Organizational outcomes, positive or negative, that accrue to certain behaviors mirror the values placed on those behaviors, values that are made manifest and salient by specific and definable patterns of sanctions. These sanctions provide guidelines that then influence some behavioral choices for organizational members.

In the current case, it can be argued that employees in organizations with few contingencies between harassing behaviors and negative sanctions may regard harassment as a manifestation of an organizational culture that permits dominance of certain groups of employees over other groups. Such dominance is not reflected only or mainly in formal supervisory or control relationships but may take the form of male employees using putdowns, unwanted physical contact, verbal harassment, verbal threats, and sexual coercion to establish dominance over female employees. The "rules" governing such behavior may be well known to most organizational members, and the behaviors may even be highly scripted to follow these rules. Similarly, a lack of formal or

Lack of policy may give permission to Harass

informal contingencies between harassing behaviors and outcomes may be perceived as permission for those who may feel threatened by women entering previously all-male work groups to retaliate by behaving aggressively or threateningly toward the interlopers.

As we emphasize above, the realization that a lack of organizational sanctions for harassing behavior reflects the dominant values of the organization may lead directly to job stress and other negative outcomes whether or not the focal employee is herself a target of harassment. That is, wondering whether one will be the next target, or watching one's coworkers treated as pariahs or "whistle-blowers" while their harassers go unpunished, may be nearly as stressful as being the actual target of a harassing episode.

Although the psychological processes involved in the translation of such perceptions of organizational climate into employee response patterns have yet to be fully explicated, it seems reasonable to argue that they are learned by organizational members via observation, modeling, and other standard acquisition processes; reflect organizational reality to some degree; and are, as well, cognitive representations of likely consequences of specific behaviors. Empirical support for this position is summarized in Pryor and Whalen (in press). Contingencies thus serve as guides to individuals in organizations—or particular work groups—for behavioral choices as they negotiate the thickets of conflicting pressures, norms, and beliefs about permitted and sanctioned organizational behaviors.

Objective contingencies between behaviors and outcomes are communicated formally to organizational members in a variety of ways as well as indirectly (but effectively) through repeated examples. Informal communications within groups and departments provide additional information about contingencies that may or may not reflect "objective" organizational realities. Myths, stories, legends, and other forms of oral history (Green, 1972) represent important sources by which contingencies may become part of an organization's culture and climate. Communications about such contingencies take place during the organizational indoctrinations and "boot camps" that represent rites of passage from outsider to organizational member (Van Maanen, 1988).

Summary. In this section of the chapter, we have attempted to anchor the literature on organizational influences on sexual harassment within the more general literature on organizational climate and culture. We argue that employee perceptions of the contingencies between sexually harassing behaviors and outcomes (for both target and perpetrator) facilitate or inhibit such behavior as well as other related behaviors (e.g., reporting) and outcomes. We label these perceived contingencies *organizational tolerance for sexual harassment,* which we conceptualize as a specific dimension of the broader concept of organizational climate. The remainder of our chapter describes the development and preliminary validation of an inventory to assess this construct: the *Organizational Tolerance for Sexual Harassment Inventory* (OTSHI).

DEVELOPMENT OF CLIMATE MEASURE

We begin by assuming that sexual harassment of female employees is likely to exist to some degree in all organizations. Such harassment can range from (common) misogynistic comments made directly to women or in their presence, through jokes more cruel than funny, unwanted sexual attention, the solicitation of sexual cooperation in return for favorable job outcomes, to the relatively rare instances of outright physical and sexual assault. Empirical estimates of incidents of sexual harassment of working women typically average approximately 50% (Fitzgerald, 1993; Gutek, 1985; Koss et al., 1994; U.S. MSPB, 1981, 1988) with estimates in some organizations running considerably higher (e.g., Martindale, 1990; Schneider & Swan, 1994). Given this base rate, it is likely that some degree of sexual harassment exists in all large organizations, occurring more frequently in some organizations than others. It is a major premise of our theory that organizational climate is a primary explanatory variable in such differential prevalence rates. These acts of harassment, their interpretations by harassers and recipients alike, the sanctions meted out for harassers, the reaction to those who complain about harassment, and related social-organizational phenomena are grist for the mills of the observers. Overall perceptions of the climate of organizations or of the work groups embedded in them are based on cognitive representation of such events.

Development of Item Pool

Our assessment of climate focuses on the likely outcomes—that is, organizational repercussions—to both a target and a perpetrator following a complaint of sexual harassment. Items were written based on a facet analysis of harassing incidents that suggested two major facets:

organizational role of the harasser and *type of harassing behavior.* With respect to the harasser role, we focused on supervisors and colleagues/ coworkers; we excluded subordinates as harassers because of the low frequency with which such incidents are reported in the literature. Given practical considerations of instrument length, we also excluded harassment by clients, customers, and other, less included, organizational members—reasoning that organizations that tolerate sexual harassment on the part of supervisors or coworkers would also tolerate it on the part of less included organizational members. We note, however, that this is an empirical question that deserves further examination especially in service organizations in which interactions with clients or customers may represent the majority of employee's work-related interactions. Examples such as flight attendant, waitress, and nurse come readily to mind.

The second facet focused on the type of harassment experienced by a target; for this aspect of our design, we employed the model developed in the Illinois studies of sexual harassment (Fitzgerald, Gelfand, & Drasgow, 1995; Gelfand, Fitzgerald, & Drasgow, 1995). This model, which enjoys strong empirical support, identifies three general categories of behavior as necessary and sufficient to account for all specific manifestations of harassment: gender harassment, unwanted sexual attention, and sexual coercion.

Gender harassment is characterized by insulting, misogynistic, and degrading remarks and behavior. Although not designed to elicit sexual cooperation, such behavior is typically highly sexualized (via the use of derogatory sexual terminology, insulting names for women's body parts, and so on) in a way that conveys hostility and degrading attitudes about women. *Unwanted sexual attention* consists of unwelcome sexual behavior that is unwanted and unreciprocated by the recipient but that is not tied to any job-related reward or punishment. *Sexual coercion* refers to implicit or explicit threats or promises of job-related outcomes conditioned on sexual cooperation. Sexual coercion is thus the behavioral equivalent of the legal concept of *quid pro quo,* whereas unwanted sexual attention and gender harassment constitute the two aspects of a *hostile work environment.*

Our facet analysis generated a six-cell design, crossing two harasser roles (supervisor, coworker) with three types of harassing behavior (gender harassment, unwanted sexual attention, sexual coercion). Sexual harassment vignettes were written for each of these six cells, depicting either a supervisor or a coworker engaging in one of the three types of harassment behaviors. In each case, the target of the harassing behavior was a female employee; this design results in minimal loss of generality because women are overwhelmingly more likely than men to be the targets of sexual harassment (Berdahl, Magley, & Waldo, 1994; Fitzgerald et al., 1988; Gutek, 1985; U.S. MSPB, 1981, 1988). Following each item, respondents were asked to indicate the probable outcomes if a woman in their department were to complain about such behavior. We focused on the outcomes of *complaints* about the harassment rather than those directly contingent upon the harassment itself because organizational managers and supervisors have more control over the former, thus making it a more logical indicator of organizational climate.

Specifically, we asked respondents to rate the *risk* to a woman who complained about different kinds of harassment by different organizational members, what would be *the likelihood that she would be taken seriously,* and what would be the *likely consequences for the supervisor or coworker* who had engaged in the harassment behavior. The first two of these response scales sample perceptions of general responses by managers and coworkers (that might define organizational risk for complaining) and more specific responses by managers (taking the complaint of harassment seriously). The final scale, assessing perceptions of what might happen to the harasser, is the most problematic from the Naylor, Pritchard, and Ilgen (1980) perspective; it defines an outcome several steps removed from the complaint and is the result of a lengthy and tangled administrative process. Nonetheless, perceptions of the likelihood of some negative outcomes for the harasser should be part of the perceptions by organizational members of relevant contingencies.

This crossed design has disadvantages as well as advantages. The formal facet analysis helps ensure that no relevant aspects of a sexual harassment episode will be ignored in our assessments. The sampling of specific behaviors is limited, however, and with few items sampled, there are correspondingly greater chances of biasing the results (for example, by inadvertently describing more extreme harassment by supervisors than by coworkers). In the current case, we believe this possibility is unlikely. Not only did we take care to balance the scenarios closely, but we also possess some empirical evidence that this attempt was successful. Specifically, in the original version of the scale, we included two scenarios for each type of harassment and job level of the harasser but found no reliable response differences that could be attributed to the specific episodes. Rather, variance in responses was due to systematic differences in types of harassment (gender harassment, unwanted sexual attention, sexual coercion), job level of the harasser (supervisor, coworker), and gender of the respondent; trivially small amounts of variance were contributed by the specific examples of harassing behaviors depicted in the scenarios. Further examination of the individual items composing the replication factor revealed few differences in correlations that could be attributed to specific items. Thus we are confident that our scenarios tap general categories rather than representing idiosyncratic examples.

Table 7.1 contains six of the scenarios and the three response scales that were used with each. The six scenarios and their replications provided 12 item stems with three responses per stem; these 36 item responses permitted us to partition the variance of the responses into the proportion due to work role of the harasser (a random effect), the proportion due to type of harassment (a fixed effect), the proportion due to response scales (nested within scenarios), as well as interactions.

Pilot Research

This original 36-item version was included in two of three forms of a questionnaire distributed to graduate students in four departments at a large midwestern state university. An initial phone call soliciting cooperation and a chance to win a lottery prize (one $50 prize given for every 50 respondents who returned the questionnaire) generated approximately a 40% response rate for women and 46% response rate for men. Two female graduate students were sampled for every male student. The final sample of 520 contained approximately 67% women and 33% men, of which 263 respondents received one of the forms of the questionnaire containing the organizational climate items; only these respondents are included in the analyses reported here.

Internal consistency. Internal consistency estimates (coefficient α's of the response scales created by summing the three types of contingency perceptions (risk, taken seriously, likelihood of sanctions) across the 12 scenarios were .90, .91, and .94. Coefficient α for the overall climate score, created by summing across all 36 responses, was .96.

Although the individual scales demonstrated very high internal consistency, there was little discriminant validity among them, as each scale was correlated between .92 and .95 with the sum of all responses. The sums of the items assessing perceived risk, chances of being taken

Table 7.1. Scenarios and Response Scale Assessing Organizational Tolerance for Sexual Harassment

Work Role of Harasser	*Gender Harassment*	*Unwanted Sexual Attention*	*Quid Pro Quo or Sexual Coercion*
Supervisor	A supervisor in your department makes reference to "incompetent women trying to do jobs they were never intended to do and taking jobs away from better qualified workers." He makes all women in the department feel incompetent and unwanted.	A supervisor in your department talks a great deal about his sex life and tries to get his female subordinates to tell him about their personal lives also.	A supervisor in your department has said several times that the way for women to get good job assignments is to be "more friendly and nice" to him.
Coworker	One of the employees in your department makes frequent remarks about incompetent women doing jobs they are incapable of doing and refers to them as "affirmative action" hires and "bitches with attitudes" in their presence.	An employee in your department continues to pressure the women in the department to go out with him after they have made it clear that they are not interested.	An employee in your department has implied that he can make life on the job very difficult for a female employee by withholding information and interfering with her work unless she has sex with him.

NOTE: Response scales repeated for all six of these scenarios were as follows: Perceptions of *risk* if a woman in the department made a formal complaint. Options ranged from *It would be extremely risky* . . . scored as (5) to *It would not be any risk* . . . scored as (1). Likelihood of complainant being taken seriously. Options ranged from *There is almost no chance she would be taken seriously* (5) to *There is a very good chance she would be taken seriously* (1). What would be done if a woman made a formal complaint? Options ranged from *Nothing* . . . (5) to *There would be very serious consequences for him; he would be disciplined* (1).

seriously, and chances that action would be taken against the harasser were intercorrelated between .56 and .81 in the combined sample. Perceptions that an organization tolerates one kind of sexual harassment—say, gender harassment—are thus accompanied by perceptions that it tolerates other kinds of sexual harassment as well. Some of the correlations discussed below involving relations between perceptions of victims being taken seriously and chances that some action will be taken against the harasser, however, suggest some advantages for analyzing the three response scales separately.

Substantive findings. An examination of the 36 by 36 correlation matrix derived from the responses reveals several trends. First, as noted above, the three response scales were substantially correlated within-scenario; consistently, however, the highest correlations were between perceived likelihood that the complainant would be taken seriously and the perception that some action would be taken against the harasser. This trend was observed within all 12 scenarios. One interpretation of these consistent correlations is that they reflect some degree of perceived causality. That is, the perception that organizations must take a complaint seriously before anything can be done about it may be responsible for the correlations. Alternatively, the consistently high correlations may be based on respondents' perceptions of past chains of events. That risk of reporting was less highly correlated with the other two scales suggests retaliation against targets for reporting may be somewhat independent of whether the complaint is taken seriously or the perpetrator is punished. Given that retaliation can (and often does) come from coworkers as well as management, this finding is intuitively reasonable. Such post hoc explanations for the relationships among the three scales need further testing, however.

In general, analyses partitioning the variance of the responses suggested a moderate degree of construct validity. Across scales, gender of the respondent accounted for approximately 5% of the response variance ($\omega^2 = .05$, $\eta^2 = .04$; as ω^2 and η^2 yielded nearly identical results in all cases, η^2 values will be reported). Job level of the harasser accounted for approximately 28% of the variance, type of harassment accounted for approximately 5%, and the harasser job level by type of harassment interaction accounted for 9% of the variance.

The mean differences responsible for the variance accounted for by these variables contained few surprises. Female graduate students perceived the university as more tolerant of sexual harassment than did the male students, and both groups perceived the university as more toleran when a harasser is a supervisor rather than a coworker. In addition students of both sexes perceived their university as most tolerant o gender harassment and least tolerant of sexual coercion. An interaction accounting for 9% of the response variance, involved differences between perceptions of male and female students of tolerance for differen types of harassment by supervisors and coworkers. Whereas the male students perceived the university as being less tolerant of gender harassment by supervisors than of unwanted sexual attention, female students perceived the university as equally (and more) tolerant of harassment, regardless of harassers' job levels or type of harassment.

As described above, we examined the data to determine whether the specific incidents (i.e., scenarios) within each type of harassment accounted for unique variance in responses; given that no differences were found, the scales were shortened by eliminating one of the scenarios in each cell, leaving one scenario describing each type of harassment by a supervisor and one by a coworker. This reduced the number of items from 36 to 18; such a reduction appears justified by the overall reliability of the total score (= .96), the lack of important differences attributable to the replication factor, and the practical value of shortening the scale.

Results From a Public Utility Organization

The final version of the OTSHI (six scenarios with three response scales each) were subsequently administered to a 50% sample (N = 1,188) of individuals employed by a West Coast public utility, along with other scales assessing job attitudes, job stress, incidents of sexual harassment and hazing, organizational withdrawal, and other attitudinal and behavioral responses to organizational and job characteristics. The study, conducted as part of the organization's efforts to develop a harassment-free workplace, was described to employees as a workplace environment survey that was part of a series of such studies conducted by the authors as independent researchers, not consultants retained by the organization. An eight-person team administered the questionnaires during a five-day period; questionnaires were administered at the employees' work sites to groups ranging from 1 to 78, under conditions of guaranteed confidentiality and anonymity.

These procedures resulted in a total of 1,156 usable questionnaires, 697 from male employees and 459 from female employees. The reliability of the 18-item total scale was .96 for the female sample, .95 for the male sample, and .96 overall. Consistent with our pilot results, the three subscales were correlated between approximately .60 and .80 within the male and female samples, as well as in the combined sample. Also consistent with our previous findings, items assessing perceptions

Table 7.2. Subscale Intercorrelations, Reliability Indexes, Means, and Standard Deviations for Men and Women for Perceived Risk, Chances of Being Taken Seriously, and Likelihood of Action Being Taken Against Harasser—Public Utility Organization

				Scales Means		*SD*		*Coefficient* α	
Scale	*1*	2	3	*Male*	*Female*	*M*	*F*	*M*	*F*
1. Risk	—	.80	.62	11.2	13.2	5.0	5.9	.89	.94
2. Serious	.66	—	.80	10.4	12.7	4.4	5.6	.91	.94
3. Action	.57	.82	—	11.7	14.8	4.9	5.5	.91	.93

NOTE: Correlations from men are shown below the diagonal; correlations from women are shown above the diagonal. For male employees, $N = 645$; for female employees, $N = 418$. All correlations are significant, $p < .01$.

that the complainant would be *taken seriously* and perceptions of *harasser sanctions* were more highly correlated with each other than with perceptions of victim *risk for complaining*. The intercorrelations of the three subscales, and their coefficient α, means, and standard deviations, appear in Table 7.2.

Table 7.3 presents the mean perceived tolerance scores across gender of respondent, job level of harasser, and type of harassment. These results generally parallel the results of the pilot study. Female employees perceived the organization as more tolerant of sexual harassment than did male employees ($\eta^2 = 6.5\%$, the comparable estimate from the pilot study being 5%). Overall, the employees reported that their organization was more tolerant of sexual harassment by supervisors than by employees ($\eta^2 = 15\%$; the comparable estimate from the pilot study was 28%). Type of harassment accounted for 6.5% of the variance in responses in this organization, compared with 5% for the university sample. A harasser level by type of harassment interaction accounted for 10% of the variance, compared with 9% in the pilot study.

With respect to coworker harassment, the organization was seen as being most tolerant of gender harassment, less tolerant of unwanted sexual attention, and least tolerant of sexual coercion (quid pro quo harassment). For harassment by supervisors, gender harassment was also perceived to be the most likely to be tolerated, but there were no differences between unwanted sexual attention and sexual coercion.

Table 7.3. Means and Standard Deviations for Perceptions of Tolerance for Each Type of Harassment by Job Level of Harasser and Sex of Respondent—Public Utility Organization

	Supervisor			*Employee*		
Respondent	*Gender Harassment*	*Unwanted Sexual Attention*	*Quid Pro Quo*	*Gender Harassment*	*Unwanted Sexual Attention*	*Quid Pro Quo*
Male	5.8	5.6	6.0	5.6	5.6	4.7
	(2.6)	(2.5)	(2.7)	(2.2)	(2.3)	(2.1)
Female	7.4	6.9	6.9	6.9	6.6	5.8
	(3.2)	(2.8)	(3.0)	(2.8)	(2.6)	(2.7)

NOTE: For male employees, $N = 645$; for female employees, $N = 418$.

These results should be considered with some caution, given that type of harassment is represented by only one item in these analyses. The results are shown graphically in Figure 7.2.

Despite differences in some scales, the most striking feature of the results is their similarity across the two studies. The internal structure of the responses and the homogeneity estimates are remarkably similar; the intercorrelations of response scales within the six scenarios, as well as those obtained by collapsing across the scenarios, are also similar across the two organizations. These results suggest that the psychometric properties and internal structure of the items and scales are reasonable and consistent across organizations, types of respondents, and even types of supervisors (professor versus formal supervisors). A number of substantive results are presented below that are relevant to the validity and usefulness of the scale.

Substantive results. In this public utility organization, we found small but statistically reliable differences in perceptions of organizational tolerance between employees assigned to office locations and those assigned to field locations. Employees of both sexes who work in administrative offices viewed the organization as more tolerant of sexual harassment than their counterparts in the field ($p < .10$). Because organizational efforts to eliminate sexual harassment had up to that time been concentrated on field sites (which were perceived by management

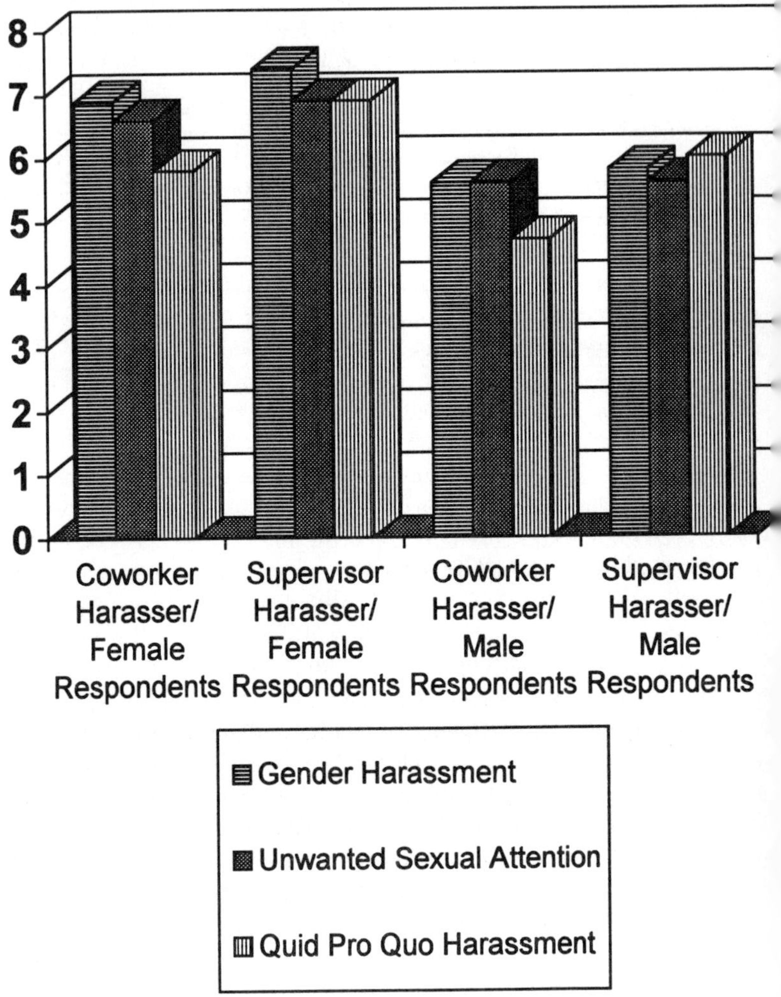

Figure 7.2. Tolerance for Sexual Harassment by Type of Harassment, Gender of Respondent, and Job Level of Harasser for Public Utility Organization

as having more problems), it is reasonable to suppose that the results may reflect these efforts, suggesting that the OTSHI may be sensitive to training and prevention efforts by management.

A second finding had to do with the sex of supervisor; female employees with a male supervisor viewed the organization as more toleran than did their counterparts who were supervised by women ($p < .05$). In addition, women who reported that they were one of the first female employees in their job category viewed the organization as being more tolerant of sexual harassment than did other female employees. These differences account for very small amounts of variance (1%); however, they are consistent and suggest that women in positions where harassment is more likely to occur (i.e., those with a male supervisor and those who are in nontraditional jobs) view the organization as more willing to tolerate such behavior.

The correlations between individual employees' reports of incidents of sexual harassment and their perceptions of organizational tolerance of such harassment were .45 for reports of gender harassment, .38 for reported incidents of unwanted sexual attention, and .19 for reports of sexual coercion. When corrected for unreliability, the correlations are .51, .43, and .30; all three of these correlations are reliably different than zero ($p < .01$). The relative sizes of the relationships may reflect true differences, base rate differences in the items assessing different kinds of harassment, or both. The correction for unreliability adjusts, only in part, for the effects of base rates in the responses to the items composing the scales. The total scale scores of reported unwanted sexual attention and sexual coercion episodes are badly skewed relative to the scores for gender harassment. Such skewed distributions will introduce downward biasing effects on the correlation.

Finally, there is an intriguing finding in the data from this organization. Several outcome measures were included in the questionnaire to assess the impact of sexual harassment on the employees who experienced it; these included assessments of psychological well-being, symptoms of anxiety and depression, physical health, job withdrawal, work withdrawal, job stress, and other related responses. In the sample of female employees, assessments of psychological climate (i.e., perceptions of organizational tolerance scored at the individual level) consistently accounted for *more* variance in job withdrawal, life satisfaction, psychological well-being, anxiety and depression, physical health conditions, and health satisfaction than did reports of sexual harassment episodes obtained from the Sexual Experiences Questionnaire (SEQ). These findings were unexpected; although we had thought that a tolerant climate might affect women negatively, we had assumed that sexual harassment would be by far the more powerful variable. Our results may reflect apprehension and fear on the part of women who perceived they are working in a hostile and threatening work environment, feelings that may be triggered by a perception that the organization tolerates harassment and the inference of managerial values consistent with this kind of climate, *without the necessity of being personally harassed.* Women in such organizations have to live with these perceptions every day, and the findings may reflect this chronic effect. They may also reflect reactions to beliefs that female employees who complain about harassment are treated as "whistle-blowers" whereas little is done to their harassers.

We were initially surprised by these findings and considered them somewhat counterintuitive, expecting as we did that harassment itself would result in considerably more negative effects. Recent evidence, however, suggests that they are not anomalous; Culbertson, Rodgers, and Rosenfeld (1994) recently reported conceptually similar results in a study of Navy personnel, using different instruments to assess both harassment and climate. And Hirschman (1995) has recently proposed a legal theory that argues that harassment of one or a few women chills the work environment for all female employees, whether they are themselves personally harassed or not. This is an important area for further research.

Conceptual Issues and Questions

There are several issues that we have not addressed in this chapter due to space limitations and, in some cases, a lack of data. One of these is the appropriate referent for measures of climate. We have reported here results based on what is more properly termed *psychological* climate rather than organizational or work group climate (Naylor et al., 1980). The referent for our results is thus the individual, rather than aggregations of individuals representing work groups or entire organizations. This is simply because we would have had an *N* of 2 if we had aggregated our measure to the level of organization to create climate assessments and because administrative and ethical concerns prevented us from creating intact work groups from the measure we had available to us from the public utility. Our original intent was to aggregate scores to the level of the work group, with each individual receiving a climate score based on the aggregated scores of coworkers, sans his or her own personal score. Thus scores would reflect an employee's immediate working environment and colleagues' perceptions of tolerance for sexual harassment. Among the many advantages of this procedure is that relationships between climate and outcomes are not contaminated by response bias; this use of the measures should be pursued. Zickar (1994) has reported some preliminary results based on the OTSHI scores as a measure of psychological climate and as a measure of work group climate. Both are promising.

A second conceptual problem is raised by our finding of significant differences between the climate perceptions of male and female employees. Such a difference is, of course, understandable and very likely reflects differences in existing attitudes, expectations, beliefs, and experiences; however, if we pursue this finding to its logical conclusion, we have two work group climates rather than one. If we want to predict the responses of a female employee, which is conceptually better: a measure derived from her entire work group, or one derived from only the female members (sans her own score)? Neither solution is conceptually neat; both need to be pursued empirically. Empirically stronger relations between one measure of climate rather than the other would suggest differential relevance of the two measures and also provide some clarification of the appropriate bases for aggregated climate measures.

IMPLICATIONS FOR ORGANIZATIONAL PRACTICE

A recent Second Circuit Court of Appeals decision, which was denied *certiorari* (i.e., appellate review) by the Supreme Court of the United States (*Karibian v. Columbia University,* 1994), raises several issues with direct implications for the theory and scales of organizational climate that we describe in this chapter. The essence of the decision, which currently applies only in the Second Circuit, is that actions taken after the discovery of patterns of sexual harassment may not be sufficient to prevent claims of substantial damages by the targets of such harassment. Nor are plaintiffs who were targets of quid pro quo harassment required to demonstrate actual economic losses. Given these judicial admonitions, the prevention of harassment by aggressive intervention programs would appear to be the best defense organizations have to reduce their liability exposure.

Our data suggest a link between reports of sexual harassment on the job and perceptions of an organization's tolerance for the sexual harassment of its employees. The content of the OTSHI reflects the perceived risk for targets of sexual harassment who report harassing incidents, the chances that they will be taken seriously by management, and the likelihood that something will be done to the harasser. Each of these contingencies can be influenced and, at least partially, controlled by organizational managers and supervisors. Establishing and communicating contingencies between sexual harassing behaviors and negative outcomes for harassers, establishing procedures that minimize the risk of reporting sexual harassment (i.e., retaliation), and establishing procedures that ensure complainants, or grievants, will be taken seriously can do a great deal to improve the climate for sexual harassment in an organization. Our data also suggest a spread of affect such that perceptions of a tolerant organizational climate lead to negative outcomes for female employees—negative outcomes that do not appear to require sexually harassing incidents to trigger their occurrence. If organizations now must prevent the occurrence of sexual harassment to reduce their liability exposure (*Karibian v. Columbia University,* 1994), the scales described in this chapter may offer an assessment and diagnostic approach with much promise as early warning signals as well as being useful for designing programs aimed at preventing sexual harassment.

NOTE

1. Strictly speaking, of course, organizations as such are neither tolerant nor intolerant; more accurately, organizations have (or do not have) policies and procedures that are enforced (or not) by managers and supervisors. Policies may be strong or weak; managers and supervisors may be tolerant or intolerant of sexual harassment. It is these factors that are perceived and responded to by individuals that generate the climate of the organization.

REFERENCES

Berdahl, J., Magley, V., & Waldo, C. R. (1994). *The sexual harassment of men: A concep in search of definition.* Paper presented at the Symposium on Sexual Harassment at the Ninth Annual Conference for the Society of Industrial and Organizational Psychology Nashville, TN.

Bond, M. E. (1988). Division 27 sexual harassment survey: Definitions, impact, an environment context. *Community Psychologist, 21,* 7-10.

Bularzik, M. (1978). Sexual harassment at the workplace: Historical notes. *Radica America, 12,* 25-43.

Culbertson, A. L., Rodgers, W., & Rosenfeld, P. (1994, August). *Organizational change The case of sexual harassment.* Paper presented at the annual meeting of the America Psychological Association, Los Angeles.

Dansky, B., & Kilpatrick, D. (in press). Effects of sexual harassment. In W. O'Donohu (Ed.), *Sexual harassment: Theory, research and treatment.* New York: Allyn & Baco

Fitzgerald, L. F. (1993). Sexual harassment: Violence against women in the workplace. *American Psychologist, 48,* 1070-1076.

Fitzgerald, L. F., Gelfand, M., & Drasgow, F. D. (1995). Measuring sexual harassment: Theoretical and psychometric advances. *Basic and Applied Social Psychology, 17,* 425-445.

Fitzgerald, L. F., Hulin, C. L., & Drasgow, F. D. (1995). The antecedents and consequences of sexual harassment in organization: An integrated model. In G. Keita & J. J. Huvvell, Jr. (Eds.), *Job stress in a changing workforce: Investigating gender* (pp. 55-73). Washington, DC: American Psychological Association.

Fitzgerald, L. F., & Ormerod, A. L. (1993). Breaking silence: The sexual harassment of women in academia and the workplace. In F. I. Denmark & M. A. Paludi (Eds.), *Psychology of women: A handbook of issues and theories* (pp. 553-582). Westport, CT: Greenwood.

Fitzgerald, L. F., & Shullman, S. L. (1993). Sexual harassment: A research analysis and agenda for the 1990s. *Journal of Vocational Behavior, 42,* 5-27.

Fitzgerald, L. F., Shullman, S. L., Bailey, N., Richards, M., Sweeker, J., Gold, Y., Ormerod, A. J., & Weitzman, L. (1988). The incidence and dimensions of sexual harassment in academia and the workplace. *Journal of Vocational Behavior, 32,* 152-175.

Fitzgerald, L., Swan, S., & Fisher, K. (1995). Why didn't she just report him? The psychological and legal implications of women's responses to sexual harassment. *Journal of Social Issues, 51,* 117-138.

Gelfand, M. J., Fitzgerald, L. F., & Drasgow, F. (1995). The structure of sexual harassment: A confirmatory analysis across cultures and settings. *Journal of Vocational Behavior, 47,* 164-177.

Green, A. (1972). *Only a miner.* Urbana: University of Illinois Press.

Gutek, B. A. (1985). *Sex and the workplace.* San Francisco: Jossey-Bass.

Gutek, B. A., & Koss, M. P. (1993). Changed women and changed organizations: Consequences of and coping with sexual harassment. *Journal of Vocational Behavior, 42,* 28-38.

Hesson-McInnis, M., & Fitzgerald, L. F. (1995). *Modeling sexual harassment.* Unpublished paper, under review.

Hirschman, L. (1995, April). Paper presented at "Women, Sexuality, and Violence: Revisioning Public Policy," Annenberg Public Policy Center, Philadelphia.

Hulin, C. L. (1993, April). *A framework for the study of sexual harassment in organizations: Climate, stressors, and patterned responses.* Paper presented at the Society of Industrial and Organizational Psychology meeting, San Francisco.

Hulin, C. L., & Roznowski, M. A. (1985). Organizational technologies: Effects on organizations; characteristics and individuals' responses. In B. Staw & L. L. Cummings (Eds.), *Research in organizational behavior* (Vol. 7). New York: Academic Press.

Karibian v. Columbia University, 14 F.3d 773 (2nd Cir.), *Cert Denied* 114 S. Ct. 2693 (1994).

Koss, M. P. (1990). Changed lives: The psychological impact of sexual harassment. In M. Paludi (Ed.), *Ivory power: Sex and gender harassment in the academy* (pp. 73-92). New York: SUNY Press.

Koss, M. P., Goodman, L. A., Browne, A., Fitzgerald, L. F., Keita, G., & Russo, N. F. (1994). *No safe haven: Male violence against women at home, at work, and in the community.* Washington, DC: American Psychological Association.

Martindale, M. (1990). *Sexual harassment in the military, 1988.* Arlington, VA: Defense Manpower Data Center.

Naylor, J. C., Pritchard, R. D., & Ilgen, D. R. (1980). *A theory of behavior in organizations.* New York: Academic Press.

Perrow, C. (1965). Hospitals, technology, structure, and goals. In J. G. March (Ed.), *Handbook of organizations.* Chicago: Rand McNally.

Pryor, J. B. (1987). Sexual harassment proclivities in men. *Sex Roles, 17,* 269-290.

Pryor, J. B. (1992, March). The social psychology of sexual harassment: Person and situation factors which give rise to sexual harassment. In *Proceedings* of the First National Conference on Sex and Power Issues in the Workplace, Bellevue, WA.

Pryor, J. B., Giedd, J. L., & Williams, K. B. (1995). A social psychological model for predicting sexual harassment. *Journal of Social Issues, 51,* 69-84.

Pryor, J. B., LaVite, C. M., & Stoller, L. M. (1993). A social psychological analysis of sexual harassment: The person/situation interaction. *Journal of Vocational Behavior, 42,* 68-83.

Pryor, J. B., & McKinney, K. (in press). Sexual harassment. *Basic and Applied Social Psychology.*

Pryor, J. B., & Stoller, L. M. (1994). Sexual cognition processes in who are high in the likelihood to sexually harass. *Personality and Social Psychology Bulletin, 20,* 163-169.

Pryor, J. B., & Whalen, J. J. (in press). A typology of sexual harassment: Characteristics of harassers and the social circumstances under which sexual harassment occurs. In W. O'Donohue (Ed.), *Sexual harassment: Theory, research and treatment.* New York: Allyn & Bacon.

Schein, E. H. (1990). Organizational culture. *American Psychologist, 45,* 109-119.

Schneider, K. (1995, March). *The development of a sexual harassment bystander stress scale.* Paper presented at the annual meeting of the Association for Women in Psychology, Indianapolis, IN.

Schneider, K. T., & Swan, S. (1994). *Job-related psychological, and health-related, outcomes of sexual harassment.* Paper presented at the Symposium on Sexual Harassment at the Ninth Annual Conference for the Society of Industrial and Organizational Psychology, Nashville, TN.

Triandis, H. C. (1972). *The analysis of subjective culture.* New York: John Wiley.

Trist, E. L., & Bamforth, L. W. (1951). Some social and psychological consequences of the long-wall method of goal getting. *Human Relations, 4,* 3-38.

U.S. Merit Systems Protection Board. (1981). *Sexual harussment of federal workers: Is it a problem?* Washington, DC: Office of Merit Systems Review and Studies/ Government Printing Office.

U.S. Merit Systems Protection Board. (1988). *Sexual harassment in the federal government: An update.* Washington, DC: Office of Merit Systems Review and Studies/ Government Printing Office.

Van Maanen, J. (1988). *Tales of the field.* Chicago: University of Chicago Press.

Woodward, J. (1965). *Industrial organization: Theory and practice.* London: Oxford University Press.

Woodward, J. (1970). *Industrial organization: Behavior and control.* London: Oxford University Press.

Zickar, M. (1994). *Organizational antecedents of sexual harassment.* Paper presented at the Symposium on Sexual Harassment at the Ninth Annual Conference for the Society of Industrial and Organizational Psychology, Nashville, TN.

8

Sexual Harassment Types and Severity: Linking Research and Policy

JAMES E. GRUBER
MICHAEL SMITH
KAISA KAUPPINEN-TOROPAINEN

Do women of different occupations or nationalities experience similar types of sexual harassment? And is the impact or severity of the different forms of sexual harassment similar across groups? The research literature suggests that there may be a universality in harassment experiences and severity. Recent works that review the conceptualization and measurement of harassment experiences and create typologies are discussed. The literature on severity is discussed in terms of five factors that affect impact: source, frequency or duration, directness, averseness, and threat. Research on types and severity is discussed within the context of analyses of the experiences of American, Canadian, and European women. The results of the analyses provide a basis for a discussion of the universality of sexual harassment as well as for conceptualization and measurement issues that need to be addressed in the future. The implications of universal types and severity for policy and legal standards that emphasize an objective "reasonable person" perspective are discussed.

Since the emergence of sexual harassment as a social and legal issue in the late 1970s, two issues that have generated considerable discussion are the range of experiences that might be defined as harassment and the impact of these experiences on women. The federal government provided researchers and policy analysts with both a legal (Equal Employment Opportunity Commission [EEOC], 1980) and a research (U.S. Merit Systems Protection Board [MSPB], 1981) framework for such a discussion. The latter developed seven harassment types, categorized them in terms of severity ("Most Severe," "Severe," and "Less Severe"), and analyzed the targets and the impact of each. The U.S. MSPB study was one of the first of a large number of research endeavors, many of which generated their own definitions and measures of sexual harassment, that attempted to determine what-happens-to-whom-and-with-what-effect during the last decade. The lack of uniform conceptualizations and measurements stymied an understanding of the full range of harassment types and, relatedly, the impact of the different forms on targets. Many of these problems (see Gruber, 1990, and Fitzgerald & Shullman, 1993, for overviews) have been addressed recently by the development of more rigorous categories of sexual harassment and more detailed analyses of severity.

The body of research accumulated since the late 1980s suggests that there may be universality in the types of harassment that women experience and in the severity, or emotional impact, of these experiences. Specifically, we believe that the likelihood of women experiencing a particular form of sexual harassment (e.g., sexual touching, date requests) is similar for women of different occupations, organizations, and nationalities. Likewise, we believe the degree of emotional impact or distress (i.e., the "severity") created by the different forms of harassment is common (or "universal") to women irrespective of job type or culture. The research literature we have reviewed, as well as our own analysis that is included in this chapter, strongly suggests that there are not a variety of sexual harassment experiences that are unique to different categories of working women: There is no "blue-collar sexual harassment" that is distinguishable from the harassment of upper-middle-class professionals or clerical workers; nor is there an "American sexual harassment experience" that is distinct from the harassment of European or Canadian women. In terms of range and prevalence of experiences, and the emotional impact of each type of experience, there is simply sexual harassment.

In this chapter, we will discuss the issues and problems that have been addressed to arrive at such an understanding as well as those that still curtail our ability to comprehend the complexity and range of harassment experiences. Each issue—the types of harassment and the severity of these—has presented unique problems: for the first (types), delineating the range of experiences that are considered by policy and research experts as "sexual harassment" and translating this knowledge into survey items; for the second (severity), determining the conditions under which research participants perceive a situation to be more or less severe sexual harassment, or accurately assessing the emotional impact that harassment has on its targets. Survey results from American, Canadian, and European women will be used to illustrate the problems of and the potential for understanding sexual harassment universality.

The attempt to discover the typical or universal nature of harassment types and severity serves at least two important functions. First, a determination of the universality of sexual harassment types may prevent the use of different standards of evaluation or scrutiny for women in different jobs. For example, a fairly common assumption that has been reinforced by some court decisions (e.g., *Rabidue v. Osceola Refining Co.*, 1986; *Robinson v. Jacksonville Shipyards*, 1991) is that gender interactions in blue-collar environments are more offensive and hostile than those of other occupations. An unsubstantiated viewpoint such as this may force many blue-collar women either to endure unwanted sexual attention or to quit their jobs because much of the harassment is regarded as a normal job aspect. Second, the discovery that the emotional impact of each type of sexual harassment is similar (or "universal") for women in very different occupational or geographic locations may facilitate the development of an objective standard of harm. Courts typically require plaintiffs in sexual harassment cases to establish both a subjective and an objective element: She must prove that she was adversely affected by the harassment, and the court must be shown that a reasonable person (or in some courts, a reasonable woman) would have been affected similarly (see Paetzgold & O'Leary-Kelly, this volume, for a discussion). Without a research-based objective standard, the courts are forced to create their own, often using assumptions about gender interactions that are stereotyped (Gutek & O'Connor, in press). Assumptions about harm often intersect with those about occupational differences (e.g., *Rabidue v. Osceola Refining Co.*, 1986): Blue-collar environments are presumed to be "rougher" and women in these jobs are expected to have a greater tolerance of offensive conduct. More generally, the lack of an objective standard may result in the plaintiff's perceptions of sexual harassment receiving closer scrutiny than the defendant's alleged behavior (Gutek, 1995).

Two recent examples of research that was developed to tap the variety and impact of sexual harassment experiences are the Sexual Experiences Questionnaire (SEQ) of Fitzgerald and her colleagues and the Inventory of Sexual Harassment (ISH) developed by Gruber (1992a). Both have sorted through an array of confusing definitions presented in legal opinions, policy statements, and research conceptualizations to present a range of harassment types. Also, both have addressed the issue of qualitative differences in sexual harassment experiences—for example, being the focus of sexual jokes versus being the object of sexual stares—by considering the relative seriousness of individual forms of harassment. Finally, both have used their research to cut across diverse status or occupational groups and, most recently, across national boundaries (Fitzgerald & Gelfand, 1994) to discover the common features of sexual harassment experiences. Gruber's critique of sexual harassment measurement and sampling problems (1990) was followed by the development of 11 types of sexual harassment (1992a) and, later, by the creation of questionnaire items to measure these in surveys of American, former Soviet, and Canadian women.

TYPES OF SEXUAL HARASSMENT EXPERIENCES

The issue as to whether there is substantial uniformity in the types of harassment that women in different jobs or organizations receive has not been answered definitively, largely because of methodological and sampling problems. These problems include variations in the terms used to describe similar forms of harassment from study to study; categories that were too inclusive (e.g., several distinct forms subsumed under one category); typologies that were not exhaustive, especially with regard to "hostile environment" forms of harassment; and paucity of attempts to distinguish the severity of the different forms of harassment. The number of harassment categories used in 18 surveys varied from three to eight, and the percentages of women who had experienced at least one kind of harassment ranged from 28% to 75%. Also, researchers generally sampled narrowly from discrete occupations, populations, or geographic areas (Gruber, 1990).

A critical analysis of 18 sexual harassment surveys found that when disparate categories of sexual harassment were compared and subsumed under general headings, "sexual commentary" (e.g., jokes, emotional come-ons) was the most prevalent form of harassment, followed by "sexual posturing" (e.g., leaning, following), "sexual touching," and "relational pressures" (Gruber, 1990, Table 4). This order persisted in spite of large differences among these surveys in the percentages of women who indicated that they had been sexually harassed.

Evidence from European surveys suggests a similar ranking, again despite differing methodologies. Surveys of French, Spanish, and English women found that verbal abuse or suggestive comments were the most frequent forms of harassment, followed by nonverbal harassment (touching, following, leering), and relational or sexual pressures (Rubenstein, 1992). Two surveys with items that were very similar to those used in the Merit Systems surveys of American federal employees revealed comparable results. Verbal comments were the most frequent forms of harassment, followed by sexual posturing, sexual touching, sexual bribery, and sexual assault, respectively (Hagman, 1988; Hogbacka, Kandolin, Haavio-Mannila, & Kauppinen-Toropainen, 1987). These European surveys, however, shared most of the same measurement and sampling problems exhibited by their American counterparts.

This chapter will study the universality of sexual harassment by comparing the rankings of the percentages of women in different occupational categories in three geopolitical regions who have experienced one or more of the forms of sexual harassment described by Gruber (1992a). A brief overview of these types and the corresponding survey items are presented in Table 8.1.

SEXUAL HARASSMENT HIERARCHIES AND SEVERITY

A substantial body of research that addresses the issue of harassment severity has developed over the past decade and a half. This research, which analyzes the factors that affect laypersons' perceptions of how severe, offensive, or inappropriate a hypothetical situation is, provides valuable insights into the experiences of actual harassment targets. Harassment severity is related to both the manner in which women

Table 8.1. Sexual Harassment Types and Related Survey Items[a]

Types of Harassment	*Survey Items*
Verbal requests	
sexual bribery	A man hinted that you could lose your job (or could have a better job) if you did not (or did) have a sexual relationship with him (Canada)
	Pressure for sexual favors with a threat or promise of a reward (U.S., former Soviets)
sexual advances	Not asked (Canada).
	Pressure for sexual favors but with no threat or promise of a reward (U.S., former Soviets)
relational advances	Repeatedly asking for a date or relationship (Canada)
	Pressures for dates or a relationship (U.S., former Soviets)
subtle pressures/ advances (sex life)	Asking you questions about your sex life (Canada).
	Subtle hints, innuendos, suggestions, or references of a sexual nature (U.S., former Soviets)
Verbal comments	
personal remarks	Insulting sexual jokes or remarks about you in your presence (Canada)
	Sexual teasing, jokes, or remarks (U.S., former Soviets)
subjective objectification (objectify)	Insulting sexual jokes or remarks about you behind your back (Canada)
	Discussing behind your back your body, sexuality, or personal life (U.S., former Soviets)
sexual categorical remarks	Insulting jokes or remarks about women in general in your presence (Canada)
	Men openly making offensive comments about the bodies, sexuality, or personal lives of other women (U.S., former Soviets)
Nonverbal displays	
sexual assault	Grabbed you or tried to grab you using physical force (Canada)
	Actual or attempted rape or sexual assault (U.S., former Soviets)
sexual touching	Touched you suggestively (e.g., brushed against, patted, hugged, pinched, kissed) (Canada)
	Deliberate touching, leaning over, cornering, or pinching (U.S., former Soviets)
sexual posturing	Sexually suggestive gestures in your presence (Canada)
	Sexually suggestive looks or gestures (U.S., former Soviets)
sexual materials	Sexual material such as pornography or degrading drawings of women displayed in or around your workplace (Canada)
	Notes, letters, pictures, posters, or objects of a sexual nature (U.S., former Soviets)

a. The items under each heading are ranked by severity with the most severe forms presented first. These rankings appear in Gruber (1992a).

respond to harassment (Brooks & Perot, 1991; Gruber & Bjorn, 1986) and to psychological, health-related, and work-related outcomes stemming from harassment (Canadian Human Rights Commission [CHRC], 1983; U.S. MSPB, 1981, 1988). Severity may also provide important information about organizations' responses to, or tolerance of, sexual harassment (Fitzgerald & Shullman, 1993; Pryor, LaVite, & Stoller, 1993). Finally, the distinctions between what laypersons or harassment recipients regard as serious versus less severe harassment may provide legal experts and policy analysts with what a "reasonable person" (or a "reasonable woman") would regard as sexual harassment. For example, such research may prevent some forms of harassment from being dismissed as "horseplay" or, relatedly, prevent women who are affected adversely by harassment from being labeled as "hypersensitive" or "neurotic."

Knowledge about the factors that influence judgments of severity has come from three sources. One source is surveys that ask respondents to judge whether a specific behavior constitutes sexual harassment and then uses the extent of agreement among respondents to determine severity (e.g., Gutek, 1985; Schneider, 1982; Terpstra & Baker, 1987; U.S. MSPB, 1981). A second source uses written scenarios to elicit judgments from survey participants about the degree of seriousness, offensiveness, or coerciveness of a particular situation (e.g., Fitzgerald & Hesson-McInnis, 1989; Fitzgerald & Ormerod, 1991). The third source, with roots in the research of Weber-Burdin and Rossi (1982) and Reilly, Carpenter, Dull, and Bartlett (1982), asks respondents to evaluate the seriousness or inappropriateness of written or visual scenarios in which the context of the harassment has been carefully manipulated (e.g., Gutek, Morasch, & Cohen, 1983; Pryor & Day, 1988; Pryor et al., 1993).

What do we know about severity? Gruber's (1992a) typology of sexual harassment was ordered in terms of severity. These rankings were developed on the basis of five factors found to affect severity ratings in the research studying perceptions of sexual harassment: (a) source (e.g., supervisor versus coworker), (b) frequency or duration, (c) directness, (d) averseness, and (e) threat (Gruber, 1992b). Conduct by a person in a position of authority is more apt to be perceived as sexual harassment than that by a peer or subordinate (Bursik, 1992; Fitzgerald & Weitzman, 1990; Gutek et al., 1983; Pryor, 1985; U.S. MSPB, 1981). Defining conduct as sexual harassment was also related to its frequency or duration. Apparently, some acts attain a high or severe rating with only limited occurrences (e.g., sexual assault or sexual propositions) and other acts *become* harassing with repetition. For example, only 24% of the heterosexual women in Schneider's (1982) survey agreed that a single date request was sexual harassment, compared with over 90% who believed that a single sexual proposition or pinch was harassment. Repeated incidents of gender harassment, the least severe form in Fitzgerald's typology, increased the severity of these experiences (Brooks & Perot, 1991). More recently, Stockdale, Vaux, and Cashin (1995) found that women were more apt to define their experiences as sexual harassment when these were frequent and pervasive. The view that some forms of conduct must be more enduring or pervasive to cross a threshold of "sexual harassment" has been supported by federal policy (EEOC, 1990) as well as by higher court decisions (*Harris v. Forklift Systems, Inc.*, 1993; *Robinson v. Jacksonville Shipyards,* 1991).

The directness of experiences separates those that are "personal" from ones that are "environmental" (Gruber, 1992a). In general, environmental forms of harassment are regarded by legal and policy statements (e.g., EEOC, 1988) as less severe than personal harassment. Research supports this distinction: As sexual comments become focused on an individual as opposed to generic women or womanhood (Rossi & Weber-Burdin, 1983), or when graffiti contains explicit references to a particular individual (Baker, Terpstra, & Larntz, 1990), research subjects are more apt to define these occurrences as sexual harassment. The range of experiences along a directness dimension, however, has not been studied in detail. For example, little is known about the impact of "bystander harassment," where women witness the harassment of other female coworkers (EEOC, 1988), or of subjective objectification (Gruber, 1992a), where, for example, a woman is the target of sexual rumors. Each of these falls on a continuum between the direct and personal (e.g., sexual propositions) and sexualized work environments (Gutek, Cohen, & Konrad, 1990) in which sexual bantering and displays are commonplace.

Averseness (degree of offensiveness) and threat (hostility) are key elements of most policy and research definitions of sexual harassment. Despite the centrality of offensiveness and hostility or intimidation to nearly all conceptualizations of sexual harassment, researchers generally have not asked harassment recipients or research participants in perception studies to indicate explicitly how offensive, how hostile, or how intimidating they found various experiences or vignettes to be, and then compared the differences. Vaux (1993) argued recently that distinctions should be drawn between harassment forms in which power is conveyed through sexuality from those in which sexuality or sexual interest are conveyed with few power implications. Conceptualizations and corresponding measures of threat or intimidation that are separate from those of inappropriateness or offensiveness could help clarify this distinction.

Most types of sexual harassment probably vary considerably in terms of offensiveness or threat depending upon the language or behavior that is part of the experience. For example, a sexual comment directed at a woman may be a crude attempt at flattery (e.g., "Your body really turns me on") or one that contains sexually graphic terms. It may be that sexual advances are perceived as more severe harassment than date requests (Fitzgerald & Hesson-McInnis, 1989; U.S. MSPB, 1981) because of the greater inappropriateness or offensiveness of requests that involve sex. A general approach used by researchers that seems to include a notion of offensiveness has asked research participants to rate both the inappropriateness of an act and its seriousness (e.g., Bursik, 1992; Jones & Remland, 1992; Popovich, Gehlauf, Jolton, Somers, & Godinho, 1992). These studies find that the source and the explicitness of an act influence judgments of appropriateness. Perceptions of what is appropriate or inappropriate, however, may differ from that which is defined as offensive, hostile, or sexual harassment (Gutek, 1995). A recent study by Gervasio and Ruckdeschel (1992) is unique in its attempt to correlate the perceived appropriateness of a variety of sexual terms or expressions and the degree to which they are judged as "sexual harassment." They found that a subset of terms or expressions that were deemed inappropriate or offensive were also perceived as sexually harassing. Specifically, women rated sexual euphemisms and obscenity (e.g., *whore, tits*) as harassing while expressions that objectified women (e.g., whistling) or belittled women's competency (e.g., *honey, babe*) were described as inappropriate. A similar approach might also prove useful for determining distinctions among different forms of nonverbal behaviors—for example, to determine which types of "crude" gestures or sexual materials are not merely offensive but are sexually harassing as well. Recently, Gruber (1994) developed a pilot study that explicitly asked respondents to evaluate the offensiveness, hostility, intimidation, and embarrassment of 12 written vignettes. He found that offensiveness or embarrassment, particularly for women, were stronger predictors than either hostility or intimidation for perceiving a wide range of acts as "sexual harassment."

If "threat" is denoted by acts that can potentially affect a woman's psychological or economic well-being, then some types of sexual harassment are highly threatening and, relatedly, very severe as well. Sexual bribery, which generally originates from someone who has authority over the target, is an obvious example of a high-threat type, and one that is perceived by both men and women to constitute severe harassment. Fitzgerald and Hesson-McInnis (1989), for example, found sexual bribery to have higher levels of perceived psychological coercion than other forms of harassment. Sexual contact (e.g., grabbing, fondling) is also perceived as severe sexual harassment, perhaps because the invasiveness and aggressiveness of such behaviors distinguish them from touches that have sexual overtones. Again, Fitzgerald and Hesson-McInnis (1989) provide insight in this regard: The coercion ratings of a professor's behavior increased significantly when he was described as making "*forceful* attempts" to touch or fondle. More generally, physical contact, even if it is nonsexual, increases the probability that verbal comments will be perceived as sexually harassing (Gutek et al., 1983; Reilly et al., 1982). It also appears that threat or invasiveness may be a factor explaining why verbal requests are generally perceived to be more severe than verbal comments, and why gestures or stares are less severe than physical contact (Baker et al., 1990; Rossi & Weber-Burdin, 1983). Threat or intimidation may be a function of the content of a harassing act or its context, such as verbal tone, body language, or taboo sexual expressions. In addition to source and physical intrusiveness, perceived pervasiveness of sexual harassment in an organization is related to severity (Stockdale et al., 1995). The fact that women in nontraditional work environments, or ones in which there are skewed sex ratios, report more harassment may be related in part to the greater level of general hostility or intimidation experienced by many women in these environments.

RESEARCH FOCUS

Our analysis will explore the universal or widespread nature of sexual harassment types and severity by comparing the ranks of (a) frequency for different harassment types and (b) average distress level for each type of harassment among women in different occupations in three geopolitical regions. This analysis will provide a vehicle for discussing the underlying dimensions of severity of different forms of harassment.

The hierarchy of severity presented by Gruber (1992a) and summarized in Table 8.1 is based on the notion that some experiences were highly severe because they were direct, threatening, and offensive (e.g., sexual bribery, assault). In contrast, other experiences were less severe because they were environmental rather than personal (e.g., sexual materials, categorical remarks) and probably less threatening as well. Subtle hints or pressures, for example, are not blatantly personal, are less offensive, and are less threatening because either the target or the purpose of such statements is generally obscure.

Our analysis and discussion will focus upon the severity dimensions of directness, averseness, and threat as potential factors underlying rank-order differences in severity. To eliminate differences in severity that may result from source or frequency, our analysis will focus upon only those women who have had few experiences with each type of harassment and whose harassment has been from peers rather than persons in positions of power.

TWO CROSS-NATIONAL SURVEYS OF SEXUAL HARASSMENT

The comparisons drawn in this chapter come from two large surveys comprised entirely of working women, which were conducted between 1989 and 1991 in Europe, the United States, and Canada. The American-European survey targeted a small number of nontraditional occupations and selected many of the respondents through nonrandom methods. Also, most of the items focused on economic, social, and psychological aspects of work. One group of women, former Soviet engineering technicians ($N = 54$), were drawn from the motor vehicle assembly plant in Kamaz, Russia. The American autoworkers ($N = 130$) worked in final assembly plants in southeastern Michigan. The Canadian data are from a representative sample of women in a variety of jobs across Canada. The survey focused on public harassment (e.g., stalking, obscene phone calls) as well as workplace harassment. Telephone interviews of Canadian women who were employed or had been employed during the previous year were conducted in 1992 under the direction of the second author. More complete information on the American-European sample and survey can be found in Gruber and Kauppinen-Toropainen (1994). Details of the Canadian survey are presented in Gruber and Smith (1994).

Survey items were developed to correspond to the subcategories of three major forms of sexual harassment: sexual requests, sexual remarks, and sexual nonverbal displays (see Gruber, 1992a, for a full description). The items are described in Table 8.1. Because the development of these measures occurred over a two-year period, the wording of several items in the earlier U.S.-European project differs slightly from that of the later Canadian survey. The women in both research projects were asked how often they had experienced one or more of 13 forms of "uninvited sexual attention" in the past 12 (Canada) or 24 (United States, Europe) months. Several of these items were later combined to form the variables described in Table 8.1.

Sexual harassment severity was determined by how distressing the uninvited sexual attention was. Canadians who had experienced one or more forms of uninvited attention were asked, "How upset were you?" (Possible responses were very upset, fairly upset, or not at all upset). The Americans and former Soviets were asked, "What effects did this unwanted sexual attention have on you?" and presented with five statements: I felt like quitting or transferring; I found it difficult to go to work; I lost my enthusiasm for my job; I stayed home from work; and I worried about losing my job. The items were combined and transformed to a 10-point scale. Similar items that were factor analyzed and scaled to tap severity were labeled "distress" (Stockdale et al., 1995) and "work/school consequences" (Stockdale, Cashin, & Shearer, 1995), respectively.

Are Sexual Harassment Types Universal?

The two surveys provide a unique opportunity to address the question of universality of harassment types and severity because they asked nearly identical questions. A perusal of the rankings in Table 8.2 reveals that verbal remarks (categorical remarks and personal jokes or comments) are the most frequent forms of harassment. In contrast, coercive behavior—bribery and assault—are relatively infrequent. Requests are less frequent than remarks, and only subtle pressures rank highly. In terms of average ranks across the five national-occupational groupings, four harassment types have middling ranks: touching (5.2), relational advances (5.8), sexual materials (5.8), and posturing (4.8). Three of these are "nonverbal displays." Subjective objectification, a harassment type that has not received a great deal of attention from researchers, is

Table 8.2. Ranks of Percentages of Women Who Have Experienced Each Type of Sexual Harassment[a]

	Canadians			*Americans*	*Former Soviets*
Ranks	*Total* (*N* = 1,990) %	*Professionals & Managers* (*N* = 242) %	*Blue-Collar* (*N* = 173) %	*Autoworkers* (*N* = 130) %	*Engineering Technicians* (*N* = 102) %
1	Categorical 46	Categorical 46	Categorical 41	Jokes 75	Jokes 24
2	Jokes 21	Jokes 22	Jokes 24	Categorical 72	Posturing 19
3	Sex life 14	Materials 14	Materials 16	Posturing 62	Sex life 17
4	Touching 13	Sex life 9	Sex life 15	Sex life 59	Categorical 14
5	Dates 12	Touching 8	Dates 14	Touching 57	Dates 12
6	Materials 11	Posturing 7	Touching 13	Dates 48	Touching 11
7	Posturing 10	Objectify 5	Posturing 12	Objectify 46	Objectify 9
8	Objectify 8	Dates 5	Objectify 9	Materials 42	Materials 6
9	Bribery 3	Bribery 1	Bribery 2	Bribery 16	Bribery 5
10	Assault 2	Assault 1	Assault 1	Assault 10	Assault 1

a. Only those items that appear in all three surveys (Canadians, Americans, and former Soviets) are ranked.

relatively infrequent (7.4). Is the relative frequency of sexual harassment types consistent across countries and occupational categories? Spearman's rank-order coefficients were computed for each pair of groups to address this question. The strength (.62 to .95) and statistical significance of the coefficients give an emphatic yes to the question at hand. It should be noted that these correlations persisted in spite of variations in the wording of some of the survey items. For example, the differential ranking of gestures between the Canadian and American-European surveys is most probably the result of item content (i.e., "gestures" versus "looks or gestures").

Also, the rank-order correlations persisted despite significant differences in cultural standards regarding open discussions of sexual matters and in sensitization to the issue of sexual harassment. We have discussed elsewhere (Kauppinen-Toropainen & Gruber, 1993) that former Soviets and American autoworkers seemed to be at opposite ends of a continuum in terms of their willingness to discuss events of a sexual nature with our interviewers and in their understanding of "unwanted or uninvited sexual attention." The former Soviets were reluctant to talk about their interactions with men. Also, they did not label some forms of conduct that they found offensive as "unwanted" because they believed that these were aspects of normal male behavior. The low percentages among the former Soviets compared with the Americans and Canadians is most probably a function of these differences in reporting.

Is Severity of Sexual Harassment Universal?

Severity ratings for each category for the United States and Canada were computed. Because the items used to determine severity were not asked of most of the former Soviets, their figures are not included. Rank-order correlations computed for the categories in Table 8.3 reveal that there is a very strong similarity of rankings across the four groups. These four diverse groups of women are affected in very similar ways by each form of sexual harassment. A perusal of the average rankings in Table 8.3 reveals four clusters of harassment types. Physical contact—assault and touching—fill the top two severity ranks for all four groups. The second cluster, with midlevel average severity ranks, consists of sexual posturing (4.50), date or relational advances (4.00), and subjective objectification (3.75). Subtle hints/pressures (6.25) and jokes or personal remarks (6.75) constitute the second least severe cluster. The least severe kinds are sexual categorical types (8.00) and sexual materials (8.25). These rankings reflect the degree to which harassing acts are personal and invasive. Physical contact has the greatest repercussions. On the other hand, conduct that is not targeted—especially remarks about other women or womanhood and sexual materials—have less impact. Although personal remarks and subtle pressures are direct, apparently they are less threatening than they are offensive (Gruber, 1994). Also, subtle pressures may be less threatening than relational pressures, which are more overt and often force women to respond more assertively. An unanticipated outcome of our analysis

Table 8.3 Numerical Ranks and Means of Severity for Nine Types of Sexual Harassment for American and Canadian Women[a]

	Canadians			*Americans*	
Type of Sexual Harassment[b]	*All Others*	*Professionals & Managers*	*Blue-Collar Workers*	*Autoworkers*	*Average Rank*
Verbal requests					
sexual bribery[c]					
relational advances	4 (5.89)	3 (6.25)	4 (5.92)	5 (4.33)	4.00
subtle pressures	6 (5.37)	6 (5.13)	7 (5.00)	6 (4.18)	6.25
Verbal remarks					
personal remarks	7 (4.92)	7 (4.60)	5 (5.71)	8 (3.79)	6.75
subjective objectification	5 (5.74)	4 (6.00)	3 (6.25)	3 (5.20)	3.75
sexual categorical	8 (4.44)	8 (4.31)	9 (4.34)	9 (3.44)	8.00
Nonverbal displays					
sexual assault	1 (8.51)	1 (8.91)	1 (8.72)	1 (8.01)	1.00
sexual touching	2 (6.45)	2 (6.82)	2 (7.59)	2 (6.16)	2.00
sexual posturing	3 (6.13)	5 (5.83)	6 (5.45)	4 (4.58)	4.50
sexual materials	9 (4.08)	9 (3.96)	8 (4.61)	7 (4.01)	8.25

NOTE: Spearman rank-order correlations are as follows: Others with Professionals & Managers (.92), Blue-Collar (.82), Autoworkers (.93); Professionals & Managers with Blue-Collar (.93), Autoworkers (.91); Blue-Collar with Autoworkers (.86). All correlations are significant where $p < .01$.
a. Only harassment by peers and low-frequency experiences were analyzed.
b. Severity ranks are presented as numerals; means are in parentheses.
c. Sexual bribery figures are omitted because nearly all cases involved supervisors.

was the high average ranking (third) of subjective objectification. A pilot study (Gruber, 1994) that presented undergraduate students with a vignette that portrayed a woman who was the victim of rumoring found that it was perceived as more offensive, hostile, and intimidating than relational advances, subtle pressures, sexual posturing, and sexual categorical remarks. Perhaps the severity of subjective objectification points to another factor that affects the impact of some forms of harassment: how public the offensive or hostile conduct is. Such conduct may function as a form of "identity stripping" (Goffman, 1977) in two ways: by making the private (i.e., sexuality) a matter of public discourse and by negating a woman's ability to control or influence the discourse (Benokraitis & Feagin, 1986; Gruber, 1992a).

SUMMARY AND DISCUSSION

What We Know and What It Means: An Emerging Universality of Sexual Harassment Types and Severity?

The course of research over the last two decades has gradually produced a determination of the types of experiences that constitute sexual harassment from a legal or policy standpoint, as well as the severity or impact of these experiences. Although early research, because of definitional and methodological problems, may have created a sense that sexual harassment experiences differ widely from group to group, more recent research suggests that the types of experiences women have are similar. Researchers who used the Merit Systems (1981) categories found fairly similar arrays of experiences—some types of experiences were consistently more common than others—although the percentage of women who experienced a particular form of harassment (e.g., touching) varied from one study to another (e.g., Hagman, 1988; Stringer-Moore, 1982; Verba, DiNunzio, & Spaulding, 1983). The cross-national data presented here provide further evidence for the universality of sexual harassment experiences.

Based on our analyses, the severity of different types of sexual harassment also appears to be universal. The severity rankings of different types of harassment experiences seem to be a function of one or more of five factors: source, frequency or duration, directness, threat, and offensiveness. The impact of each factor on severity is largely speculative at this point because researchers have not analyzed the unique contribution of each factor to the severity ratings of a particular harassment experience. What we have shown is that a "typical" experience of one kind (e.g., touching) is more or less severe than typical experiences of other types (e.g., assault, jokes). For example, experiences that are environmental (materials and categorical remarks) have lesser impact, and directed comments or queries that are apparently not highly threatening (jokes or subtle pressures) have more. In contrast, physical assertion by the harasser has a very severe impact.

The Tasks Before Us: Old Problems and New Directions

There is considerable research that shows that women who have had experiences that are defined objectively as sexual harassment often do not perceive these as sexual harassment (e.g., Fitzgerald, Weitzman,

Gold, & Ormerod, 1988; Stockdale et al., 1995). Perhaps this is the case because current survey techniques that ask respondents about unwanted sexual attention do not fully account for the wide range in content (and therefore in severity) that many experiences have. Also, although research on perceptions has been notable in its attention to the effects of content or context on severity, or acknowledgment of an experience as sexual harassment, little attention has been given to measures that explicitly tap differences in offensiveness and threat. As a result, it is often difficult to determine precisely why one experience is perceived as more serious than another. Specifically, it may be that one or more dimensions (e.g., directness, offensiveness) have greater impact in determining severity than others. It may be, for example, that Tata's (1993) finding that source did not affect whether sexual coercion, bribery, or assault (three of Fitzgerald's SEQ categories) were perceived as severe sexual harassment is a function of the very high levels of threat or offensiveness that these types of conduct already have.

Perceptions research that asks lay observers to make judgments about hypothetical situations, as well as research that asks women about their actual experiences, needs to include measures that tap a greater variety of harassment dimensions, such as the ones described in this chapter. Specifically, an understanding of sexual harassment severity can be enhanced by the following:

(1) Developing thresholds for frequency or duration. Although it seems clear that some experiences attain high severity with only limited repetition (e.g., bribery or assault), there is little research that establishes how often the less severe (and more prevalent) types of experiences must occur before they become significantly more severe. It may be, as Fitzgerald and Shullman (1993) argue, that the impact of some types of harassment is cumulative.

(2) Creating supplementary scales to tap offensiveness and threat. Because harassment experiences differ widely in content and context, a more solid link between type of experience and the severity of the experience might be made by evaluating the relative offensiveness and threat of these. A pilot study of respondents' reactions to vignettes conducted by the first author found that items that tapped offensiveness, hostility, embarrassment, and intimidation were uniquely related to perceptions of sexual harassment. A fairly common survey strategy that asks women to describe in detail either a recent event or

the one that had the greatest impact could be enhanced by asking recipients to indicate levels of offensiveness or intimidation.

(3) Expanding the content of offensive and threatening experiences. Which types of language or behavior *are* offensive or threatening? Gervasio and Ruckdeschel (1992) have filled a void with their analysis of various sexual expressions. Specifically, researchers often use terms such as *crude, vulgar,* or *offensive* to describe language or behavior without clarifying which words or deeds they are referring to. This creates the obvious problem of leaving the meaning of *crude* or *vulgar* to the imagination of the respondent. It seems that research that studies perceptions through the use of vignettes could easily accommodate these changes by inserting different forms of sexual language or gestures and then asking respondents to indicate the offensiveness and threat of each. For survey researchers who use types of experiences (e.g., SEQ, ISH), the problem is more difficult. The most feasible approach seems to be to present open-ended questions following each sexual harassment survey item and ask the respondent to provide precise information on the words and behavior. The researcher could then content analyze the open-ended responses and create a continuum of experiences that fall under each specific harassment type.

(4) Exploring aspects of directness. Often, surveys have asked a woman if she has experienced comments or gestures without specifying whether these were directed to her, at other women, or about her as a target of public scorn. Directness is rarely treated systematically. For example, the "gender harassment" category of the highly regarded Sexual Experiences Questionnaire (Fitzgerald et al., 1988) includes such response items as "suggestive stories or offensive jokes" and "crudely sexual remarks" without specifying whether these were directed at her or at women in general. The ISH (Gruber, 1992a) was developed to account for such differences—such as personal remarks versus sexual categorical remarks and subjective objectification. These distinctions revealed another aspect that has not been studied systematically: how public the harassment was. For example, the public nature of rumoring may contribute to its relatively high severity ranking (Table 8.3). In general, it may be that some types of harassment that occur before an "audience" may have greater impact than similar conduct that is one-to-one.

(5) Exploring the totality of sexual harassment experiences. We concur with others who have noted recently that harassment experiences are rarely of one type (Fitzgerald & Shullman, 1993; Gutek & Koss, 1993). Although pervasiveness is a component of sexual harassment policies, as well as of recent court decisions focusing on hostile environment claims, there is little research available that could be used to inform policy or legal processes (Gutek, 1995). The data from the Canadian survey that were explored in this chapter revealed that the typical recipient had been a target of more than four types of sexual harassment. Furthermore, recipients of severe harassment (e.g., touching, bribery) experienced more different types of harassment than those who experienced less severe harassment (e.g., jokes). To accompany an analysis of frequency or duration of a particular type of harassment, researchers also need to measure the number of different types of harassment a woman has experienced. Perhaps hierarchical scaling techniques could be used to determine whether types of harassment, based on their severity, are cumulative. For example, it is possible that a woman who has experienced a harassment type of a given level of severity has also experienced most of the harassment types below it in severity. Such an approach might provide insights into the *process*—such as escalation of requests or of physical overtures—that is an important, though understudied, aspect of many sexual harassment experiences.

Research, Harassment Policies, and Legal Standards: Universality Among Women . . . and Men

We have argued that experiences and severity of sexual harassment are common to women in a wide range of cultural and occupational contexts. The evidence we have presented may provide a research-supported framework for the development of objective legal standards. On one hand, a universality of harassment experiences may function as a benchmark for evaluating the atypicality of incidents for some women or work environments. Specifically, we may be able to provide substance for issues of whether certain women or work environments are marked by unusual harassment experiences. We cannot determine whether a particular work environment is unusually harassing unless we have, among other things, a standard of what is typical or "universal." On the other hand, our discussion of the universality of severity may serve in the creation of an objective standard of harm. Without research-based criteria of harm, the courts' use of the "reasonable" standard may force judges and juries to tap stereotypical beliefs or personal experiences to develop such a perspective. A research-based objective standard could provide the court with a basis of determining whether the impact of harassment on particular individuals was typical.

As a final note on the universality of sexual harassment, we would like to point out increasing evidence that suggests parallels between the experiences and perceptions of women *and* men. First, recent studies have found that what men and women perceive as harassment, or as more or less severe harassment, is similar (see Gutek, 1995, for a review). Gender differences in perception are diminished further when men are asked to take the perspective of the victim (woman) portrayed in a vignette (Pryor & Day, 1988). Second, there are similarities in types of harassment experiences as well in responses to harassment by women and men. Although working women experience harassment more frequently, the sexes are likely to experience similar kinds. For example, the most common harassment experiences of women in the U.S. MSPB (1981) survey (sexual remarks, suggestive looks, and deliberate touching, respectively) were also the most prevalent for men. Gender similarities in experiences were also found in more recent research (e.g., Fitzgerald et al., 1988; McKinney, 1990; Roscoe, Goodwin, Repp, & Rose, 1987; Vaux, 1993). Also, it appears that men and women respond to their harassers in similar ways, typically ignoring the behavior or avoiding the harasser (U.S. MSPB, 1981). The impact of harassment is substantially greater for women, however (U.S. MSPB, 1981; Vaux, 1993).

From a policy or legal standpoint, the research on gender differences suggests that both women and men may be able to determine objectively whether or not "sexual harassment" occurred if they are asked to take the perspective of the "reasonable victim" (Gutek & O'Connor, in press). Based on our interpretation of the research, however, it appears that men who are asked to evaluate the severity or harm of harassment may need to be provided with information that informs them of the differential impact of similar types of sexual harassment on women.

REFERENCES

Baker, D. D., Terpstra, D., & Larntz, K. (1990). The influence of individual characteristics and severity of harassing behavior on reactions to sexual harassment. *Sex Roles, 2*[illegible] 305-326.

enokraitis, N., & Feagin, J. (1986). *Modern sexism.* Englewood Cliffs, NJ: Prentice-Hall.
rooks, L., & Perot, A. R. (1991). Reporting sexual harassment: Exploring a predictive model. *Psychology of Women Quarterly, 15,* 31-47.
ursik, K. (1992). Perceptions of sexual harassment in an academic context. *Sex Roles, 27,* 401-412.
anadian Human Rights Commission (CHRC). (1983). *Unwanted sexual attention and sexual harassment.* Montreal: Minister of Supply and Services of Canada.
qual Employment Opportunity Commission (EEOC). (1980). Guidelines on discrimination because of sex. *Federal Register, 45,* 74676-74677.
qual Employment Opportunity Commission (EEOC). (1988, October 25). *EEOC policy guidance* (N-915.035.5168; 6472-89). Washington, DC: Author.
qual Employment Opportunity Commission (EEOC). (1990). *Policy guidance on current issues of sexual harassment* (Notice N-915-050). Washington, DC: Author.
itzgerald, L., & Gelfand, M. (1994, August 16). *Sexual harassment in Latin America: Prevalence and perceptions in Brazil.* Paper presented at the annual meeting of the American Psychological Association, Los Angeles.
itzgerald, L. F., & Hesson-McInnis, M. (1989). The dimensions of sexual harassment: A structural analysis. *Journal of Vocational Behavior, 35,* 309-326.
itzgerald, L., & Ormerod, A. (1991). Perceptions of sexual harassment: The influence of gender and academic context. *Psychology of Women Quarterly, 15,* 281-294.
itzgerald, L. F., & Shullman, S. L. (1993). Sexual harassment: A research analysis and agenda for the 90's. *Journal of Vocational Behavior, 42,* 5-29.
itzgerald, L. F., & Weitzman, L. M. (1990). Men who harass: Speculation and data. In M. Paludi (Ed.), *Ivory power: Sexual harassment on campus.* Albany: SUNY Press.
itzgerald, L. F., Weitzman, L. M., Gold, Y., & Ormerod, M. (1988). Academic harassment: Sex and denial in scholarly garb. *Psychology of Women Quarterly, 12,* 329-340.
ervasio, A., & Ruckdeschel, K. (1992). College students' judgments of verbal sexual harassment. *Journal of Applied Social Psychology, 22,* 190-211.
offman, E. (1977). The arrangement between the sexes. *Theory of Society, 4,* 301-331.
ruber, J. E. (1990). Methodological problems and policy implications in sexual harassment research. *Population Research and Policy Review, 9,* 235-254.
ruber, J. E. (1992a). A typology of personal and environmental sexual harassment: Research and policy implications for the 1990's. *Sex Roles, 26,* 447-464.
ruber, J. E. (1992b, March 20-21). The sexual harassment experiences of women in nontraditional jobs: Results from cross-national research. *Proceedings of the First National Conference on Sex and Power Issues in the Workplace,* Bellevue, WA.
ruber, J. E. (1994, April 10). *Dimensions of sexual harassment: Perceptions of averseness and hostility.* Paper presented at the annual meeting of the Southern Sociological Society, Raleigh, NC.
ruber, J. E., & Bjorn, L. (1986). Women's responses to sexual harassment: An analysis of sociocultural, organizational, and personal resource models. *Social Science Quarterly,* 814-825.
ruber, J. E., & Kauppinen-Toropainen, K. (1994, August 16). *Sexual harassment experiences and outcomes: A comparison of American and European women.* Paper presented at the annual meeting of the American Psychological Association, Los Angeles.
ruber, J. E., & Smith, M. (1994, August 6). *Women's responses to sexual harassment: Results from a national survey of Canadians.* Paper presented at the Third Annual Conference of Sociologists Against Sexual Harassment, Los Angeles.

Gutek, B. A. (1985). *Sex and the workplace: The impact of sexual behavior and harass- ment on women, men and organization.* San Francisco: Jossey-Bass.

Gutek, B. (1995). How subjective is sexual harassment? An examination of rater effects *Basic and Applied Social Psychology, 17,* 447-468.

Gutek, B., Cohen, A., & Konrad, A. (1990). Predicting social-sexual behavior at work: A contact hypothesis. *Academy of Management Journal, 33,* 560-577.

Gutek, B., & Koss, M. (1993). Changed women and changed organizations: Consequence of and coping with sexual harassment. *Journal of Vocational Behavior, 42,* 28-48.

Gutek, B. A., Morasch, B., & Cohen, A. G. (1983). Interpreting socio-sexual behavior i a work setting. *Journal of Vocational Behavior, 22,* 30-48.

Gutek, B., & O'Connor, M. (in press). The empirical basis for the reasonable woma standard. *Journal of Social Issues.*

Hagman, N. (1988). *Sexual harassment on the job.* Helsinki, Finland: Wahlstrom & Widstrand.

Harris v. Forklift Systems, Inc., 114 S.Ct. 367 (1993).

Hogbacka, R., Kandolin, I., Haavio-Mannila, E., & Kauppinen-Toropainen, K. (1987) *Sexual harassment in the workplace: Results from a survey of Finns.* Helsinki, Finlanc Ministry for Social Affairs and Health.

Jones, T., & Remland, M. (1992). Sources of variability in perceptions of and response to sexual harassment. *Sex Roles, 27,* 121-141.

Kauppinen-Toropainen, K., & Gruber, J. (1993). The antecedents and outcomes o women-unfriendly behavior: A study of Scandinavian, former Soviet, and America women. *Psychology of Women Quarterly, 17,* 431-456.

McKinney, K. (1990). Sexual harassment of university faculty by colleagues and student *Sex Roles, 23*(7-8), 421-438.

Popovich, P., Gehlauf, D., Jolton, J., Somers, J., & Godinho, R. (1992). Perceptions c sexual harassment as a function of sex of rater and incident form and consequence. *Se Roles, 27,* 609-615.

Pryor, J. B. (1985). The lay person's understanding of sexual harassment. *Sex Roles, 1* 273-286.

Pryor, J. B., & Day, J. D. (1988). Interpretations of sexual harassment: An attribution analysis. *Sex Roles, 18,* 405-417.

Pryor, J. B., LaVite, C. M., & Stoller, L. M. (1993). A social psychological analysis c sexual harassment: The person/situation interaction. *Journal of Vocational Behavio 42,* 68-81.

Rabidue v. Osceola Refining Co., 805 F.2d 611 (6th Cir. 1986).

Reilly, M. E., Carpenter, S., Dull, V., & Bartlett, K. (1982). The factorial survey: A approach to defining sexual harassment on campus. *Journal of Social Issues, 3* 99-110.

Robinson v. Jacksonville Shipyards, 760 F. Supp. 1486 (M.D. Fl., 1991).

Roscoe, B., Goodwin, M., Repp, S., & Rose, M. (1987). Sexual harassment of universi students and student-employees: Findings and implications. *College Student Journa 21,* 254-273.

Rossi, P., & Weber-Burdin, E. (1983). Sexual harassment on the campus. *Social Scienc Research, 12,* 131-158.

Rubenstein, M. (1992). Combatting sexual harassment at work. *Conditions of Wo Digest, 11,* 285-290.

Schneider, B. (1982). Consciousness about sexual harassment among heterosexual and lesbian women workers. *Social Issues, 38,* 75-98.

Stockdale, M., Cashin, J., & Shearer, V. (1995). *Moderators of associations between sexual harassment severity and consequences: Gender and coping mechanisms.* Unpublished manuscript.

Stockdale, M., Vaux, A., & Cashin, J. (1995). Acknowledging sexual harassment: A test of alternative models. *Basic and Applied Social Psychology, 17,* 469-496.

Stringer-Moore, D. (1982). *Sexual harassment in the Seattle city workforce.* Seattle, WA: Office for Women's Rights.

Tata, J. (1993). The structure and phenomenon of sexual harassment: Impact of category of sexually harassing behavior, gender, and hierarchical level. *Journal of Applied Social Psychology, 23*(3), 199-211.

Terpstra, D. E., & Baker, D. D. (1987). A hierarchy of sexual harassment. *Journal of Psychology, 121,* 599-605.

U.S. Merit Systems Protection Board. (1981). *Sexual harassment in the federal workplace: Is it a problem?* Washington, DC: Office of Merit Systems Review and Studies/Government Printing Office.

U.S. Merit Systems Protection Board. (1988). *Sexual harassment in the federal government: An update.* Washington, DC: Office of Merit Systems Review and Studies/Government Printing Office.

Vaux, A. (1993). Paradigmatic assumptions in sexual harassment research: Being guided without being misled. *Journal of Vocational Behavior, 22,* 116-135.

Verba, S., DiNunzio, J., & Spaulding, C. (1983). *Unwanted attention: Report on a sexual harassment survey* (Report to the Faculty Council). Cambridge, MA: Harvard University.

Weber-Burdin, E., & Rossi, P. H. (1982). Defining sexual harassment on campus: A replication and extension. *Journal of Social Issues, 38,* 111-120.

effects of SH on organization + individual

9

An Integrated Framework for Studying the Outcomes of Sexual Harassment: Consequences for Individuals and Organizations

KATHY A. HANISCH

Studying multiple stressors including sexual harassment and their multiple consequences for individuals and organizations is the focus of this chapter. Past research on sexual harassment has primarily focused on single outcomes of sexual harassment; a summary of past research and arguments for studying multiple outcomes of sexual harassment are presented. Five general outcome categories of organizational stressors and particularly of sexual harassment are identified; they are health condition, work role attitudes, work withdrawal, job withdrawal, and litigation (see Figure 9.1). Specific research directions for studying multiple stressors and multiple outcomes as well as an integrated framework (see Figure 9.2) for studying organizational stressors and their relation to employee attitudes and behaviors are described. The identification of multiple attitudinal and behavioral outcomes of individuals who are experiencing stress is the first step in understanding the impact of the stressors on employees in organizations. Subsequent research, after a comprehensive and empirical identification of the consequences of stressors, should evaluate the dollar costs of the multiple outcomes to individuals and organizations. Sexual harassment should be a concern for organizations because of its impact on organizational profits and overall effectiveness as well as on individuals' lives.

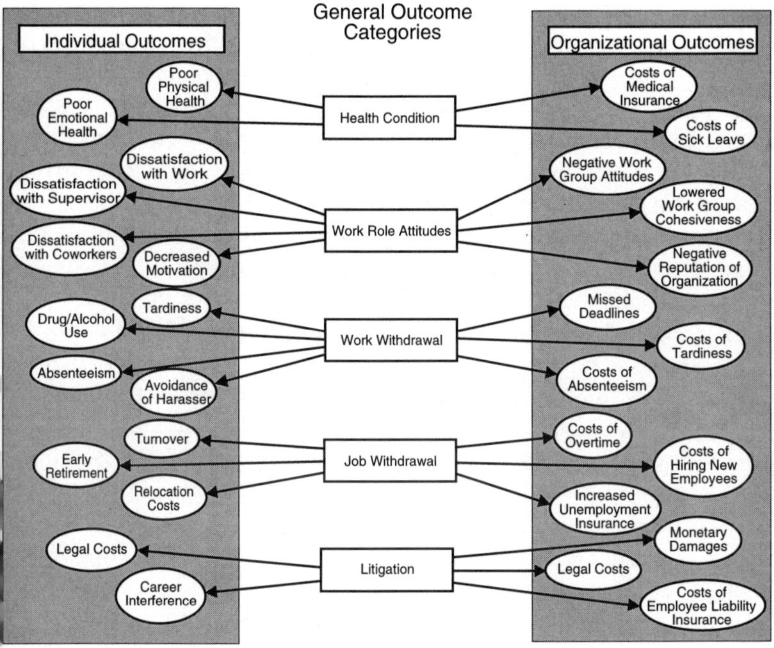

Figure 9.1. Individual and Organizational Outcomes of Sexual Harassment

Sexual harassment in the workplace affects the well-being of employees and the productivity of organizations (Gutek, 1985). Identification of the multiple and varied consequences of sexual harassment for both individuals and organizations is needed to understand the effects on employees and implications for managers. Management needs to view sexual harassment as an area of concern because it is expensive and affects the overall effectiveness of organizations. The corporate world typically associates lawsuits and the grievance process with sexual harassment (Gutek, 1985). Other as or more expensive consequences of sexual harassment result from, for example, employees' increased use of sick leave, decreased productivity and motivation, and turnover (e.g., Wagner, 1992). This chapter is organized around Figure 9.1, which shows *multiple outcomes* or costs of sexual harassment for *both individuals and organizations*—costs that are relevant to some degree to virtually all organizations. Understanding the costs of sexual harassment may (a) encourage individuals to report incidents of sexual harassment because of the negative personal consequences to them and (b) encourage managers in organizations to actively support policies and procedures and to take preventive measures with regard to sexual harassment because they are concerned about profits, organizational effectiveness, and their human resources, and not out of fear of lawsuits or compliance with legislation.

The purpose of this chapter is to present and discuss multiple outcomes of sexual harassment for individuals and organizations, suggest additional outcomes or consequences of sexual harassment that have not been examined or assessed, and present future research directions for studying the outcomes of sexual harassment by integrating sexual harassment into the organizational stressors and withdrawal literatures. Organizational withdrawal, discussed in detail below, comprises behaviors employees use to adapt to their stressors and negative attitudes (Hanisch, in 1995a). Realizing that employees can respond in multiple ways to events or stimuli in their organizations and that stress experienced as a result of sexual harassment can interact with other organizational stressors is important as we attempt to understand a complicated and difficult experience for individuals and organizations.

BACKGROUND

The foundation for studying sexual harassment has been laid. It consists of research documenting the frequency and severity of harassment primarily of women in the United States (Fitzgerald & Shullman 1993) but in many other countries as well (Webb, 1994). In addition research on sexual harassment has focused on identifying individuals who are likely to experience sexual harassment in the workplace (U.S. Merit Systems Protection Board [MSPB], 1981, 1988); traditional versus nontraditional work roles for women (Gruber & Bjorn, 1982) possible explanatory models of sexual harassment (Tangri, Burt, & Johnson, 1982); characteristics of complainants who file sexual harassment charges with the Equal Employment Opportunity Commission (EEOC) or a state human rights agency (Terpstra & Cook, 1985), as well as characteristics of the perpetrators, behaviors, and agency action (Coles, 1986); the similarity of sexual harassment to other workplace disputes (Lach & Gwartney-Gibbs, 1993); and the potenti neglect of the sexual harassment of men (Vaux, 1993). These issues are all important.

A topic that has received relatively little *systematic* assessment and evaluation by sexual harassment researchers is the multiple outcomes or consequences of sexual harassment for individuals *and* organizations. Some of the effects of sexual harassment have been identified and they are best documented at the individual level (Gruber & Bjorn, 1982; Gutek, 1985; Gutek & Koss, 1993; Lach & Gwartney-Gibbs, 1993; U.S. MSPB, 1981, 1988). Researchers have, for example, asked individuals who have been sexually harassed about its effects on personal and work-related outcomes (e.g., Gutek, 1985; U.S. MSPB, 1981, 1988), but the assessment of different types of outcomes varies greatly by study. Controlled, comprehensive studies of sexual harassment in the workplace have rarely been conducted and we do not know the conditions that cause certain types of outcomes (Gutek & Koss, 1993). Finally, direct evidence about the outcomes of sexual harassment is lacking and outcomes are assumed rather than systematically measured; future research and theory needs to explicitly incorporate and study outcomes of sexual harassment (Vaux, 1993). There are a few studies that have identified and assessed somc of the effects of sexual harassment on individuals and estimated the corresponding costs to organizations; they provide a good, albeit tentative, beginning base for this important topic (i.e., Faley, Knapp, Kustis, & Dubois, 1994; U.S. MSPB, 1981, 1988).

In this chapter, *outcomes* is a broad-based term that will refer to the consequences of sexual harassment for individuals and organizations. Figure 9.1 outlines general outcome categories of sexual harassment and presents examples of individual and organizational outcomes associated with the general categories. Figure 9.2 expands this framework to illustrate the importance of evaluating multiple organizational stressors and their relations to multiple employee attitudes and behaviors; it is an extension of a causal model empirically evaluated by Hanisch and Hulin (1991). The variables in ovals connected by darkened arrows are the primary constructs; the specific attitudes and organizational stressors included in the figure are examples of their respective, relevant constructs. The basic premise underlying both Figures 9.1 and 9.2 is that employees' work environments are complex, multifaceted systems and employees' responses to their environment, including reactions to unwanted sexual attention, will also be multiple, varied, and complex. We need to begin a more comprehensive examination of these relations

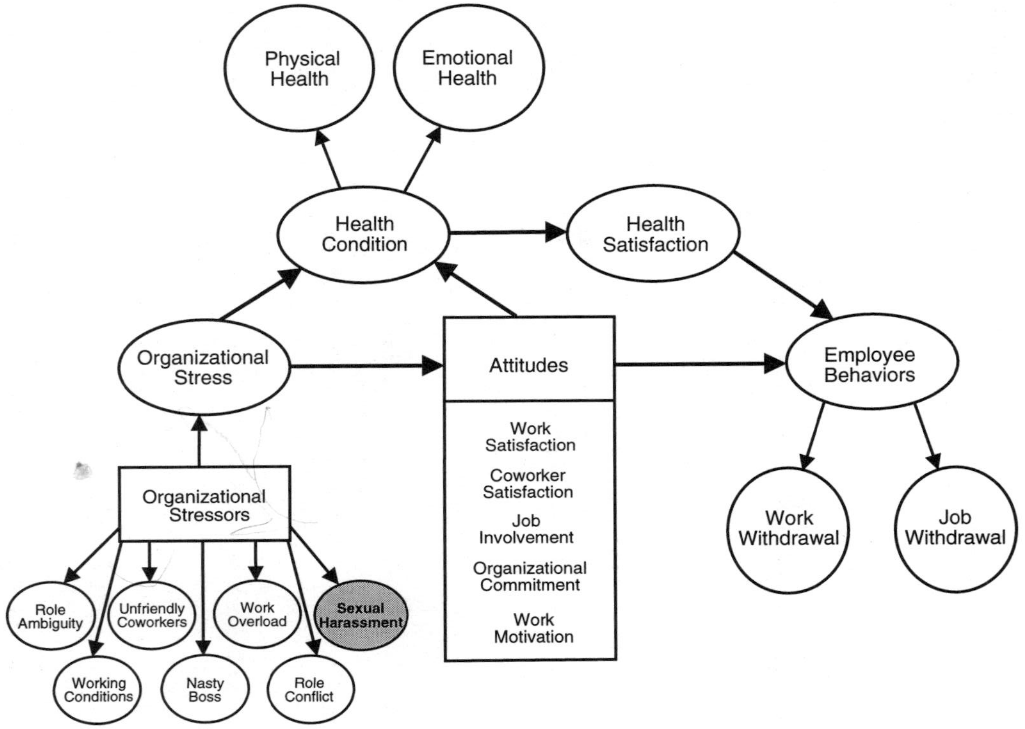

Integrated Framework for Studying Sexual Harassment as an Organizational Stressor

to allow a better understanding of employees who compose our organizations. In addition, the consequences to organizations of sexual harassment, as one of many stressors, can be costly in terms of their impact on the productive functioning of their human resources.

OUTCOMES OF SEXUAL HARASSMENT

General outcome or reaction categories of the effects of sexual harassment that have been described, but not systematically evaluated from both the individual and the organizational perspective, include work performance and attitudes, psychological health, and physical health (Crull, 1982); cognitive/affective, physiological, behavioral, and work-related outcomes (Terpstra & Baker, 1989); psychological, somatic, and work outcomes (Gutek & Koss, 1993); physical violation and psychological harm (Vaux, 1993); and job-related, psychological, and health outcomes (Fitzgerald & Shullman, 1993). Figure 9.1 shows general outcome categories that summarize and expand some of the earlier categories; they are health condition, work role attitudes, work withdrawal, job withdrawal, and litigation. The general categories are based on past research on employees' attitudes and behaviors and focus primarily on direct outcomes to individuals who experience sexual harassment and the consequences to organizations. Additional outcome categories are possible such as the effects of sexual harassment on individuals' life satisfaction or interpersonal relationships, but the focus here is primarily on outcomes that are directly associated with consequences to organizations. All of the categories in Figure 9.1 are assumed to be important because of the likely impact they can have on organizations' profits or effectiveness and on individuals' lives.

The first step in effectively studying the outcomes of sexual harassment involves identifying, assessing, and attempting to evaluate exhaustively the multiple outcomes experienced by individuals. The next step is to identify the effect or impact these outcomes have on individuals and organizations, followed by a calculation of the dollar values associated with these organizational outcomes. Scientific identification and expansion of the number and types of individual and organizational outcomes associated with sexual harassment needs to be done prior to calculating the costs to organizations.

Three research studies have associated costs with some of the outcomes of sexual harassment for individuals and organizations. Two of the studies were conducted by the U.S. Merit Systems Protection Board (1981, 1988) and the other, more recent study was reported by Faley et al. at the 1994 Society for Industrial and Organizational Psychology Conference. The U.S. MSPB studies examined the costs and effects of sexual harassment on federal merit system employees over two-year time periods (i.e., 1978 to 1980 and 1985 to 1987) and Faley et al.'s study examined 1993 sexual harassment costs to active-duty Army employees using 1988 survey data. Although the studies provide useful discussions of some of the outcomes of sexual harassment and associated costs, none of the studies provide sufficient detail and information to allow one to evaluate whether there are errors in the cost estimates. Specifically, limitations of the studies include the following: a lack of clarity regarding what the cost estimates were based on and how they were determined; no employee population size provided in any of the studies; no discussion or clarification of the implications of the sampling of employees who participated in the studies (e.g., oversampling of women and minorities in the Faley et al. study), the specific content and perceptual nature of the survey questions, and the possible problems associated with perceptions when extrapolating from a sample to a population. In addition, the reported results do not allow comparisons of the cost estimates across the studies because the costs include different outcomes; some of the similar outcomes are differently measured (e.g., absenteeism is equated with use of sick leave versus all voluntary and involuntary absences); different employee sizes, and different types of organizations and levels of jobs that are associated with variable costs. Although questions can be raised with regard to the reported costs, these are the only research studies that have attempted to tackle the issue of assigning costs to the outcomes of sexual harassment for individuals and organizations. These issues raised, however, should be addressed before additional cost studies are conducted and reported.

Previously studied and possible additional outcomes of sexual harassment will be reviewed using the general outcome categories presented in Figure 9.1; where reported, dollar values for the organizational outcomes will be given with specific details presented where available (see references for complete details). For ease of presentation, specific individual and organizational outcome examples (see Figure 9.1) are associated with a single general category, although several could be associated with two or more general categories.

Health Condition

Individual outcomes. Individuals who experience sexual harassment ranging from offensive language to sexual assault have exhibited a deterioration of both their physical and their psychological or emotional health: 21% to 82% of women reported a decrease in their physical and/or emotional conditions as a result of sexual harassment (Koss, 1990); 33% of women and 21% of men reported their emotional or physical condition became worse (U.S. MSPB, 1981).

Physical health symptoms reported by individuals who have been sexually harassed include inability to sleep, tiredness, appetite disturbances (e.g., loss of appetite, binge eating), jaw tightness, grinding of teeth, headaches, crying spells, urinary tract infections, weight loss, and nausea (Crull, 1982; Gutek, 1985; Koss, 1990; Webb, 1994). In a sample of 92 women who had written the Working Women's Institute's Information, Referral, and Counseling Service for assistance regarding sexual harassment, 63% reported physical stress symptoms (Crull, 1980). In addition, individuals may be physically injured from a sexual assault attack.

Anger (Gutek, 1985; Tong, 1984), disgust, fear, depression, anxiety, irritability, lowered self-esteem (Gruber & Bjorn, 1982; Koss, 1990; McCormack, 1985), feelings of humiliation and alienation, a sense of helplessness and vulnerability, low self-confidence (Gutek, 1985; Tong, 1984), nervousness, and stress (Crull, 1982; Gutek, 1985; Koss, 1990) have been identified as negative psychological or emotional health outcomes of sexual harassment. Mixed results have been found for the effect of sexual harassment on individuals' feelings of competency (Gruber & Bjorn, 1982; McCormack, 1985). Crull (1982), in her sample of 92 women seeking assistance for sexual harassment and 170 client counseling records at the Women's Institute's Information, Referral, and Counseling Service, found that 90% had experienced emotional stress symptoms and about 12% of them had sought psychological therapy as a result of being sexually harassed.

Organizational outcomes. An increase in employees' health problems for organizations is associated with an increase in the costs of sick leave, medical insurance, and disability for employers (e.g., U.S. MSPB, 1988; Webb, 1994). Additionally, the deterioration of employees' physical or emotional health may also partially cause a decrease in individual and work group productivity. The U.S. Merit System Protection Board (1988) estimated that from 1985 to 1987 the costs of sick leave for federal employees who stayed on the job despite being sexually harassed was $26.1 million. In addition, they estimated the costs of emotional stress at $5 million (U.S. MSPB, 1988). An earlier study conducted from 1978 to 1980 estimated the costs of extra sick leave resulting from sexual harassment at $7.9 million for federal employees (U.S. MSPB, 1981).

Work Role Attitudes

Individual outcomes. Employee work role attitudes are caused by and have been related to a variety of individual and organizational variables including organizational stressors (e.g., sexual harassment, uncertainty of work role tasks, working conditions), disposition, and work tasks (e.g., Judge, Hanisch, & Drankowski, 1995). Specifically, sexual harassment has been found to have a negative impact on satisfaction with coworkers and supervisors (Gruber & Bjorn, 1982; O'Farrell & Harlan, 1982) and organizational commitment (Culbertson, Rosenfeld, Booth-Kewley, & Magnusson, 1992). Work/job satisfaction (Gutek, 1985; Kissman, 1990; O'Farrell & Harlan, 1982) and intrinsic job satisfaction (Gruber & Bjorn, 1982) were negatively related to sexual harassment, although Gruber and Bjorn (1982) did not find a relationship between global job satisfaction and sexual harassment in a sample of blue-collar workers. It has also been related to individuals' decreased work motivation, work distraction, dreading work (Jensen & Gutek, 1982), and morale (Webb, 1994). In general, the U.S. MSPB (1981) reported that 54% of their sample reported their feelings about work became worse as a result of sexual harassment. The employee attitudes discussed above are costly because they have been shown to be antecedents of employees' health condition and withdrawal behaviors (e.g., absenteeism, quitting) that have a negative impact on individuals and organizations (Hanisch & Hulin, 1990, 1991); organizational withdrawal will be discussed below.

Organizational outcomes. The consequences to organizations of negative employee attitudes are typically indirect, with the direct costs being employees' negative behaviors and poor health (Hanisch & Hulin, 1991). Three rarely studied but logical outcomes of work role attitudes caused by sexual harassment include the negative effect on work group attitudes, work group cohesiveness (Fitzgerald & Shullman, 1993), and the reputation or image of the organization. Specifically, damage to employee relations as well as damage to an organization's public image can result from the negative press of sexual harassment (Gutek, 1985; Wagner, 1992). The aftermath of the harassment also affects the work group of the individual who was harassed, including lowered morale (U.S. MSPB, 1988).

These negative attitudes can also result in reduced productivity including a reduction in job efficiency and effectiveness (Webb, 1994). They have been shown to have an indirect negative effect on work performance resulting from a lack of sharing of knowledge or support from coworkers or supervisors for individuals who experience sexual harassment (DiTomaso, 1989).

Organizational Withdrawal

Organizational withdrawal is a construct that comprises work and job withdrawal—two employee behavioral families (Hanisch, in 1995a). Work and job withdrawal, shown in Figures 9.1 and 9.2, are two broad categories of behaviors that include the behaviors that have been studied in relation to sexual harassment; they also suggest additional outcomes of sexual harassment that have never been studied. A discussion of job withdrawal as it relates to sexual harassment follows the presentation of work withdrawal outcomes.

Work Withdrawal

Individual outcomes. This behavioral category has been defined and assessed as behaviors individuals engage in to avoid their work tasks and minimize work role inclusion while retaining organizational membership (Hanisch, 1995a). Behaviors that have been identified as work withdrawal include tardiness, absenteeism, and unfavorable work behaviors (e.g., missing meetings, drinking alcohol/using drugs before or after work; Hanisch, 1990; Hanisch & Hulin, 1990, 1991).

Relevant work withdrawal behaviors associated with sexual harassment include avoiding the harasser (Crull, 1982; Livingston, 1982) possibly by missing work meetings or making excuses to leave one's workplace. Being late for work, using alcohol or drugs before work, and other work withdrawal behaviors are among several possible responses to sexual harassment that have not been studied and are potentially costly behaviors to individuals and organizations. These negative behaviors might also reduce the potential for forming friendships or work alliances with coworkers.

Absenteeism, a work withdrawal behavior, has received some attention in the sexual harassment literature. For example, the U.S. MSPB (1988) asked federal employees to report whether they had used annual leave or leave without pay after experiencing sexual harassment. They found that 6% of harassed individuals reported taking leave without pay and 12% took annual leave. The leave without pay translated into a cost of $9.9 million in salaries for these individuals. Studies have examined a very limited number of these types of behaviors; the behaviors within the work withdrawal category seem likely reactions to sexual harassment and should be assessed systematically.

Organizational outcomes. The costs to organizations of employees' behaviors such as tardiness, absenteeism, alcohol and drug use, or employees who avoid their coworkers or supervisors as a result of being sexually harassed are likely to be very expensive. Of the many possible behaviors from the work withdrawal category that employees could choose to relieve their stress and deal with the harassment, only absenteeism has received specific and direct attention from sexual harassment researchers. Costs of absenteeism as a result of sexual harassment were estimated by Faley et al. (1994) to be almost $9 million in 1993 dollars based on 1988 survey results from active-duty U.S. Army enlisted personnel and officers. Although Faley et al. (1994) mention additional costs of absenteeism to organizations such as the costs of supervisory time spent dealing with the impact of the absences (e.g., finding a replacement, doing the work themselves, missed deadlines), they did not include them in their cost estimates. The U.S. MSPB (1981, 1988) in their two studies estimated the costs of absenteeism among federal employees due to sick leave (described earlier in the health condition outcome category), but did not include tardiness at work or absenteeism that was *not* due to sick leave. All of these are clearly relevant outcomes that need to be empirically and comprehensively examined if we are to understand the effect of sexual harassment on individuals and organizations.

Job Withdrawal

Job withdrawal has been defined and assessed as behaviors individuals engage in to remove themselves from their organization and its implied organizational role as opposed to their work tasks (Hanisch, 1995a). Job withdrawal includes quitting and retiring early (see Hanisch & Hulin, 1990, 1991). In addition, choosing to be laid off and interdepartmental transfers have been hypothesized to be components of job withdrawal (Hanisch, in 1995b).

Individual outcomes. Several studies report the number of individuals who quit (Gutek, 1985; U.S. MSPB, 1981) or who quit, transferred, were reassigned (e.g., demoted), or fired as a result of sexual harassment (Coles, 1986; Crull, 1982; U.S. MSPB, 1988). Gutek (1985) reported that over 20% of women and 3% of men reported quitting, transferring, or being fired because they were sexually harassed. In a sample of 92 women who were seeking help for sexual harassment and who responded to a questionnaire, 24% indicated they had been fired and 42% stated they had been forced to quit their jobs (Crull, 1980).

The personal impact of sexual harassment on employees may be manifest in long-term career damage or a complete change of career. If an employee is forced from his or her job because of sexual harassment, he or she may experience the stigma of being fired that can affect future employment opportunities and employment references. Additionally, the costs of relocating to begin a new job can be expensive and are often paid by the person who was harassed (Gutek, 1985). Given that sexual harassment has been experienced by employees of all ages (e.g., Crull, 1980; U.S. MSPB, 1981), early retirement, although it has not been studied, may be a viable alternative to individuals who are sexually harassed who wish to remove themselves from an uncomfortable and dissatisfying environment. Additionally, if individuals are given the option, they may choose to be laid off from their organizations for the same reasons.

Organizational outcomes. The costs of employee turnover and transfers within organizations of individuals who have been harassed have been examined by a few researchers. The expenses associated with employees who quit or are terminated involve, at a minimum, recruiting applicants, background checks on potential employees, and training for new employees. Other potential expenses include overtime costs paid to employees who must work to complete the job duties and work not finished by employees who quit or are terminated.

The costs of turnover for federal employees in the U.S. MSPB study (1981) from 1978 to 1980 were estimated at about $27 million, which included the costs to offer a job, background checks, and training. Using these same categories to determine the costs of turnover from 1985 to 1987, these costs were conservatively estimated at $36.7 million when 36,647 federal employees were estimated to have quit their jobs as a result of sexual harassment (U.S. MSPB, 1988). The cost estimates in the U.S. MSPB (1981, 1988) studies are conservative because it was assumed that the first person offered the job accepted it, and they do not include costs associated with having the job vacant (e.g., work not done, overtime for other employees), or administrative costs. Faley et al. (1994) conservatively estimated 1988 (reported in 1993 dollars) employee separation costs at approximately $6.6 million, recruitment expenses at about $165 million, and training costs of approximately $282 million for officers and enlisted personnel in the active-duty U.S. Army based on a sample percentage who stated they were going to quit their jobs as a result of sexual harassment at work. Transfer costs of employees as a result of experiencing sexual harassment in the U.S. Army were also estimated by Faley et al. (1994) to be approximately $25 million per year.

In addition, some states have required organizations to pay unemployment wages to individuals who have been sexually harassed because they maintain that sexual harassment creates a nonvoluntary reason for leaving a job (MacKinnon, 1979); this consequently may increase organizations' unemployment insurance rates.

Litigation

Individual outcomes. The legal costs of a lawsuit against an organization by an employee who has been harassed can be substantial and may prohibit an employee from pursuing this response (Webb, 1994). Additionally, individuals' career advancement (Gutek, 1985) or career interference can occur while they engage in legal activities.

Organizational outcomes. If individuals who are sexually harassed pursue legal action, organizations must defend themselves, and the costs may be substantial. The costs of litigation for organizations may include legal fees (e.g., attorney fees) and monetary damages or settlement costs. Given the interpretation of the 1991 U.S. Civil Rights Act based on court cases that allow individuals who have experienced sexual harassment to have remedies for pain and suffering, to have jury trials, and to file class action suits, the resulting costs to organizations are anticipated to be much higher than prior to the 1991 legislation (Webb, 1994). Employers may be accountable to government oversight agencies and face civil suits in which they can be liable for extensive punitive damages. Prior to 1991, punitive damages and remedies for mental suffering were not discussed; the basic focus was to restore employees to their status prior to the harassment (or discrimination) that might include back pay, reinstatement to the job, or attorney's fees (Webb, 1994). Although there are currently caps (ranging from $50,000 to $300,000) on monetary damage awards as a function of the number of employees in an organization, legislation is pending to remove the caps entirely, which would make organizations more vulnerable to expensive lawsuits (Webb, 1994). Court cases also have costs in the form of lost work hours, lowered morale, and disruption of work (Gutek, 1985).

Employment practice liability coverage, separate from general liability insurance that most organizations have for employee accidents and injuries, is a relatively new type of insurance that is aimed at protecting organizations against race, age, and sex discrimination suits filed by employees. Some organizations have decided to subscribe to this type of insurance because of the expenses associated with the defense for discrimination suits if a case goes to trial.

Other Costs or Outcomes

Outcomes of sexual harassment that are not included in Figure 9.1 because they are a composite of potentially multiple employee attitudes and behaviors and because they are currently difficult to quantify include incident costs, which are the dollar value of the working time lost by the harasser and the person harassed as a result of the incident itself (Faley et al., 1994), and a decrease in productivity of the individual who was harassed or the harasser that may include a reduction in quantity and quality of work as well as their lack of ability to work with others (e.g., Gruber & Bjorn, 1982; Tangri et al., 1982; U.S. MSPB, 1988). Additional effects on individuals who are sexually harassed may include poor decision making, feelings of distrust and betrayal, work disruption, and a hostile environment (Vaux, 1993). Others discuss the possibility of an increased risk of retribution from harassers and the organization (Fritz, 1989), as well as retaliation in the form of psychological abuse, lowered performance evaluations, shunning of coworkers, and withdrawal of social support (Salisbury, Ginorio, Remick, & Stringer, 1986).

The time involved in the harassing episode(s) can be costly. At least two employees are wasting valuable work time during an incident. It has been documented that incidents of sexual harassment are not just one-time occurrences or passing events. In fact, most individuals reported being subjected to repeated harassment that lasted more than a week and in many cases longer than six months (U.S. MSPB, 1981). It has also been reported that individuals believed that their harasser had behaved in a similar way to other employees (U.S. MSPB, 1981). Faley et al. (1994) estimated incident costs, using conservative time estimates that would apply to both the harasser and the person being harassed, to be $9 million per year for officers and enlisted personnel in the active-duty U.S. Army.

In the U.S. MSPB (1981) study of federal employees, 21% of the individuals reported that their quantity of work became worse, 20% stated their quality of work became worse, and 30% said their ability to work with others was worse as a result of being sexually harassed. The authors estimated the costs due to individual lost productivity of those who had been harassed at about $72 million, and $77 million for work group productivity (U.S. MSPB, 1981). Faley et al. (1994) also estimated productivity-reduction costs by asking individuals who were harassed to report the frequency of each harassing experience and its impact on their productivity. The total estimated annual productivity-reduction costs for the active-duty U.S. Army in 1988 (reported in 1993 dollars) was $36 million.

Summary of Organizational Outcomes or Costs

The federal government conservatively estimated a loss of $189 million as a result of sexual harassment—$102 million for women and $87 million for men—from 1978 to 1980 (U.S. MSPB, 1981), and $267 million from 1985 to 1987 (U.S. MSPB, 1988) due to federal employee job turnover, medical insurance claims, sick leave payments as a result of absenteeism, and reduced individual and work group productivity. Faley et al. (1994) estimated the U.S. Army's costs of sexual harassment per year in 1988 (reported in 1993 dollars) to be almost $533 million, which included productivity reduction, incident, absenteeism, separation, replacement, transfer, and miscellaneous costs. They did not include costs of litigation or medical and counseling services associated with sexual harassment.

The possible additional costs or outcomes of sexual harassment, described above using the general outcome categories, that have never been studied and were not included in the U.S. MSPB (1981, 1988) or Faley et al. (1994) studies lead to the conclusion that the costs of sexual harassment are potentially much higher than any of the reported studies that have estimated the organizational costs of sexual harassment. The three studies that have calculated some of the costs of sexual harassment have widely diverse values (i.e., $189,000,000 versus $267,000,000 versus $533,000,000). As previously mentioned, the differences are likely due to the assessment of outcomes, components of the various costs, exhaustiveness of the costs, type of organization (e.g., job levels), number of employees, and possibilities of errors in estimates. Therefore, no cost equating across studies is possible in these three studies. However, these studies do indicate some of the expenses associated with sexual harassment and also attest to the costs of sexual harassment to employees (e.g., poor physical and emotional health, lost pay).

Identification, accurate assessment, and detailed reporting of the many outcomes of sexual harassment are needed so that when costs are estimated in different organizations with different types of employees, they will be based on the same outcomes and can be reported on a per employee basis. If these could be achieved, studies evaluating the outcomes and costs to individuals and organizations could be more accurately and appropriately compared. Future research should strive to report all pertinent details so we can fully understand the costs of sexual harassment; this will enable sexual harassment to be more effectively dealt with in organizations. Sexual harassment as one of many organizational stressors that have consequences or outcomes for individuals and organizations is discussed below.

SEXUAL HARASSMENT AS AN ORGANIZATIONAL STRESSOR

This section relates sexual harassment to the general category or construct to which it belongs, namely, organizational stressors. An organizational stressor has been defined as an antecedent condition within one's job or the organization that requires adaptive responses on the part of an employee (Beehr & Newman, 1978). Organizational stress has been defined as the uncomfortable feelings derived from forces found in the workplace that an individual experiences when he or she is forced to deviate from normal or desired patterns of functioning (Summers, DeNisi, & DeCotiis, 1989). Given the earlier review of individual outcomes of sexual harassment, it is clear that sexual harassment has been found to cause employees to feel uncomfortable and to engage in adaptive behaviors that have costly consequences to organizations. Brown (1991) states that individuals who are sexually harassed are exposed to and undergo multiple abnormal stressors. The work stress literature describes various stressors including role conflict and ambiguity (e.g., Kahn, Wolfe, Quinn, Snoek, & Rosenthal, 1964), work overload (e.g., French & Caplan, 1970), and situational constraints imposed on the employee by the organization (e.g., Peters & O'Connor, 1980). Figure 9.2 presents examples of stressors, including sexual harassment, that employees may experience in their organizations.

Empirical research on organizational stressors has identified the following employee outcomes or reactions that, in turn, affect organizations' profit-making or effectiveness goal: cardiovascular disease, hypertension, depression, decreased self-esteem and emotional well-being, dysfunctional family relationships, anxiety/tension, high levels of frustration, job dissatisfaction, low organizational commitment, low job involvement, poor work performance, reduced work effort, substance abuse, increased absenteeism, increased turnover intentions, and quitting (Jex & Beehr, 1991). These consequences clearly mirror the presentation of the general outcome categories of sexual harassment shown in Figure 9.1.

Of some irony, because of their importance to organizations' profits and effectiveness, is that the multiple behavioral responses, in general, to organizational stressors have been the least studied (Jex & Beehr, 1991); this is also true of sexual harassment as an organizational stressor. The costs of job stress to the U.S. economy were estimated to range between $75 and $90 billion dollars annually (Ivancevich & Matteson, 1980), although what exactly constitutes this estimate is never described. Macro-level estimates such as these do not, for example, include costs of increased turnover and absenteeism or decrements in performance as organizational consequences of stress; stress costs associated with individual consequences, such as high blood pressure and heart disease, also are not included (Summers et al., 1989). Employee organizational withdrawal behaviors, although infrequently examined, that would however also increase the costs of stress to organizations, include, for example, accidents, moonlighting on the job (as a way to avoid one's work), wandering around looking busy at work (as a way to avoid the source of stress), abuse of sick leave, lateness, early retirement, missing meetings, and substance abuse. These behaviors, as well as decreased job performance and increased absenteeism and turnover, need to be simultaneously and more exhaustively studied than they currently are to provide evidence to managers of the costs of sexual harassment and other stressors. General or macro-level costs, although staggering, do little to encourage managers to take action to decrease organizational stress for their employees.

As mentioned before, several organizational stressors are included in the integrated framework for studying sexual harassment shown in Figure 9.2. These stressors, including sexual harassment, work overload, unfriendly coworkers, role ambiguity, working conditions, nasty boss, and role conflict, are examples of some of the many stressors employees may encounter in organizations. Stressors in addition to those shown in Figure 9.2 are undoubtedly encountered, with stress experienced by employees. The purpose of including several stressors is to exemplify the idea that more than one stressor should be evaluated in our research studies because it is likely true that employees at any point in time and particularly over time are experiencing stress from more than one stressor. Two stressors may interact and result in a different kind of stress than that caused by each stressor in isolation. Studying a single stressor, such as sexual harassment, will provide an incomplete and inaccurate understanding of the complexity of the relations among organizational stressors, employee attitudes, and behaviors. Examining multiple stressors should provide a greater understanding of employees' attitudes and behaviors.

MULTIPLE STRESSORS AND MULTIPLE OUTCOMES

Both the sexual harassment and the organizational stressors literatures have focused infrequently on multiple outcomes or costs to organizations and individuals within one study. A logical question is, Why have so few researchers evaluated multiple organizational stressors and multiple outcomes of these stressors? There are several possible explanations, but three are likely: (a) the difficulty of assessing multiple outcomes and multiple stressors relative to a single outcome or behavior and specific stressor; (b1) the desire to affect or control one response or behavior for practical purposes (e.g., reduce absenteeism) and (b2) the desire to isolate one stressor and assume it is more important because of individual, organizational, or societal issues, or has a greater impact than the multiple stressors employees encounter within organizations (even though there still remains a lack of understanding and potentially a misspecification of the outcome or stressor of interest); and (c) not explicitly recognizing the multiple determinants of organizational behaviors and that employees may react to organizational stressors by forming attitudes that lead to their engaging in multiple behaviors over time. Researchers need to begin focusing on additional manifestations of employees' responses or behaviors and the multiple causes (e.g., stressors, attitudes) of their behaviors. Continuing to focus on isolated, individual responses and stressors will contribute but little to our understanding of employees' behaviors in organizations. It will also have less impact on organizational managers who need to acknowledge the various costs of organizational stressors including sexual harassment and take preventive measures to ensure the productivity and health of their human resources.

SPECIFIC DIRECTIONS FOR FUTURE RESEARCH ON SEXUAL HARASSMENT

The current approach of evaluating one outcome, such as quitting, and relating it to sexual harassment, a single stressor, although initially useful as a base of information, is no longer appropriate because of the complexity of employees and their work environments. Studies that examined one or two behaviors or health perceptions were useful, but the time has come to evaluate within a single study many possible responses to sexual harassment. The relations among multiple organizational stressors and attitudes and their impact on organizational outcomes need to be evaluated empirically to build a realistic understanding of the interactions among important organizational constructs.

Specifically, researchers need to begin to systematically assess multiple outcomes experienced by individuals who are exposed to multiple organizational stressors. As an initial study to examine multiple stressors and multiple outcomes, at least two stressors should be evaluated such as work overload and sexual harassment. Given a large enough sample size, individuals could be categorized as experiencing significant stress from both stressors, being low on one stressor and high on the other, and vice versa, and experiencing little to no stress from either stressor. This would result in a 2 × 2 design with high and low stress for each stressor. There are obviously a variety of ways to define the study, but the critical feature is to include two or more stressors and relate these stressors to many individual responses. Individual and specific stressors can also be evaluated in this framework, but the neglected and much needed focus should be on the effects of more than one stressor on individuals and organizations.

A specific research direction for examining multiple outcomes could begin by assessing responses from each of the general outcome categories shown in Figure 9.1. Several items should be generated to tap into the health condition, work role attitudes, work withdrawal, job withdrawal, and litigation categories. Individuals could be asked, in either interview or survey form, their responses (e.g., tardiness, intentions to quit their job, alcohol use) to organizational stressors—in this case, sexual harassment and work overload—or the perceived effects on attitudinal or health outcomes (e.g., commitment to their organization, work satisfaction, difficulty sleeping, severe headaches). A reasonable starting point would be to assess several of the variables reviewed in the discussion of each general category to begin to evaluate the relations among and between the different outcomes experienced by individuals.

Individuals' reactions to sexual harassment and their relevant coping skills are worth investigating, but they should be tied to bottom line profits and effectiveness within organizations if we want our research to result in improvements in the workplace. A complicating feature is that employees do not necessarily experience stressors in the same manner, and individual differences (e.g., age, education, psychological disposition) will determine those stressors that are problematic for one employee and those that are neutral or even positive for another employee (Newton, 1989). In other words, a given situation, event, object, or process can be differentially stressful to different employees. It is therefore important to assess each employee with regard to whether or not a particular stressor creates problems for him or her, what type of problems it creates, how much trouble the employee has coping with the stressor, and why he or she has trouble coping with the stressor (Newton, 1989). In this way only can stress researchers determine the relevance of their constructs and measurements to their samples.

Research that examines integrated, well-specified causal models is also needed to understand the complexity of employees' behaviors and impact on organizations' bottom lines. Focusing on one or two of the consequences to individuals who experience stress or very broad macro-level costs, such as the costs of turnover to an industry or the U.S. economy, will result in a lack of understanding of the effects on individuals and will have minimal impact on the behaviors of organizational managers. The integrated framework for studying sexual harassment, shown in Figure 9.2, offers scientific utility, practical advantages, and an increase in understanding of the relations among critical constructs in organizations.

CONCLUSION

Gutek (1985) reported that up to the time of her study, most women did not report being sexually harassed to anyone in their organization for a variety of reasons. She stated that managers should appreciate that for every woman who complains about harassment, there are probably two, or four, or perhaps eight more who were harassed but did not complain. Although the women may not have complained or filed a grievance, they were likely reacting in some way, and these responses were, although perhaps unknowingly, translated into costs to individuals and the organization.

In multiple studies, one out of ten women reported leaving their jobs as a result of sexual harassment (Gutek & Koss, 1993). The prevalence of sexual harassment within organizations has been estimated to be between 42% and 67% (Gutek, 1993). It could be concluded then that approximately four out of the nine women who did not quit their jobs were sexually harassed. A question that needs to be addressed concerns the behaviors or responses of the remaining women who were sexually harassed but did not quit their jobs.

As an illustration, let us assume that there were four women who were sexually harassed who did not leave their jobs, based on prevalence statistics (Gutek, 1993). Using the earlier discussion of individual outcomes of sexual harassment, the following describes the possible attitudes and behaviors of the four women. One woman, as a reaction to the stress she experienced at work, was dissatisfied with her supervisor, took several sick days, and missed company meetings. As responses to their stress, two other women were late for work, were depressed, and tried to avoid their harasser by wandering around their workplace looking busy. Another woman began to make arrangements to transfer to another department, did not produce quality work, and used her accumulated vacation days to decrease the stress she was experiencing. All of the women were reacting in multiple ways that had as their potential effect a decrease or reduction in the stress they were experiencing. Researchers assume that a specific behavior serves a function for employees; we need to go a step further and focus on the identification and function of multiple behaviors across and within employees as they adapt to stressful work situations, with subsequent effects on organizations.

Sexual harassment as an issue for individuals and organizations shows no sign of decreasing. A poll of 160 New York area executives conducted in 1992 resulted in sexual harassment being ranked as the third most critical workplace employment issue behind benefits and job security; in 1991, sexual harassment ranked 14 (Webb, 1994). The pervasiveness and likelihood of expansion of the problem of sexual harassment may come about because of technological progress and the information superhighway. Computer mail or electronic mail (e-mail) may provide an additional unique forum for individuals to harass co-workers or subordinates; this issue will undoubtedly have to be dealt with by the court systems in the years to come (Webb, 1994).

Awareness of sexual harassment in the workplace around the globe has increased dramatically in the last few years as a result of research, media attention, court cases, and legislation. This increased awareness may or may not translate into an understanding of sexual harassment and concern about its effects on individuals and organizations. Emphasizing the behaviors of employees who are sexually harassed that affect the bottom line and overall effectiveness of organizations may be the approach necessary to obtain managers' attention and action. Arguing for sexual harassment policies, training, or educational programs as solutions to sexual harassment because organizations should care about their employees and be desirous of such programs and policies is nearsighted. If individually focused issues are given undue emphasis, they may have a major disadvantage of diverting attention away from the problems within organizations and toward employees. Organizations may have sexual harassment policies and implement training programs, but management must feel committed to the ideals of the training and policies if they are to have a chance at successfully altering harassers' behaviors. If organizational managers understand the costs of sexual harassment and other stressors that accrue to organizations and their employees, including all forms of *work* and *job withdrawal,* they may condemn instances of sexual harassment by their actions as well as support those employees who experience various organizational stressors including sexual harassment.

It behooves organizations to have policies and procedures to discourage sexual harassment because of the noted potential high costs associated with legal fees, insurance, health of employees, work and job withdrawal, negative attitudes, and decreased productivity that directly affect their effectiveness and bottom lines. Organizations need to be serious about eliminating sexual harassment by creating sanctions against it in their reward systems. Without managers' attention and action, changes to reduce or curtail sexual harassment or other stressors will come slowly. The potential costs of organizational outcomes caused by stressors, including the consequences of employees' attitudes and behaviors, can be used as leverage to encourage managers to recognize and solve problems in their organizations.

Sexual harassment affects the productivity of an organization and the job satisfaction and health of its employees. We initially need to achieve the most complete and exhaustive identification and understanding of the individual and organizational outcomes of sexual harassment through controlled, systematic studies. Following this, we would be ready to conduct studies to associate dollar values with the identified multiple outcomes, and preferably report the costs on a per employee basis for purposes of generalizing across studies as well as reporting the total costs to the organization. The dollar values will then provide useful information for scientists and practitioners to help organizations better assess the need for and relative benefits of training programs and preventive measures aimed at alleviating sexual harassment.

REFERENCES

Beehr, T. A., & Newman, J. E. (1978). Job stress, employee health, and organizational effectiveness: A facet analysis, model, and literature review. *Personnel Psychology, 31,* 665-699.

Brown, L. S. (1991, March). *Psychological evaluation of victims of sexual harassment.* Paper presented at the National Conference to Promote Men and Women Working Productively Together, Bellevue, WA.

Coles, F. S. (1986). Forced to quit: Sexual harassment complaints and agency response. *Sex Roles, 14,* 81-95.

Crull, P. (1980). The impact of sexual harassment on the job: A profile of the experiences of 92 women. In D. A. Neugarten & J. M. Shafritz (Eds.), *Sexuality in organizations: Romantic and coercive behaviors at work* (pp. 67-71). Oak Park, IL: Moor.

Crull, P. (1982). Stress effects of sexual harassment on the job: Implications for counseling. *American Journal of Orthopsychiatry, 52,* 539-544.

Culbertson, A. L., Rosenfeld, P., Booth-Kewley, S., & Magnusson, P. (1992). *Assessment of sexual harassment in the Navy: Results of the 1989 Navy-wide survey* (TR-92-11). San Diego, CA: Navy Personnel Research and Development Center.

DiTomaso, N. (1989). Sexuality in the workplace: Discrimination and harassment. In J. Hearn, D. L. Sheppard, P. Tancred-Sheriff, & G. Burrell (Eds.), *The sexuality of organizations* (pp. 71-90). London: Sage.

Faley, R. H., Knapp, D. E., Kustis, G. A., & Dubois, C. L. Z. (1994, April). *Organizational cost of sexual harassment in the workplace.* Paper presented at the Ninth Annual Conference of the Society for Industrial and Organizational Psychology, Nashville, TN.

Fitzgerald, L. F., & Shullman, S. L. (1993). Sexual harassment: A research analysis and agenda for the 1990s. *Journal of Vocational Behavior, 42,* 5-27.

French, J. R. P., & Caplan, R. D. (1970). Psychosocial factors in coronary heart disease. *Industrial Medicine, 39,* 383-397.

Fritz, N. R. (1989). Sexual harassment and the working woman. *Personnel, 66,* 4-8.

Gruber, J. E., & Bjorn, L. (1982). Blue-collar blues. *Work and Occupations, 9,* 271-298.

Gutek, B. A. (1985). *Sex and the workplace: The impact of sexual behavior and harassment on women, men, and organizations.* San Francisco: Jossey-Bass.

Gutek, B. A. (1993). Responses to sexual harassment. In S. Oskamp & M. Costanzo (Eds.), *Gender issues in social psychology: The Claremont Symposium on Applied Social Psychology* (pp. 197-216). Newbury Park, CA: Sage.

Gutek, B. A., & Koss, M. P. (1993). Changed women and changed organizations: Consequences of and coping with sexual harassment. *Journal of Vocational Behavior, 42,* 28-48.

Hanisch, K. A. (1990). *A causal model of general attitudes, work withdrawal, and job withdrawal, including retirement.* Unpublished doctoral dissertation, University of Illinois at Urbana-Champaign.

Hanisch, K. A. (1995a). Organizational withdrawal. In N. Nicholson (Ed.), *The dictionary of organizational behavior.* Oxford: Blackwell.

Hanisch, K. A. (1995b). Behavioral families and multiple causes: Matching the complexity of responses to the complexity of antecedents. *Current Directions in Psychological Science, 4,* 156-162.

Hanisch, K. A., & Hulin, C. L. (1990). Job attitudes and organizational withdrawal: An examination of retirement and other voluntary withdrawal behaviors. *Journal of Vocational Behavior, 37,* 60-78.

Hanisch, K. A., & Hulin, C. L. (1991). General attitudes and organizational withdrawal: An evaluation of a causal model. *Journal of Vocational Behavior, 39,* 110-128.

Ivancevich, J. M., & Matteson, M. T. (1980). *Stress and work: A managerial perspective.* Glenview, IL: Scott, Foresman.

Jensen, I., & Gutek, B. A. (1982). Attributions and assignment of responsibility for sexual harassment. *Journal of Social Issues, 38,* 121-136.

Jex, S. M., & Beehr, T. A. (1991). Emerging theoretical and methodological issues in the study of work-related stress. *Research in Personnel and Human Resources Management, 9,* 311-365.

Judge, T. A., Hanisch, K. A., & Drankowski, R. D. (1995). Human resource management and employee attitudes. In G. R. Ferris, S. D. Rosen, & D. T. Barnum (Eds.), *Handbook of human resource management* (pp. 574-596). Oxford: Blackwell.

Kahn, R. L., Wolfe, D. M., Quinn, R. P., Snoek, D., & Rosenthal, R. A. (1964). *Organizational stress: Studies in role conflict and ambiguity.* New York: John Wiley.

Kissman, K. (1990). Women in blue-collar occupations: An exploration of constraints and facilitators. *Journal of Sociology and Social Welfare, 17,* 139-149.

Koss, M. P. (1990). Changed lives: The psychological impact of sexual harassment. In M. A. Paludi (Ed.), *Ivory power: Sexual harassment on campus* (pp. 73-92). Albany: SUNY Press.

Lach, D. H., & Gwartney-Gibbs, P. A. (1993). Sociological perspectives on sexual harassment and workplace dispute resolution. *Journal of Vocational Behavior, 42,* 102-115.

Livingston, J. A. (1982). Responses to sexual harassment on the job: Legal, organizational, and individual actions. *Journal of Social Issues, 38,* 5-22.

MacKinnon, C. A. (1979). *Sexual harassment of working women: A case of sex discrimination.* New Haven, CT: Yale University Press.

McCormack, A. (1985). The sexual harassment of students by teachers: The case of students in science. *Sex Roles, 13,* 21-32.

Newton, T. J. (1989). Occupational stress and coping with stress: A critique. *Human Relations, 42,* 441-461.

O'Farrell, B., & Harlan, S. L. (1982). Craftworkers and clerks: The effects of male co-worker hostility on women's satisfaction with non-traditional jobs. *Social Problems, 29,* 252-264.

Peters, L. H., & O'Connor, E. J. (1980). Situational constraints and employee affective reactions: The influences of a frequently overlooked construct. *Academy of Management Review, 5,* 391-397.

Salisbury, J., Ginorio, A. B., Remick, H., & Stringer, D. M. (1986). Counseling victims of sexual harassment. *Psychotherapy, 23,* 316-324.

Summers, T. P., DeNisi, A. S., & DeCotiis, T. A. (1989). Attitudinal and behavioral consequences of felt job stress and its antecedent factors. *Journal of Social Behavior and Personality, 4,* 503-520.

Tangri, S. S., Burt, M. R., & Johnson, L. B. (1982). Sexual harassment at work: Three explanatory models. *Journal of Social Issues, 38,* 33-54.

Terpstra, D. E., & Baker, D. D. (1989). The identification and classification of reactions to sexual harassment. *Journal of Organizational Behavior, 10,* 1-14.

Terpstra, D. E., & Cook, S. E. (1985). Complainant characteristics and reported behaviors and consequences associated with formal sexual harassment charges. *Personnel Psychology, 38,* 559-574.

Tong, R. (1984). *Women, sex, and the law.* Totowa, NJ: Rowman & Allanheld.

U.S. Merit Systems Protection Board. (1981). *Sexual harassment in the federal workplace: Is it a problem?* Washington, DC: Office of Merit Systems Review and Studies/Government Printing Office.

U.S. Merit Systems Protection Board. (1988). *Sexual harassment in the federal government: An update.* Washington, DC: Office of Merit Systems Review and Studies/Government Printing Office.

Vaux, A. (1993). Paradigmatic assumptions in sexual harassment research: Being guided without being misled. *Journal of Vocational Behavior, 42,* 116-135.

Wagner, E. J. (1992). *Sexual harassment in the workplace: How to prevent, investigate, and resolve problems in your organization.* New York: Creative Solutions, Inc.

Webb, S. L. (1994). *Shockwaves: The global impact of sexual harassment.* New York: MasterMedia Limited.

10

The Real "Disclosure": Sexual Harassment and the Bottom Line

DEBORAH ERDOS KNAPP
GARY A. KUSTIS

Several studies have attempted to compute the organizational costs of sexual harassment at work, in both the private and the public sectors. Unfortunately, the studies included only a subset of the total possible costs of sexual harassment and none of the studies has developed an underlying model or conceptual framework with which the cost of sexual harassment may be determined across many organizational settings. As a result, a comprehensive, general model for estimating the organizational costs of sexual harassment in the workplace is proposed along with specific costing formulas associated with the model.

It's used for all sorts of purposes—as a way of relating, a way of placating, as a weapon, as a threat. It can be quite complicated the way sex is used. Haven't you found that to be true?

—Michael Crichton, *Disclosure*

About half of all women (and between 14% and 17% of men; Martindale, 1988; Mazer & Percival, 1989; U.S. Merit Systems Protection Board [U.S. MSPB], 1981, 1988) will experience sexual harassment during their lives (Fitzgerald & Shullman, 1993; Gutek, 1985). Although the number of sexual harassment complaints escalating to litigation has increased over recent years (Castellow, Wuensch, & Moore, 1990), the number of litigated cases does not come close to the actual incidence of sexual harassment. The costs of litigation and associated settlements can be devastating, however, reportedly running as high as $15 million for a single case (Garvey, 1986). In addition to litigation, there are a wide range of other responses available to targets of sexual harassment, which include everything from ignoring the harassment to leaving the organization. As the individual and organizational costs of sexual harassment continue to increase, the research imperative for the development of theoretical perspectives with which to estimate the costs of sexual harassment also escalates.

Sexual harassment has been a topic of intense investigation and empirical exploration. The issues addressed in the literature have been primarily descriptive in nature and the topic has been analyzed from a number of perspectives. These include perception and its effect on individual assessments of sexual harassment, the legal and ethical issues involved, the frequency and extent of sexual harassment, the structure of sexual harassment, coping responses to sexual harassment, and the impact of context. Moreover, sexual harassment has been shown to have significant negative consequences for the targets of such behavior. Targets of sexual harassment may experience career interruption, lower productivity, less job satisfaction, lower self-confidence, loss of motivation, deterioration of interpersonal relationships, and loss of commitment to work and employer (Benson & Thomson, 1982; Collinson & Collinson, 1989; Crull, 1982; DiTomaso, 1989; Fitzgerald et al., 1988; Gruber & Bjorn, 1982; Gutek, 1985, 1993; Gutek & Dunwoody, 1988; Gutek & Koss, 1993; Gutek & Nakamura, 1982; Silverman, 1976-1977; U.S. MSPB, 1981, 1988).

Although the previous discussion underscores the fact that approaches to the study of sexual harassment have been quite variable, the consensus of the literature appears to be that sexual harassment not only is a widespread phenomenon but one that is damaging to organizations as well as individuals. As a result, sexual harassment has become a legitimate and serious workplace issue that cannot be dismissed as an innocuous or infrequent occurrence.

THE COST OF SEXUAL HARASSMENT

As research evidence revealing the widespread nature of sexual harassment increases, researchers have begun to call attention to a broader range of associated organizational costs (Terpstra, 1986; Terpstra & Baker, 1986). For example, the results of surveys of sexual harassment targets have indicated that harassment can lead to increases in absenteeism, turnover, requests for transfers, and the use of mental health services, as well as decreases in work motivation and productivity (Gutek & Koss, 1993; Martindale, 1988; U.S. MSPB, 1981, 1988). Some of these outcomes have multiple associated cost components. For example, turnover involves both separation and replacement costs (including additional recruitment, hiring, and training costs). Such a variety of costs can quickly add up to a substantial dollar amount when aggregated across a large number of employees.

Several studies have attempted to compute the organizational costs of sexual harassment at work, in both the private and the public sectors. The first attempt to determine the economic consequences of sexual harassment was undertaken by the U.S. MSPB in 1981. Its 1981 study surveyed over 23,000 federal employees and estimated that the total annual cost of sexual harassment for the federal workforce was $188.7 million. The study was repeated by the U.S. MSPB in 1987. In this study, the total annual cost of sexual harassment in the federal workforce was estimated to be $267.3 million. The total cost of sexual harassment was based on four categories: (a) job turnover ($36.7 million), (b) sick leave ($26.1 million), (c) individual productivity ($76.3 million), and (d) work group productivity ($128.2 million).

The strengths of the U.S. MSPB studies were twofold. First, they brought attention to the wide range of organizational costs (other than legal costs) that are associated with sexual harassment. Second, the total dollar estimates of the studies were large enough to draw attention to the magnitude of the potential financial impact of sexual harassment on organizations. Unfortunately, the studies included only a subset of the total possible costs of sexual harassment (for example, the study did not consider transfer costs or the cost of medical or emotional counseling). Moreover, the various costs involved in these studies involved a considerable amount of "guesstimation" by the researchers. Finally, none of the studies that have attempted to determine the costs of sexual harassment has developed an underlying model or conceptual framework with which the cost of sexual harassment may be determined across many organizational settings.

An attempt at costing the organizational impact of sexual harassment in the private sector came from a survey of individuals in 160 *Fortune* 500 companies, the results of which were published in *Working Woman Magazine* (Sandroff, 1988). The total annual cost to a *Fortune* 500 company with 23,750 employees was estimated to be $6.7 million. This amount included the costs associated with increased absenteeism and turnover as well as productivity losses. The scientific merit of this study is questionable because the study's methodology and other details (e.g., the sampling and costing strategies) are not available.

Although the costing-related research has made important contributions to understanding the financial impact of sexual harassment, a comprehensive framework of the determinants of the costs of sexual harassment has yet to be developed. Clearly, given the magnitude of the individual and organizational costs associated with sexual harassment, research that addresses methods for estimating the costs of such behavior to organizations is an important human resource-related issue. Therefore, the following discussion outlines a conceptual model for determining the costs of sexual harassment as well as suggestions for measuring specific model elements. Further, this model can be applied in any organizational setting.

COMPREHENSIVE BEHAVIORAL COSTING MODEL OF SEXUAL HARASSMENT

Determining the economic costs and benefits of employee action using the behavioral costing approach has been the subject of researc since the mid-1970s (Cascio, 1991). Behavior costing has been used t determine the costs of absenteeism, turnover, training, employee assis tance programs, and so on. Further, attaching a cost to employee behav ior is an effective method of demonstrating the pervasiveness of a organizational problem. Problems viewed as inconsequential to th organization are often perceived differently once their direct impact o the bottom line is more fully understood. For example, in some organi zations, sexual harassment may be viewed as an unfortunate, work related problem but, aside from the legal implications, hardly wort spending much time and money to eradicate. A behavior costing ap proach would provide such an organization with a practical method

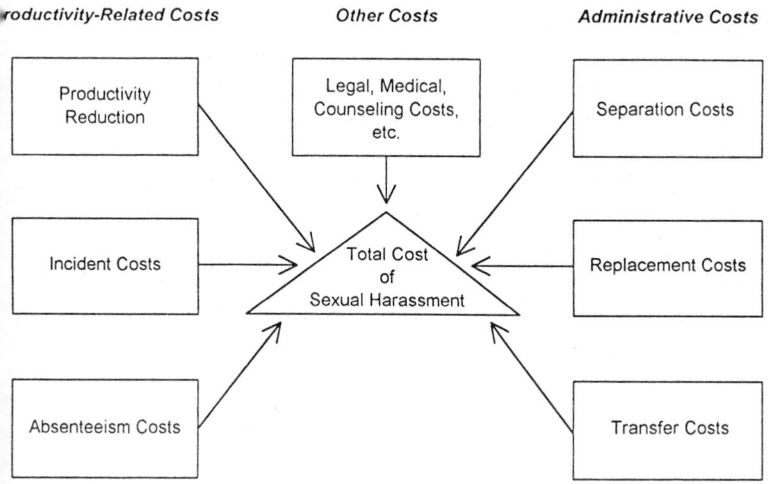

Figure 10.1. Comprehensive Behavior Costing Model of Sexual Harassment

determining the financial implications of its current approach to the problem. To explore the economic impact of sexual harassment, a comprehensive model for determining the costs of such behavior in organizations is required.

The behavioral costing model of sexual harassment described below focuses on those employee behaviors that have an economic impact on the organization (see Figure 10.1). The model is framed in terms of three broad categories of costs: productivity-related costs, administrative costs, and other costs.

Productivity-Related Costs

The productivity-related costs described below are based on the economic assumption that an employee's total compensation is a reasonable reflection of the employee's overall productivity for the firm. Productivity-related costs include actual reductions in productivity as a result of sexual harassment, the cost of the time spent during the harassing incident, and the cost of absenteeism or unplanned leave that are direct results of sexual harassment at work.

Productivity-reduction costs. Productivity-reduction costs are those costs the organization incurs when a worker's productivity is reduced by any amount for any length of time due to sexual harassment. These costs may be estimated by asking employees (a) whether any sexually harassing incidents have affected their productivity and (b) the magnitude of that impact (for example, employees may be asked to give an estimate of the percentage of reduction in their productivity compared with their normal job performance and, further, to indicate how long that reduction lasted).

The following formula may be used to estimate the total annual dollar value of the productivity-reduction costs of sexual harassment in an organization:

$$P = \sum_{i=1}^{n} t_i \; [_p(\text{Pay} + \text{Benefits})_e]$$

where P = total annual productivity-reduction costs, p = percentage of reported productivity reduction, t = length of productivity reduction, e = employee, and n = number of employees affected.

Incident costs. These costs reflect the working time lost by the harasser and harassee as a result of the harassing incident (incident costs are separate from productivity-reduction costs in that the incident itself may take time away from productive work but the individual's productivity may be unaffected after the incident occurs). Incident costs will vary based on the type of harassment involved (for example, a whistle or a catcall involves significantly less time than pressuring a person for sexual favors). A time estimate must be assigned to each harassing incident to estimate incident costs. Unfortunately, there is currently no information available in the literature regarding the time it takes to harass an individual. This is true because incidents of sexual harassment are generally performed covertly and because it is not ethical to determine this information experimentally. Therefore, reasonable estimates must be assessed when attempting to determine the cost of incidents of sexual harassment. The time-related cost of each incident of sexual harassment is equal to the dollar value of the pay and benefits of both the harasser and the harassee for the duration of the incident.

The following formula may be used to estimate the total annual dollar value of the time-related incident costs due to sexual harassment in an organization's workplace:

$$I = \sum_{i=1}^{n} t_i \quad [(\text{Pay} + \text{Benefits})_e + (\text{Pay} + \text{Benefits})_h]$$

where I = total annual incident costs, h = harasser, e = employee, t = time elapsed during incident, and n = number of employees affected.

Absenteeism costs. These reflect the costs the organization incurs as a result of employees taking unplanned leave due to the sexual harassment they experienced. This includes the direct cost to the organization of the unplanned leave as well as any associated costs, such as the dollar value of the supervisory time spent dealing with the ramifications of the absence (e.g., finding a suitable replacement, actually doing the work of the absent employee, instructing replacement employees, or inspecting the work of replacement employees). Cascio (1991) suggests that a representative sample of supervisors be interviewed to determine the average amount of time spent handling absenteeism-related issues (unfortunately, no industrywide averages are available).

The following formula may be used to estimate the total annual dollar value of the cost of absenteeism due to sexual harassment in an organization's workplace:

$$A = \sum_{i=1}^{n} h_i \quad (\text{Pay} + \text{Benefits})_e + \sum ti\,(\text{Pay} + \text{Benefits})_s$$

where A = total annual cost of absenteeism, h = hours absent (employee), t = supervisory hours required to deal with employee absenteeism, e = employee, s = supervisor, and n = number of employees affected.

Administrative Costs

Separation costs. Separation costs are the administrative costs incurred when an employee leaves the organization due to sexual harassment. These may include the costs involved in processing employee exits (e.g., exit interviews, which include the pay and benefits of the employee performing the interview multiplied by the time elapsed during that interview) and separation pay (in the sexual harassment literature, the turnover rate as a result of sexual harassment is about 1% for males and 10% for females; Gutek, 1985; Gutek & Koss, 1993; Gutek, Nakamura, Gahart, Handschumacher, & Russell, 1980). The following formula may be used to estimate the total annual dollar value of separation costs due to sexual harassment in an organization's workplace:

$$S = \sum_{i=1}^{n} (s_i + a_i)$$

where S = total annual separation costs, s = cost of separation for an employee, a = administrative costs associated with separation, and n = number of employees affected.

Replacement costs. These include the costs of recruiting and training a replacement for the employee that left the organization as a result of sexual harassment. Training costs include the variable costs of individual training, such as entry-level training and orientation as well as other specialized skills training. Recruitment costs include the variable costs of recruiting (e.g., advertising and time spent processing applications) and processing personnel (e.g., interviews, recruiting committee meetings, and testing).

The total annual dollar value of the training and recruitment costs incurred as a result of sexual harassment is estimated using the following formula:

$$R = \sum_{i=1}^{n} (t_i + r_i)$$

where R = total annual replacement costs, t = training costs for employee, r = recruitment costs employee, and n = number of employees affected.

Transfer costs. Transfer costs are those that must be borne by the organization when an employee moves to another department or another geographic location due to sexual harassment. The following formula may be used to estimate the total annual dollar value of transfer costs due to sexual harassment in an organization:

$$T = \sum_{i=1}^{n} (t_i + a_i)$$

where T = total annual transfer costs, t = cost of a move for an employee, a = associated administrative costs, and n = number of employees affected.

Other Costs

The direct "other" costs of sexual harassment include the costs of related litigation (at a minimum, a formal grievance requires expensive fact-finding and resolution-related activities by the appropriate boards and agencies) and any medical and/or professional counseling services used by targets of sexual harassment. For example, the organization can determine whether victims of sexual harassment require more medical and/or emotional counseling than nonvictims. If victims are found to require more care, the organization can estimate how this will be passed on in the form of higher insurance premiums. Indirect "other" costs include those costs associated with lowered employee morale, increased mistrust of the organization, and negative publicity that may result from sexual harassment within the employer's workplace. Myers and Flowers (1974) suggest that the cost of attitude changes may be determined using weighted attitude scores (which can be determined with attitude survey responses that are weighted by job level and tenure) that are multiplied by salary dollars. A behavior costing approach may also be used to determine the cost of attitude changes to an organization (Cascio, 1991). Responses to attitude surveys are correlated with employee behaviors (such as mistakes in production) to determine the costs or benefits to changes in employee attitudes.

The following formula may be used to estimate the total annual dollar value of "other" costs due to sexual harassment in an organization:

$$O = \sum_{i=1}^{n}(d_i + c_i)$$

where O = total annual "other" costs, d = direct "other" costs for an employee, c = indirect "other" costs for an employee, and n = number of employees affected.

Total Cost of Sexual Harassment

The aggregate of the various costs described above represents the total annual cost of sexual harassment to an organization. Based on the costing model discussed above, the following formula may be used to estimate the total annual cost of sexual harassment (SH) in an organization's workplace:

$$SH = \int [\, P + I + A + S + R + T + O \,]$$

where SH = total annual cost of sexual harassment, P = total annual productivity-reduction costs, I = total annual incident costs, A = total annual absenteeism costs, S = total annual separation costs, R = total annual replacement costs, T = total annual transfer costs, and O = total annual "other" costs.

APPLICATION OF THE MODEL

To apply the comprehensive behavior costing model of sexual harassment, organizations must systematically determine the individual elements of each of the model's formulas. This may involve the use of survey and/or interviews to determine the attitudinal and behavioral information necessary to develop an accurate estimate of the cost of sexual harassment. In addition, organizations must have accurate information concerning employee pay and benefits, training and recruitment costs for each job, and the administrative costs as described by the model. Although organizations may find it difficult to identify each costing element found in the model, they should not be dissuaded from attempting to determine the costs of sexual harassment. Clearly, even incomplete knowledge of the cost of sexual harassment is superior to being wholly unaware of the cost of sexual harassment to the organization.

Recently, this model was used to estimate the cost of sexual harassment to the U.S. Army (Faley, Knapp, Kustis, & Dubois, 1994). This research indicated that sexual harassment cost the Army approximately $533 million annually. These costs included (a) productivity reduction ($36,148,715); (b) incident costs ($9,131,293); (c) absenteeism ($8,991,637); (d) separation costs ($6,618,883); (e) replacement cost ($164,728,393); (f) training costs ($282,307,837); and (f) transfer cost ($25,013,824). Moreover, this study determined that sexual harassment not only is expensive in terms of litigation, but it may also financially affect organizations in terms of productivity-related costs, absenteeism, turnover, requests for transfer, and the use of medical and emotional counseling. Of these costs, the cost of turnover as a result of sexual harassment had the most negative financial impact. The outcome of this

Aims of policies

research adds to the growing body of evidence that indicates the legal damages associated with sexual harassment suits are minor when compared with the costs of reduced productivity and increased absenteeism and turnover (Acken, St. Pierre, & Veglahn, 1991; Frierson, 1989). Finally, although $533 million is a relatively small part of the overall annual Army budget (approximately $61 billion in 1994), it nevertheless is enough to purchase an additional 78 of the Army's advanced Black Hawk helicopters or 888 Army Tactical Missile Systems (Fulghum, 1993).

IMPLICATIONS OF THE MODEL

Implications for Policy and Training

Clearly, one of the most important uses for the model will be in determining the utility of implementing sexual harassment policies and training (this involves comparing the cost of sexual harassment with the cost of programs designed to eradicate it). Although a great number of organizations have policies concerning sexual harassment, very few have implemented comprehensive programs to address the problem. The following discussion touches on policies and training programs that might be implemented if sexual harassment is to be eliminated as a major workplace problem.

Organizational-level policy considerations. Ultimately, the goal of any sexual harassment policy is to create an atmosphere in which instances of sexual harassment are discouraged. Further, recent court decisions have indicated that the true (or legal) test of a sexual harassment policy is whether the policy is effective in preventing the behavior (Connell, 1991). Therefore, organizations may want to consider the influence that the organizational climate and the attitude of leadership toward sexual harassment have on targets and perpetrators of sexual harassment. Organizations must look beyond the traditional target-perpetrator relationship with respect to their policies and direct additional resources toward changing the organizational conditions that allow sexual harassment to exist. In other words, if unwanted sexual overtures and sexually polluted environments are facilitated by the organizational climate, then the climate should be the target of organizational change efforts.

Individual-level policy considerations. Evidence has suggested that organizations may wish to include informal procedures as part of their reporting policies (Biaggio, Watts, & Brownell, 1990; Gadlin, 1991; Lach & Gwartney-Gibbs, 1993; McKinney, Olson, & Satterfield, 1988). This is due, in part, to the fact that individuals that are harassed by someone of a greater occupational status than their own are less likely to report instances of sexual harassment, possibly as a result of fear of retaliation. Therefore, organizations may wish to institute informal reporting mechanisms as a means of counseling those individuals who fear retaliation from a superior. Informal counseling may provide the target with suggestions regarding appropriate and "safe" methods for responding to the sexual harassment.

Training considerations. Organizations may also wish to include training programs that encourage and explain in detail appropriate channels and procedures to follow when incidents of sexual harassment occur. In addition, training should include workshops to improve coping skills and self-help measures for dealing with sexual harassment. These workshops (Grieco, 1984) should train individuals to (a) recognize sexual harassment when it occurs, (b) evaluate the situation, (c) select an appropriate and effective response, and (d) take steps to decrease the likelihood that the incident will occur again.

Certainly, the scope and magnitude of these organizational change efforts imply considerable expense. If, however, significant costs were avoided as a result of the successful implementation of such programs, organizations might be more inclined to set them in motion. An effective method for establishing the utility of such programs is to apply the comprehensive behavior costing model of sexual harassment. Several organizations have used utility analyses similar to that suggested by the model to provide evidence of the bottom line impact of employee assistance programs. For example, by using a behavior costing approach, AT&T determined that its employee assistance program directed at eradicating substance abuse yielded an annual savings of $583,413 (in 1987 dollars; Cascio, 1989). Although policies, procedures, and training programs dedicated to diminishing sexual harassment may lead to increased costs in the short term (i.e., increased litigation and counseling), these programs should eventually diminish the amount of sexual harassment and therefore, in the long term, decrease the associated costs.

CONCLUSION

This model has implications for practitioners by providing them with information concerning the utility of their sexual harassment policies and awareness training programs. Numerous consultants have seized on recent and highly publicized sexual harassment scandals (e.g., Tailhook and the Hill-Thomas hearings) and quickly flooded the market with training programs that may or may not be effective. This model would enable organizations and individuals that market such programs to establish that their programs actually have a positive impact on an organization's bottom line. By facilitating individuals' attempts to cope with sexual harassment, an organization may begin to realize diminished costs with respect to sexual harassment and improve its ability to maintain a stable workforce. As suggested by Eller (1990),

> A practical and immediate solution for employers is to accept the broad realities of their responsibility, the uncertainty of an outcome in court, and their own vulnerability; they should concentrate on prevention of sexual harassment in the workplace, not just the prevention of lawsuits. (p. 87)

REFERENCES

Acken, B. T., St. Pierre, D., & Veglahn, P. (1991). Limiting sexual harassment liability. *Journal of Accountancy, 171*(6), 42-47.

Benson, D. J., & Thomson, G. E. (1982). Sexual harassment on a university campus: The confluence of authority relations, sexual interest and gender stratification. *Social Problems, 29,* 236-251.

Biaggio, M., Watts, D., & Brownell, A. (1990). Addressing sexual harassment: Strategies for prevention and change. In M. Paludi (Ed.), *Ivory power: Sexual harassment on campus* (pp. 213-230). Albany: SUNY Press.

Cascio, W. (1989). *Managing human resources: Productivity, quality of worklife, profits.* New York: McGraw-Hill.

Cascio, W. (1991). *Costing human resources: The financial impact of behavior in organizations* (3rd ed.). Boston: PWS-Kent.

Castellow, W. A., Wuensch, K. L., & Moore, C. H. (1990). Effects of physical attractiveness of the plaintiff and defendant in sexual harassment judgments. *Journal of Social Behavior and Personality, 5,* 547-562.

Collinson, D., & Collinson, M. (1989). Sexuality in the workplace: The domination of men's sexuality (pp. 91-109). In J. Hearn, D. Sheppard, P. Tancred-Sheriff, & G. Burrell (Eds.), *The sexuality of organization.* London: Sage Ltd.

Connell, D. S. (1991). Effective sexual harassment policies: Unexpected lessons from Jacksonville shipyards. *Employee Relations Law Journal, 17,* 191-206.

Crull, P. (1982). Stress effects of sexual harassment on the job: Implications for counseling. *American Journal of Orthopsychiatry, 52,* 539-544.

DiTomaso, N. (1989). Sexuality in the workplace: Discrimination and harassment. In J. Hearn, D. Sheppard, P. Tancred-Sheriff, & G. Burrell (Eds.), *The sexuality of organization* (pp. 71-90). London: Sage Ltd.

Eller, M. E. (1990). Sexual harassment: Prevention, not protection. *Cornell Hotel and Restaurant Administration Quarterly, 30*(4), 84-89.

Faley, R. H., Knapp, D. E., Kustis, G. A., & DuBois, C. L. Z. (1994, April). *Organizational costs of sexual harassment in the workplace: The case of the U.S. Army.* Paper presented at the Ninth Annual Conference of the Society of Industrial and Organizational Psychology, Nashville, TN.

Fitzgerald, L. F., & Shullman, S. L. (1993). Sexual harassment: A research analysis and agenda for the 1990s. *Journal of Vocational Behavior, 42,* 5-27.

Fitzgerald, L. F., Shullman, S. L., Bailey, N., Richards, M., Swecker, J., Gold, Y., Ormerod, M., & Weitzman, L. (1988). The incidence and dimensions of sexual harassment in academia and the workplace. *Journal of Vocational Behavior, 32,* 152-175.

Frierson, J. G. (1989). Reduce the costs of sexual harassment. *Personnel Journal, 68*(11), 79-85.

Fulghum, D. A. (1993, April 5). Comanche in jeopardy in Army budget squeeze. *Aviation Week & Space Technology,* p. 31.

Gadlin, H. (1991). Careful maneuvers: Mediating sexual harassment. *Negotiation Journal, 7,* 139-153.

Garvey, M. S. (1986). The high cost of sexual harassment suits. *Personnel Journal, 65*(1), 75-78, 80.

Grieco, A. (1984). Suggestions for management of sexual harassment of nurses. *Hospital and Community Psychiatry, 35,* 171-172.

Gruber, J. E., & Bjorn, L. (1982). Blue-collar blues: The sexual harassment of women autoworkers. *Work and Occupations, 9,* 271-298.

Gutek, B. A. (1985). *Sex and the workplace: Impact of sexual behavior and harassment on women, men, and organizations.* San Francisco: Jossey-Bass.

Gutek, B. A. (1993). Responses to sexual harassment. In S. Oskamp & M. Costanzo (Eds.), *Gender issues in contemporary society: The Claremont Symposium on Applied Social Psychology* (pp. 197-216). Newbury Park, CA: Sage.

Gutek, B. A., & Dunwoody, V. (1988). Understanding sex in the workplace. In A. Stromberg, L. Larwood, & B. Gutek (Eds.), *Women and work: An annual review* (pp. 249-269). Newbury Park, CA: Sage.

Gutek, B. A., & Koss, M. P. (1993). Changed women and changed organizations: Consequences of and coping with sexual harassment. *Journal of Vocational Behavior, 42,* 28-48.

Gutek, B. A., & Nakamura, C. Y. (1982). Gender roles and sexuality in the world of work. In E. R. Allgeier & N. B. McCormick (Eds.), *Changing boundaries: Gender roles and sexual behavior* (pp. 182-201). San Francisco: Mayfield.

Gutek, B. A., Nakamura, C. Y., Gahart, M., Handschumacher, I., & Russell, D. (1980). Sexuality in the workplace. *Basic and Applied Psychology, 1,* 255-265.

Lach, D. H., & Gwartney-Gibbs, P. A. (1993). Sociological perspectives on sexual harassment and workplace dispute resolution. *Journal of Vocational Behavior, 42,* 102-115.

Martindale, M. (1988). *Sexual harassment in the military: 1988.* Arlington, VA: Defense Manpower Data Center.

Mazer, D. B., & Percival, E. F. (1989). Ideology or experience? The relationships among perceptions, attitudes, and experiences of sexual harassment in university students. *Sex Roles, 20,* 135-147.

McKinney, K., Olson, C., & Satterfield, A. (1988). Graduate students' experiences with and responses to sexual harassment: A research note. *Journal of Interpersonal Violence, 3,* 319-325.

Myers, M. S., & Flowers, V. S. (1974). A framework for measuring human assets. *California Management Review, 16,* 5-16.

Sandroff, R. (1988). Sexual harassment in the Fortune 500. *Working Woman, 13*(12), 69-73.

Silverman, D. (1976-1977). Sexual harassment: Working women's dilemma. *Quest: A Feminist Quarterly, 3,* 15-24.

Terpstra, D. E. (1986). Organizational costs of sexual harassment. *Journal of Employment Counseling, 23*(3), 112-119.

Terpstra, D. E., & Baker, D. D. (1986). Psychological and demographic correlates of perception of sexual harassment. *Genetic, Social, and General Psychology Monographs, 112,* 459-478.

U.S. Merit Systems Protection Board. (1981). *Sexual harassment in the federal workplace: Is it a problem?* Washington, DC: Office of Merit Systems Review and Studies/Government Printing Office.

U.S. Merit Systems Protection Board. (1988). *Sexual harassment in the federal government: An update.* Washington, DC: Office of Merit Systems Review and Studies/ Government Printing Office.

SECTION IV

Responding to Harassment: Strategies for Change

11

Understanding Sexual Harassment: Contributions From Research on Domestic Violence and Organizational Change

JEANETTE N. CLEVELAND
KATHLEEN McNAMARA

In this chapter, we draw from two literatures to further our understanding of and potential to intervene in sexual harassment situations: domestic violence and organizational change. Both of these areas provide suggestions for intervention to address problems that share essential features with sexual harassment. Common themes that cut across sexual harassment and domestic violence include victim responses, power differentials between perpetrators and victims, social isolation, and perpetrator characteristics. The domestic violence literature provides parallels with sexual harassment at the individual level, and the organizational change literature shares common contextual features with sexual harassment including formal and informal power differentials and the need to focus on multiple levels for intervention. The authors conclude that interventions selected to address sexual harassment like those used in domestic violence and organizational change must be a coordinated series of multilevel interventions that hold the more powerful participants responsible for their actions.

Sexual harassment is a complex social and organization problem. It includes a range of behaviors that vary in terms of offensiveness, intensity, and consequences, and it is often characterized by power differentials between the target and the harasser (Fitzgerald & Shullman, 1993; Gutek & Koss, 1993). Certain organizational or contextual characteristics such as norms, implicit rewards and punishments, work arrangements, and processes tend to be conducive to sexual harassment. The consequences of sexual harassment are felt at multiple levels including the individual target and harasser level, and the work group and organizational levels.

The sexual harassment literature offers little in terms of techniques or interventions that might be effective in addressing the target, the harasser, or the organizational characteristics that contribute to the occurrence of sexual harassment. Therefore, an examination of various interventions for problems similar to sexual harassment may provide new insights for preventing sexual harassment in organizations.

In this chapter, the similarities between sexual harassment and domestic violence are explored. Interventions from this literature are considered for their potential in preventing sexual harassment. In addition, the organizational change and conflict resolution literature offers interventions and strategies that have been effective in other situations and are considered for their application in preventing and responding to sexual harassment.

DOMESTIC VIOLENCE AND SEXUAL HARASSMENT

Sexual harassment is believed to be tied to other forms of violence against women and female children (Fitzgerald, 1993; Goodman, Koss, Fitzgerald, Russo, & Keita, 1993). One theory suggests that sexual harassment, as well as other forms of violence against women, arises from and reinforces the subordinate position of women in society (Fitzgerald, 1993; Pagelow, 1992). Various forms of abuse against women are considered to be a consequence of gender role socialization processes that promote male dominance, the sexual objectification of women, and cultural approval of violence against women (Pagelow, 1992). From this perspective, wife battering, rape, incest, and sexual harassment are all interrelated insofar as these acts function to maintain the patriarchal structure of society.

The first section of this chapter describes numerous similarities between sexual harassment and other types of violence and abuse directed toward women, particularly domestic violence. Similarities among victim, perpetrator, and contextual factors are explored. Various intervention approaches for dealing with domestic violence are discussed in terms of their usefulness for responding to the problem of sexual harassment.

Violence and Abuse Toward Women

Although many women harbor fear of the potential rapist who may be lurking behind bushes or in dark alleyways, the greatest threat of sexual or physical harm to women is actually from people women know, usually an acquaintance, a coworker, or an intimate partner. A woman is about as likely to be murdered by her husband as she is by anyone else, and between 21% and 34% of all women will be sexually assaulted by an intimate male partner during adulthood (Frieze, Knoble, Washburn, & Zomnir, 1980; Russell, 1982). Mercy and Saltzman (1989) determined that the leading cause of injuries to women is intimate violence, and Toufexis (1987) estimated that more women are beaten by their husbands or boyfriends than are hurt in automobile accidents, rapes, or muggings. Just as the targets of sexual harassment are usually female, victims of rape, domestic violence, and emotional, physical, or sexual abuse are also usually female. Moreover, when females engage in violence, it is usually in the form of self-protection, whereas men's assaults are usually to gain control of the woman (Barnett & LaViolette, 1993; Kurz, 1993).

Sexual harassment is just one form of abuse against women that occurs in the workplace, and it shares many similarities with other forms of abuse that women might face. NiCarthy, Gottlieb, and Coffman (1993) have described various forms of emotional abuse that many women encounter at work, including insults, intimidation, and excessive or illegitimate controlling behaviors. These authors emphasize that a pattern of various power-based behaviors by a coworker or superior may be termed *emotional abuse.* Included in their list of potentially emotionally abusive behaviors are isolating a worker from other coworkers; repeatedly threatening to fire, demote, or transfer a worker without provocation; threatening to hurt or hit a worker; and saying or implying that important responsibilities will be denied if compliance with certain demands is not met. Obvious emotional abuse may precede sexual harassment, occur in response to a woman's complaint about or resistance against sexual harassment, or occur in the absence of sexual harassment per se. Although sexual harassment has gained the attention of the public and social science researchers in recent years, the broader realm of emotional abuse against women in the workplace has received little attention.

Victim Similarities

Barnett and LaViolette (1993) reviewed the current research on the characteristics of victims of wife abuse and concluded that women entering relationships that eventually become abusive do not appear to differ from their nonbattered counterparts in terms of demographic variables, histories of childhood abuse, or psychological/personality attributes. Like targets of sexual harassment, factors that victims of various forms of abuse share are fear of consequences if the offense is revealed or reported; physical, economic, or social power differentials between the perpetrator and the victim; isolation of the victim to conceal the abuse; and similar emotional responses to the victimization (Barnett & LaViolette, 1993).

Victim Responses

Victims of physical and sexual abuse, as well as targets of sexual harassment, are often fearful that when the offense is revealed, either they will not be believed or they will be blamed for the abuse. For example, wives who have been battered are commonly thought to have at least provoked the violence, and they are often "pathologized," especially if they stay in the abusive relationship (Pagelow, 1984, 1992). Even very young victims of child sex abuse have been held responsible for "provoking" incest (Herman, 1992). Similarly, targets of sexual harassment often do not report such incidents for fear of retaliation or disbelief by others (Fitzgerald & Shullman, 1993; Jensen & Gutek, 1982; Koss, 1990; Livingston, 1982).

When crimes are "personal or intimate," the culpability of the victim is more likely to be questioned. This is due, in part, to the lack of understanding of the reasons that women stay in abusive relationships or in jobs where sexual or emotional harassment occurs. A combination of fear of revenge and hope for improvement are major factors in why women decide to return to or remain in abusive situations. Barnett and

Lopez-Real (1985) found that battered women cited "hoped my partner would change" as the most frequently given reason for remaining in a violent relationship, followed by "fear of revenge" if they left the abusive partner. In addition, fear of economic penalties can be a major obstacle to a woman leaving an abusive situation. Pagelow (1981) found that women with the fewest resources (e.g., money, automobile, job) are most likely to stay with an abuser.

In terms of the psychological consequences of abuse, victims of all forms of family violence tend to experience diminished self-esteem, feelings of shame or humiliation, and negative self-images (Pagelow, 1984). Often there are feelings of self-blame and helplessness (Herman, 1992). Many victims experience what was previously termed *battered woman syndrome* (Walker, 1979, 1984) and is now called *posttraumatic stress disorder* (Goodman et al., 1993). These conditions include a wide range of cognitive and emotional symptoms that are commonly seen among victims of trauma. Gutek and Koss (1993) have described reactions to sexual harassment that are remarkably similar to the reactions evidenced by other victims of gender-based abuse including symptoms similar to posttraumatic stress syndrome.

Perpetrator Similarities

As much as we might want to think that wife batterers and sex offenders are deeply disturbed individuals, men who rape or physically abuse their wives or who have incestuous relations with their daughters are a heterogeneous group with no clearly definable clinical profile (Pagelow, 1992, 1993; Tolman & Bennett, 1990). Although some researchers have found evidence of psychopathology among spouse abusers (Hamberger & Hastings, 1986), these findings must be viewed cautiously (Pagelow, 1993; Tolman & Bennett, 1990). Even in cases where alcohol and drug abuse is involved, it is the general consensus among domestic violence researchers that alcohol abuse is not causally linked to domestic violence (Pagelow, 1984). Although there is controversy as to how much weight to place on research findings that discriminate between abusers and nonabusers, Tolman and Bennett (1990) reviewed the literature on wife batterers and reached several tentative conclusions. Consistent with research on sexual harassers (e.g., Pryor, 1987), the empirical evidence suggests that men who batter are more hostile and angrier than nonviolent men and react with higher levels of anger to conflict situations than do nonviolent men. In terms of behavioral deficits, the research suggests that batterers tend to have difficulty expressing their desires and needs in a socially appropriate manner (Maiuro, Cahn, & Vitaliano, 1986), and they are less assertive with their spouses (Dutton & Strachan, 1987). In addition, batterers, like sexual harassers, evidence heightened needs for power and control (Dutton & Strachan, 1987; Winter, 1973). Finally, consistent with social learning explanations of abuse, findings show that perpetrators often have grown up in families in which they have witnessed, and thereby learned, violence (Hotaling & Sugarman, 1986). These research findings are compatible with findings emerging in the sexual harassment literature. For example, Pryor's work (e.g., 1987; Pryor, LaVite, & Stoller, 1993) on harassers indicates that attitudinal and social factors combine to predict when sexually harassing behaviors are most likely to occur.

Power/Powerlessness

Pagelow (1984) has discussed the issue of perceived power/powerlessness as a potentially useful concept for a global explanation of family violence. Pagelow suggests that men typically have the position of greatest power within their family units; however, in their work environment beyond the family home, some men may experience significant feelings of powerlessness. Pagelow hypothesizes that when men feel powerless in their relations with others outside the family, there may be a greater potential for them to compensate by "scapegoating" (Simmel, 1904), or displacing hostilities toward family members over whom they have power and control. This would be especially true when families are socially isolated and when the power differentials between the husband and the wife are great. Studies that have examined the relationship between sex role orientation and battering (LaViolette, Barnett, & Miller, 1984; Rosenbaum, 1986) have found that batterers view themselves as low on those characteristics that are typically labeled "masculine." Tolman and Bennett (1990) have suggested that men who perceive themselves as not living up to societal notions of "masculinity" may compensate through aggressive behavior toward females. Although this explanation does not explain why only some men use scapegoating and violence as a means of coping with feelings of powerlessness and hostility and others do not, it appears to be an interesting concept worthy of investigation.

Contextual Similarities Between Domestic Violence and Sexual Harassment

Power differentials. One underlying feature that is common to all types of domestic violence, whether wife battering, incest, or marital rape, is that it involves power differentials between the perpetrator and the victim (Pagelow, 1984). One leading authority on child sexual abuse claims that "abuse tends to gravitate to the relationships of greatest power differential" (Finkelhor, Gelles, Hotaling, & Straus, 1983, p. 17). To support this claim, Finkelhor et al. (1983) point out that the most common form of sexual abuse of children involves adult males in positions of authority victimizing girls in subordinate roles. In instances of spouse abuse, Straus, Gelles, and Steinmetz (1980) reported that wives who were most likely to be abused were those who were not in the paid labor market, were excluded from family decision making, and had less education than their husbands. Conversely, the more egalitarian the relationship, the less likely it is that spouse abuse will occur.

Consistent with these findings, sexual harassment commonly occurs between a supervisor and a subordinate and the most severe form of sexual harassment (quid pro quo) usually occurs when the power imbalance is the greatest. Like sibling or peer abuse, when harassment between two coworkers occurs, there are often informal differences in power (Cleveland & Kerst, 1993). Despite presumed similar formal power bases, these informal differences in power may take the form of access to the resources of informal information networks, for example. It should be noted that coworker harassment tends to be perceived as less severe than harassment between individuals with greater power differentials (U.S. Merit Systems Protection Board, 1981).

Social isolation. Another feature common to various forms of family violence is the presence of social isolation. Families in which violence is most likely to occur are those that are most isolated from social networks such as extended family ties or community groups. Families that move frequently and are detached from community or neighborhood organizations have been found to have the highest rates of violence (Herman & Hirschman, 1980). Dobash and Dobash (1979) have shown that in studies of wife abuse, the victims are most likely to be isolated in the home with minimal friendship networks or family ties. Gelles (1980) has pointed out that when privacy is high, the degree of social control is lowered. There is a tendency to be reluctant to violate norms of appropriate behavior when it is likely to be publicly noticed. Therefore, the more embedded a family unit is in social networks, the less likely it is that abuse will occur, or if it does, the greater the likelihood that it will be revealed.

Social isolation very likely plays a role in sexual harassment as well, although its precise nature has not been well documented (Gutek, 1985). Women in male-dominated jobs may experience more social isolation because they are more likely to be excluded from informal social networks. This social isolation may make a woman more vulnerable to sexual harassment because she is not embedded in a social network that would help prevent or reveal the harassment. Female-dominated jobs are often characterized by low power; therefore, a male supervisor might easily direct a woman into an isolated work situation and thereby increase her risk for sexual harassment. For example, a woman may be requested to work late when others have left for the day, or she may be asked to perform tasks that require her to be isolated from others. Based on the role that social isolation plays in domestic violence, it could be predicted that sexual harassment would be more likely to occur in situations where a female is relatively isolated.

Cycle of violence theory. Walker (1979) has used the "cycle of violence" theory to explain how interpersonal violence intensifies in degree and frequency over time and why women stay in abusive relationships. The cycle consists of three phases. In the first, or tension-building phase, minor incidents of violence may occur along with a buildup of anger. This phase may include verbal put-downs, jealousy, threats, or breaking things, and may last an indefinite period of time. During this period, the woman herself may not define the man's behavior as abusive and may instead perceive her relationship to have problems that are not uncharacteristic of most male-female relationships. Escalation to phase two includes acute battering, a phase in which a major violent outburst occurs. This violent episode is followed by the "honeymoon or respite," in which the batterer is remorseful and afraid of losing his partner. During this phase, the batterer may make promises, ask for forgiveness, and buy gifts to regain the woman's commitment to the relationship. This last phase has been reconceptualized by some researchers to be a phase in which the violence simply ceases, and is characterized by little remorse on the part of the batterer (Campbell, 1990; Carlisle-Frank, 1991).

Although the *cycle of violence* specifically refers to violence in intimate relationships, it may generalize to sexual harassment. A victim of sexual harassment may experience numerous minor forms of harassment that she may excuse, minimize, or otherwise deny. She may be hopeful that the behaviors will cease, particularly if she ignores the problem or copes in some nonthreatening manner. When a major harassment incident occurs that she is less likely to ignore or excuse, the perpetrator may engage in compensatory behaviors to reduce the likelihood of negative consequences. If the woman fails to report the incident at this time and waits until the cycle repeats itself, she is more likely to have difficulty reporting the harassment later. Although it is unequivocally clear that she is being harassed, she fears that she will not be believed because she did not report it sooner. Indeed, if this psychological process is not understood, the victim's credibility is likely to be questioned, and there is a greater chance that she will be "pathologized" as a conspirator in her own victimization.

Domestic Violence Interventions

Traditional intervention approaches to domestic violence have focused on the individual or family as their primary target (e.g., Gelles, 1985) as opposed to power differentials between men and women and the abuse of power. The focus of treatment is less on holding the perpetrator responsible for the abuse and more on family-systems issues and diffusion of responsibility for the abuse (Barnett & LaViolette, 1993).

Responses of institutions to abuse of women may be divided into two basic categories. The first, *conciliation,* takes place outside the legal system and involves parties participating in mediation or therapy where domestic violence is treated as a relationship issue rather than as a crime. The second method is the use of *law enforcement* to punish or rehabilitate the perpetrator and to protect the victim from further acts of violence. There is considerable philosophical controversy over the usefulness of conciliation methods in resolving domestic violence. Many writers believe that the conciliation response (Kurz, 1993; Thorne-Finch, 1992) to violence may actually perpetuate violence, first, by blaming the victim and failing to treat violence as a crime not to be tolerated and, second, by failing to hold the perpetrator responsible.

Sherman and Berk (1984) conducted a widely referenced study that tested the efficacy of three different police responses to domestic violence: arrest, separation of the parties, and mediation. A six-month follow-up revealed that there was a recurrence of violence in only 10% of the cases in which an arrest had been made compared with 24% of the cases in which there had been mediation and 17% in which there had been a separation of the parties. Similar studies by Berk and Newton (1985) and Jaffe, Wolfe, Telford, and Austin (1986) have provided additional evidence that arrests are an effective deterrent.

Interventions that have focused on treating men who batter (e.g., Neidig, Friedman, & Collins, 1985) use short-term, cognitive-behavioral methods that emphasize anger control, effective communication, problem solving, and sex role stereotyping in relationships. There are few outcome studies published on these types of interventions to date (see Neidig et al., 1985; Shupe, Stacey, & Hazelwood, 1986), and of the studies that have appeared, none have used experimental designs or control groups. Therefore, although positive results have been reported by some researchers, it is difficult to draw any firm conclusions on the efficacy of these types of programs.

The form of intervention that has been by far the most widely studied is therapeutic groups for male batterers. These groups typically employ a host of cognitive-behavioral techniques embedded in a profeminist philosophical context. Programs usually involve a short-term (8 to 32 sessions) structured program. Most of the outcome studies in the literature reveal that the majority of men stop their physically abusive behavior subsequent to intervention (e.g., DeMaris & Jackson, 1987; Dutton, 1986; Edleson & Grusznski, 1988; Hamberger & Hastings, 1986). Percentages of successful outcomes range from 53% to 85% (Tolman & Bennett, 1990); however, these results must be viewed cautiously, as the vast majority of these evaluation studies did not employ experimental designs and the outcome measures are often self-report instruments. Reports by victims frequently are not obtained.

What is most strongly advocated by experts on domestic violence is the use of multisystem intervention. Educational programs for male batterers combined with strong reactions by the criminal justice system are often called for, and it is considered to be crucial that input from women victims be sought in designing programs and in measuring the efficacy of these programs. Throughout the literature, it is noted that when various systems that interface on the program of domestic violence do not coordinate and communicate effectively, they may be working at cross-purposes (Ritmeester, 1993). Unfortunately, despite the apparent importance of system coordination, it is usually the exception rather than the rule.

Implications for Sexual Harassment

With regard to sexual harassment in the workplace, it would appear that some insight might be gleaned from the intervention literature on domestic violence. First, intervention methods that cast sexual harassment as an "interpersonal problem" between a man and a woman may be similar to the conciliation approach employed in the domestic violence arena. This institutional response may actually serve to perpetuate sexual harassment insofar as it fails to communicate directly that sexual harassment is a violation on the part of the harasser and that it will not be tolerated. Second, if programs for harassers are ever implemented in a fashion similar to those for men who abuse women in other ways, it is critical that systems work effectively together and that the effectiveness of these programs ultimately be measured by the reports of victims and/or potential victims for a sufficient period of time following the conclusion of such interventions. That is, it would be inadequate to assess the outcome of an intervention by measuring changes in men's attitudes and self-reported behaviors. Reports by women who have or may have experienced sexual harassment are necessary to accurately evaluate program effectiveness. The time period of follow-up is also of importance due to the fact that harassing behavior often occurs intermittently. Short-term behavior changes may be fairly easily acquired, but long-term cessation of harassment may be much more difficult to achieve.

CONTEXTUAL ISSUES LINKING SEXUAL HARASSMENT WITH ORGANIZATIONAL CONFLICT AND CHANGE

The links between domestic violence and sexual harassment relate to the characteristics of the target and harasser and the interactions that contribute to or cause the harassment. The literature on domestic violence provides on alternative perspective and suggests interventions that address person-based explanations of sexual harassment in organizations. The individuals involved in sexual harassment are the targets for change. As indicated throughout this book, however, there are numerous contextual factors involved in sexual harassment. Organizational context (e.g., norms, culture) plays a significant role in sexual harassment in many ways: (a) how sexual harassment is demonstrated (severity, pervasiveness); (b) how people cope with it (e.g., reluctance to report sexual harassment may reflect the culture of the organization); and (c) how the organization intervenes to effect change. Organizational development, specifically, tries to introduce planned changes in the ways in which the organization works and the way members of the organization interact with one another (French & Bell, 1984). The organizational change literature provides a way of viewing sexual harassment as an organizational behavior and effectiveness problem.

Essential for the management and elimination of sexual harassment at work, both organizational conflict and change approaches recognize the need to consider multiple levels of a given organizational problem. The conflict research suggests that sexual harassment can be viewed as an interpersonal conflict with sexual content. The organizational change approach places sexual harassment within a larger context of the organization that involves structural, group, or team issues as well as individual ones. Taken together, the organizational conflict and change approaches suggest that for effective organizational and behavioral change to occur, a coordinated series of interventions need to be implemented (Thomas, 1992). These interventions would address the individual, group, and organizational components that compose the sexual harassment situation.

Because its focus specifically targets changing the context of the work environment, the organizational change approach provides the opportunity to recast sexual harassment as an organizational problem rather than exclusively as a person or interpersonal problem. Drawing from this literature, there is a shift in focus from blaming the victim (or even the harasser) to holding the organization's power holders responsible for the climate and environment of work as well as for the behaviors of its members. The shift is from thinking about sexual harassment as involving a group of bad men doing bad things to weak women, to the modification of features of the organization that shape behavior and contribute to a denigrating, abusive workplace. For example, the organization and its reward structure can be modified to reduce or eliminate opportunities to harass and to punish harassing behaviors. One implication of the organizational approach is the possibility that many or most employees have the potential to engage in harassing behaviors given a sufficiently negative and sexualized work environment. People who are predisposed to engage in negative behaviors will take advantage of opportunities to harass if they are not sanctioned by the organization. Nevertheless, one advantage of this approach is that it looks to and targets for change, the organization and work group context rather than exclusively pointing to the individual weaknesses of victims and harassers.

Multiple-level change: Unfreezing, changing, refreezing. Organizational interventions can be geared to address multiple levels of change: (a) the individual or group level including skill, values, and behaviors; (b) the organizational structures and systems including reward systems, work design, and so forth; and (c) organizational climate, including how conflict or problems are managed, how decisions are made, and so forth (Goodstein & Burke, 1991). Because resistance to change may vary at each of these levels, each level may require different change strategies or interventions (e.g., changing the performance appraisal system or securing strong top management support). Any persistent change is believed to result only when employees change their individual work behavior in response to organizational changes (Porras & Hoffer, 1986; Porras & Robertson, 1992).

Kurt Lewin, a pioneer in the field of organizational change, proposed a three-phase model of change that highlights the use of multiple methods and levels of change. The first step in any change process is to *unfreeze* the current pattern of behavior (Goodstein & Burke, 1991). The goal is to address resistance to change, usually by some type of confrontation and retraining process. The specific techniques used in the unfreezing process depend on the organizational level of change. For example, at the climate level, it might involve securing and conveying top management support (e.g., organizational policy on sexual harassment; Gutek, in press) to eliminate a hostile work environment for females. At the structural/system level, it could entail developing an evaluation and promotion system that places emphasis on managing diversity and developing all workers. At the individual level, it might involve selecting supervisors with open and positive attitudes and behaviors toward women, or firing employees engaged in harassment.

The second phase is called movement, *change,* or learning, and it involves the actual changes that are made. This includes observing individual changes in the behaviors and responses that employees have toward work. For example, a supervisor might solicit anonymous feedback from subordinates about the appropriateness of his behavior. At the structural level, supervisors who are unsupportive of female colleagues would receive lower evaluations, would not be promoted, or would be sent to workshops on sexual harassment.

Refreezing is the final stage of the change process, and it involves incorporating acquired change into the organization and ensuring that the new changes remain secure. This may involve continued and public commitment by top management to provide a positive, productive environment for all workers and, at the individual level, recruiting individuals who possess values and supervisory behaviors consistent with a positive work environment.

Applying this multiphase process of change to sexual harassment suggests that when viewed as an organizational effectiveness issue, behaviors and contexts associated with sexual harassment must first be identified and unlearned or altered. Next, new behaviors and systems must be learned and implemented. This includes not only providing incentives and rewards for positive behaviors but also removing barriers or organizational disincentives for such behaviors (i.e., fear of retribution or punishing the complainant). The organizational change approach also appropriately recognizes the complexity of sexual harassment by framing the problem in terms of climate, structure, and individual components, each requiring multiple phases of change.

Power issues in organizational conflict and change. One type of conflict identified in organizations, disruptive conflict, shares a number of features with current definitions of sexual harassment (Filley, 1975). In such conflict situations, there are no rules of behavior, and the intent is to "reduce, defeat, harm or drive away" (p. 3) the other party. This type of conflict is characterized by stress, anger, and fear (Filley, 1975), which is similar to the ways that sexual harassment has been characterized. It is an attempt to impose control and create or maintain an imbalance of power between the parties.

Power inequities undermine trust. Further, power issues are a continual and underlying theme in the research on sexual harassment and domestic violence as well as organizational change. Studies show that the greater the power differential between two parties, the more negative the attitudes of the less powerful toward the more powerful (Kipnis, 1990). The higher-power individual also tends to view the less powerful person as compliant rather than behaving in a voluntary way. This may help to explain why individuals rate sexual harassment behaviors exhibited by supervisors with a clearly stronger power base as more severe than similar behaviors exhibited by peers or subordinates. Power differentials may also inhibit communication between individuals, which may not only lead to conflict but also contribute to conflict escalation.

One goal of both conflict resolution and change interventions is to alter power imbalances. The most effective strategies are believed to be those in which both parties are working from similar power bases (Filley, 1975). Equalization of power appears to be a critical factor in the effectiveness of various conflict resolution approaches. Yet, power imbalances are inherent in most conflict situations including sexual harassment.

Organizational conflict and change theorists have suggested ways to alter power imbalance between parties within an organization (Mastenbroek, 1987). For example, supervisors can be trained to be more participative and obtain or seek more information from subordinates. They are a critical link between the organization and the employees. An alternative is a structural approach that includes altering the organization evaluation system so that supervisors are evaluated on their effectiveness in supervising all subordinates, especially those from diverse gender or ethnic groups. Finally, organizational cultural adjustments influence the power balance (Mastenbroek, 1987). These adjustments would include changing leadership roles to include more coaching and counseling, striving for consensus, skill building in mediation of interpersonal conflicts, and increasing interpersonal relations. As in sexual harassment and domestic violence, power plays a critical role in organizational change. Such issues provide the foundation for much of the resistance to change that must be addressed in the unfreezing phase of the change process. One issue in the application of this literature to sexual harassment is that power holders need to be held responsible and accountable for creating a hostile and denigrating environment for less powerful groups or individuals.

Team Building as an Example of Change at the Individual, Group, and Organizational Levels

Interventions can be geared to individual organizational members, dyads or triads of individuals, teams and groups, intergroup relations, and/or the total organization as the unit of focus. Interventions can be implemented, either prior to a sexual harassment event or subsequent to such an event, to assess and address consequences of such behaviors. There are a wide range of organization development and organizational change interventions that might be helpful in dealing with sexual harassment (e.g., process consultation, job redesign, and so forth). We will discuss one technique, team building, that is often used in combination with others to address an organizational effectiveness problem.

Team building. French and Bell (1984) suggest that the most important interventions to change people's knowledge, attitudes, and behaviors are team interventions. Although system changes (including policy changes and laws) may achieve the broadest scope of change, they may be less effective alone in the long run because an individual's knowledge and attitudes do not change. Further, system changes such as discrimination laws or affirmative action may produce negative reactions from individuals who believe their individual choices are being curtailed. Teams can consist of intact permanent work groups with a supervisor and employee members (called a family group), or they can be newly formed groups, created because of mergers or organizational restructuring (called special groups). The goal of team building is to improve team effectiveness by better managing tasks, relationships, and group processes (French & Bell, 1984). The group critiques its own performance, and attempts to develop strategies to improve its functioning. Usually, a team-building session is initiated by the supervisor along with a third party. Team building can be implemented in response to a sexual harassment incident or complaint, or it may be used to assess group culture to prevent the occurrence of such behavior. During the team-building session, action steps are taken to address specific problems. These steps include identifying incidents and examples and establishing time frames for addressing issues. Team building may be designed for problem solving regarding task accomplishment, for assessing and improving interpersonal relationships, or for managing group culture (French & Bell, 1984).

Within the team-building process, two techniques can be used to deal with members' role ambiguity or confusion about what behaviors are expected or appropriate: role analysis and role negotiation. *Role analysis techniques* are designed to clarify role expectations and responsibilities of team members to improve group effectiveness. Group members' expectations of the focal role incumbent are discussed, modified, and agreed upon by the group and the focal role person. This technique assists a work group both in norming expectations for appropriate, productive behaviors and in publicly discouraging negative behaviors such as sexual harassment.

Related to role analysis is a technique known as *role negotiation.* This may be appropriate in teams where ineffectiveness stems from people's unwillingness to change, often because it reflects a loss of power or influence for that individual within the group (French & Bell, 1984; Harrison, 1972). The general technique calls for a controlled negotiation between individuals where one party agrees to change a behavior in exchange for a change in behavior in the second party. Each member identifies behaviors for change for each of the other group members as well as improvements that they could make in their own behavior. Two individuals discuss the most important behavior change they want to see from the other person and what behavior they are willing to change in exchange. The process ends when all members are satisfied that they will receive a reasonable return on whatever they are agreeing to give (Harrison, 1972). This may be a useful technique in groups where power and influence issues are present and operate to maintain an unsatisfactory context. Such situations appear to be a frequent denominator in sexual harassment incidents.

To illustrate the application of team building in this context, consider a work group where male peers are creating a hostile work environment for female employees through inappropriate emphasis on sexuality in the workplace. They may do this by staring and leering, paying excessive attention to appearance, or displaying sexual material or imagery in the work setting. Here, a team-building intervention might involve an analysis of how the work environment affects the effectiveness of the work team. It could also be coupled with role negotiation to reduce behaviors that create this hostile and unproductive environment. Because research on sexual harassment indicates that men and women differ in their perceptions of what behaviors constitute sexual harassment (Fitzgerald & Shullman, 1993), a discussion of norms and expectations of appropriate behaviors by work group members may reveal discrepancies in perceptions. This may then result in a renegotiation of what behaviors will or will not be acceptable in the future as well as a discussion of what responses women might make when inappropriate behaviors do occur. The major contribution of the organizational change literature is that individual interventions such as role analysis or negotiation occur within the context of group (e.g., team) and organizational (e.g., reward structure) changes so that changes at different levels of a problem reinforce each other. A single intervention at one level (i.e., individual, group, organization, societal) may not be sufficiently strong to prevent or eliminate the harassment.

LINKING INTERVENTIONS WITH ANTECEDENTS AND CONSEQUENCES OF SEXUAL HARASSMENT

There are at least two points at which change techniques drawn from the domestic violence and organizational change literatures can be implemented to address issues concerning sexual harassment. Ideally prevention of sexual harassment in organizations is our goal. A number of intervention strategies suggested by theory and research on domestic violence and organizational change can be appropriately applied at this stage. Unfortunately, however, it is likely that in many organizations sexual harassment will not be prevented, so instead, interventions must be applied to address the consequences of such behaviors.

Preventive Intervention Strategies

Because both the sexual harassment and the domestic violence literatures identify power as a critical correlate for abusive behavior, interventions at the organizational level should be implemented with the alteration of such power imbalances as a primary criterion. The domestic violence literature suggests that cognitive behavior therapy techniques can be implemented to address social stereotypes and myths regarding the notions of masculinity, femininity, power, and ineffective behaviors at work. Within work groups, role analysis and role negotiation may be techniques that can clarify expectations as well as identify behaviors that are appropriate and inappropriate for peers and supervisory relations. These techniques also communicate to each group member what expectations others have about his or her role. Team building can provide a mechanism in which the work group evaluates its own health and provides an opportunity to identify ways to prevent the occurrence of negative, unproductive sexual behavior at work. Although conciliatory techniques can be used, many of the organizational change interventions are designed to alter the contingencies or rewards and punishments for behaviors within the organization and the work group. Although change techniques are not intended to be punitive, the development of new norms and culture implies that some behaviors will be viewed favorably while others will be discouraged or perhaps in some ways, sanctioned.

Team building may be effectively applied to individual correlates of sexual harassment to prevent the occurrence of such behaviors. Target correlates of sexual harassment include lower self-esteem, powerless ness, and social isolation. Harasser correlates include greater formal and informal power and sex. Team building along with role analysis may be useful ways to impart information about the destructive uses of power and exploitation of sex-role stereotypes. Both these techniques are designed to enhance interpersonal relationships. Further, training programs supplied by the conflict management literature can be designed to build supervisory as well as mediation and problem-solving skills. These skills can be effective in providing the individual with the ability to identify potentially abusive behavior or the contextual correlates of such behavior to be able to prevent its occurrence. Further, women can learn to develop assertiveness in confronting an initial sexual harassment experience. Research shows that sexual harassment behaviors such as provocative remarks or suggestive comments on appearance may be effectively stopped when the target tells the harasser to quit such behavior.

Conciliatory techniques or training for the individual harasser and target are, in our view, incomplete and doomed to fail if the organization does not enforce norms prohibiting abusive behavior and hold the more powerful harasser responsible for his actions. If such techniques instead result in the target being transferred, demoted, or dismissed for reporting sexual harassment, they will fail. Further, organizational culture and norms and supporting personnel systems must be coordinated with more conciliatory interventions for the targets and harassers to effectively prevent abusive behavior at work (Ritmeester, 1993).

Interventions to Address Consequences of Sexual Harassment

Unfortunately, a common organizational response to the report of sexual harassment is to transfer, demote, or dismiss the employee who reported it while doing little of consequence to the harasser. Typically, organizational responses suggest that sexual harassment is viewed as purely an interpersonal problem. By blaming the victim, however, abusive and unproductive work behaviors are likely to continue to plague the organization when group and organizational correlates of sexual harassment are not recognized and addressed. Therefore, in our view and in the view of others (Gutek, in press), the organization, including upper management and the employees holding power, is responsible for implementing interventions that address the target's emotional, physical, and work outcomes. This may involve a combination of conciliatory techniques such as cognitive therapies and organizational change techniques to address work outcomes. Gutek (in press) and others suggest that organizations begin by implementing policies, procedures, and training (PPT) that address sexual harassment specifically. Further, the organization needs to investigate the circumstances of the sexual harassment context and hold powerful employees responsible for their behaviors rather than directly or indirectly punishing the targets of harassment. This view is consistent with current legal interpretations (Underwood, 1987).

While assessing the situation, the key organizational investigators need to recognize that there is a reasonable man and a reasonable woman standard that may vary significantly in sexual harassment situations. Male and female coworkers differ in their perceptions of sexually inappropriate behaviors. Further, people who have been harassed before differ in their perceptions of behavior from those who have not been harassed. These factors need to be carefully considered in any organizational assessment.

Finally, if the organization has not engaged in preventive practices or has no grievance procedures and so forth in place, the organization can alter the structure of work to address power imbalances and other organizational correlates of sexual harassment. Further, personnel systems within the organization must be coordinated with an organization statement or policy (Gutek, in press) that states that sexual harassment will not be tolerated. At the outcome stage, sexual harassment interventions will be similar to those applied at the prevention stage. However, given the individual outcomes of sexual harassment episodes on the target especially but also for work group peers, the supervisor, and the harasser, there will be greater use of conciliatory intervention. It is critical, however, especially following the occurrence of sexual harassment, that the organization send a clear message to all employees, hold the more powerful parties of such behavior responsible, and follow through with appropriate actions.

CONCLUSIONS

Sexual harassment is a complex problem that is multidimensional in scope (Fitzgerald, 1993). It occurs between two people but also within a group, organizational, and societal context that allows such abusive behavior to occur between individuals. Therefore, it appears that multidimensional interventions that address both the interpersonal and the intragroup dynamics involved in sexual harassment, as well as organizational change methods, need to be employed and evaluated. The usefulness of the various methods of intervention needs to be assessed in terms of their impact on reducing the incidence of harassment by previous and potential targets and/or their effectiveness in reducing the consequences. Ultimately, the goal of any intervention for sexual harassment is to create within the organization, a system of values and norms that encourage respectful and constructive collegial behavior in the workplace. To determine if indeed this has been accomplished, the individuals who have been or may be the targets of sexual harassment must provide the input on whether or how their experiences have changed. Multidimensional interventions appear to have the most promise for ameliorating sexual harassment, and multiple measures of change are needed to assess the success of these interventions. Experimental evaluations of interventions for sexual harassment are badly needed. Perhaps this review of possible intervention methods for sexual harassment will move us closer to that goal.

REFERENCES

Barnett, O. W., & LaViolette, A. D. (1993). *It could happen to anyone: Why battered women stay.* Newbury Park, CA: Sage.

Barnett, O. J., & Lopez-Real, D. I. (1985, November). *Women's reactions to battering and why they stay.* Paper presented at the annual meeting of the American Psychological Association, Washington, DC.

Berk, R. A., & Newton, P. J. (1985). Does arrest really deter wife battery? An effort to replicate the findings of the Minneapolis spouse abuse experiment. *American Sociological Review, 50,* 253-262.

Campbell, J. C. (1990, December). Battered woman syndrome: A critical review. *Violence Update, 1,* 10-11.

Carlisle-Frank, P. (1991, July). Do battered women's beliefs about control affect their decisions to remain in abusive environments? *Violence Update, 1,* 10-11.

Cleveland, J. N., & Kerst, M. E. (1993). Sexual harassment and perceptions of power: An under-articulated relationship. *Journal of Vocational Behavior, 42,* 49-67.

DeMaris, A., & Jackson, J. K. (1987). Batterers' reports of recidivism after counseling. *Social Casework, 68,* 458-465.

Dobash, R. E., & Dobash, R. E. (1979). *Violence against wives: A case against patriarchy.* New York: Free Press.

Dutton, D. G. (1986). The outcome of court-mandated treatment for wife assault: A quasi-experimental evaluation. *Violence and Victims, 1,* 163-175.

Dutton, D. G., & Strachan, C. E. (1987). Motivational needs for power and spouse-specific assertiveness in assaultive and nonassaultive men. *Violence and Victims, 2,* 145-156.

Edleson, J. L., & Grusznski, R. J. (1988). Treating men who batter: Four years of outcome data from the domestic abuse project. *Journal of Social Service Research, 12,* 3-22.

Filley, A. C. (1975). *Interpersonal conflict resolution.* Glenview, IL: Scott, Foresman.

Finkelhor, D., Gelles, R. J., Hotaling, G. T., & Straus, M. A. (1983). *The dark side of families.* Beverly Hills, CA: Sage.

Fitzgerald, L. F. (1993). Sexual harassment: Violence against women in the workplace. *American Psychologist, 48,* 1070-1076.

Fitzgerald, L. F., & Shullman, S. L. (1993). Sexual harassment: A research analysis and agenda for the 1990s. *Journal of Vocational Behavior, 42,* 5-27.

French, W. L., & Bell, C. H. (1984). *Organization development: Behavioral science interventions for organization improvement.* Englewood Cliffs, NJ: Prentice Hall.

Frieze, I. H., Knoble, J., Washburn, C., & Zomnir, G. (1980, March). *Types of battered women.* Paper presented at the meeting of the Annual Research Conference of the Association for Women in Psychology, Santa Monica, CA.

Gelles, R. J. (1980). Violence in the family: A review of research in the seventies. *Journal of Marriage and the Family, 42,* 873-885.

Gelles, R. J. (1985). *Intimate violence.* New York: Simon & Schuster.

Goodman, L. A., Koss, M. P., Fitzgerald, L. F., Russo, N. F. & Keita, G. P. (1993). Male violence against women: Current research directions and future directions. *American Psychologist, 48,* 1054-1058.

Goodstein, L. D., & Burke, W. W. (1991, Spring). Creating successful organization change. *Organizational Dynamics,* pp. 5-17. (Reprinted in W. L. French, C. H. Bell, & R. A. Zawacki, Eds., *Organization development and transformation: Managing effective change.* Irwin: Burr Ridge, IL)

Gutek, B. A. (in press). Sexual harassment policy initiatives. In W. O'Donohue (Ed.), *Sexual harassment: Theory, research, treatment.* Boston: Allyn & Bacon.

Gutek, B. A. (1985). *Sex and the workplace.* San Francisco: Jossey Bass.

Gutek, B. S., & Koss, M. P. (1993). Changed women and changed organizations: Consequences of and coping with sexual harassment. *Journal of Vocational Behavior, 42,* 28-48.

Hamberger, L. K., & Hastings, J. E. (1986). Personality correlates of men who abuse their partners: A cross-validation study. *Journal of Family Violence, 4,* 323-341.

Harrison, R. (1972, Spring). When power conflicts trigger team spirit. *European Business,* pp. 27-65.

Herman, J. L. (1992). *Trauma and recovery.* New York: Basic Books.

Herman, J., & Hirschman, L. (1980). Father-daughter incest. In K. MacFarlane, L. L. Jenstrom, & B. M. Jones (Eds.), *Sexual abuse of children: Selected readings* (Department of Health, Education, and Welfare, Pub. No. [OHDS] 78-30161, pp. 65-77). Washington, DC: Government Printing Office.

Hotaling, G. T., & Sugarman, D. B. (1986). An analysis of risk markers in husband to wife violence: The current state of knowledge. *Violence and Victims, 1,* 101-124.

Jaffe, P., Wolfe, D. A., Telford, A., & Austin, G. (1986). The impact of police charges on incidents of wife abuse. *Journal of Family Violence, 1,* 37-49.

Jensen, I. W., & Gutek, B. A. (1982). Attributions and assignment of responsibility of sexual harassment. *Journal of Social Issues, 38,* 121-136.

Kipnis, D. (1990). *Technology and power.* New York: Springer-Verlag.

Koss, M. P. (1990). Changed lives: The psychological impact of sexual harassment. In M. Paludi (Ed.), *Ivory power: Sexual harassment on campus* (pp. 73-92). Albany: SUNY Press.

Kurz, D. (1993). Social science perspectives on wife abuse: Current debates and future directions. In P. B. Bart & E. G. Moran (Eds.), *Violence against women: The bloody footprints* (pp. 252-269). Newbury Park, CA: Sage.

LaViolette, A. D., Barnett, O. W., & Miller, C. L. (1984, August). *A classification of wife abusers on the Bem Sex Role Inventory.* Paper presented at the Second Annual Conference on Research and Domestic Violence, Durham, NH.

Livingston, J. A. (1982). Responses to sexual harassment on the job: Legal, organizational, and individual actions. *Journal of Social Issues, 38,* 5-22.

Maiuro, R. D., Cahn, T. S., & Vitaliano, P. P. (1986). Assertiveness deficits and hostility in domestically violent men. *Violence and Victims, 4,* 279-289.

Mastenbroek, W. F. G. (1987). *Conflict management and organization development.* New York: John Wiley.

Mercy, J. A., & Saltzman, L. E. (1989). A study of battered women presenting in an emergency department. *American Journal of Public Health, 79,* 65-66.

Neidig, P. H., Friedman, D. H., & Collins, B. S. (1985). Domestic conflict containment: A spouse abuse treatment program. *Social Casework, 66,* 195-204.

NiCarthy, G., Gottlieb, N., & Coffman, S. (1993). *You don't have to take it! A woman's guide to confronting emotional abuse at work.* Seattle, WA: Seal.

Pagelow, M. D. (1981). Factors affecting women's decisions to leave violent relationships. *Journal of Family Issues, 2,* 391-414.

Pagelow, M. D. (1984). *Family violence.* New York: Praeger.

Pagelow, M. D. (1992). Adult victims of domestic violence. *Journal of Interpersonal Violence, 7,* 87-120.

Pagelow, M. D. (1993). Response to Hamberger's comment. *Journal of Interpersonal Violence, 8,* 137-139.

Porras, J. I., & Hoffer, S. J. (1986). Common behavior changes in successful organization development. *Journal of Applied Behavior Science, 22,* 477-494.

Porras, J. I., & Robertson, P. J. (1992). Organizational development: Theory, practice and research. In M. D. Dunnette & L. M. Hough (Eds.), *Handbook of industrial and organizational psychology* (Vol. 3). Palo Alto, CA: Consulting Psychologists Press.

Pryor, J. B. (1987). Sexual harassment proclivities in men. *Sex Roles, 17,* 269-290.

Pryor, J. B., LaVite, C. M., & Stoller, L. M. (1993). A social psychological analysis of sexual harassment: The person/situation interaction. *Journal of Vocational Behavior, 42,* 68-83.

Ritmeester, T. (1993). Batterers' programs, battered women's movement, and issues of accountability. In E. Pence & M. Paymar (Eds.), *Education groups for men who batter* (pp. 169-178). New York: Springer.

Rosenbaum, A. (1986). Of men, macho, and marital violence. *Journal of Family Violence, 1,* 121-130.

Russell, D. E. H. (1982). *Rape in marriage.* New York: Macmillan.

Sherman, L. W., & Berk, R. A. (1984). The specific deterrent effects of arrest for domestic assault. *American Sociological Review, 49,* 261-272.

Shupe, A., Stacey, W. A., & Hazelwood, L. R. (1986). *Violent men, violent couples.* Lexington, MA: Lexington.

Simmel, G. (1904). *Conflict and the web of group affiliation.* Glencoe, IL: Free Press.

Straus, M., Gelles, R., & Steinmetz, R. (1980). *Behind closed doors: Violence in the American family.* New York: Doubleday.

Thomas, K. W. (1992). Conflict and negotiation processes in organizations. In M. D. Dunnette & L. M. Hough (Eds.), *Handbook of industrial and organizational psychology* (Vol. 3, pp. 651-717). Palo Alto, CA: Consulting Psychologists Press.

Thorne-Finch, R. (1992). *Ending the silence: The origins and treatment of male violence against women.* Toronto: University of Toronto Press.

Tolman, R. M., & Bennett, L. W. (1990). A review of quantitative research on men who batter. *Journal of Interpersonal Violence, 5,* 87-118.

Toufexis, A. (1987, December, 21). Home is where the hurt is: Wife beating among the well-to-do no longer a secret. *Time,* p. 68.

Underwood, J. (1987, April). End sexual harassment of employees (sic), or your board could be held liable. *American School Board Journal,* pp. 43-44.

U.S. Merit Systems Protection Board. (1981). *Sexual harassment in the federal workplace: Is it a problem?* Washington, DC: Office of Merit Systems Review and Studies/Government Printing Office.

Walker, L. E. (1979). *The battered woman.* New York: Colophon.

Walker, L. E. (1984). *The battered woman syndrome.* New York: Springer.

Winter, D. G. (1973). *The power motive.* New York: Free Press.

12

Dealing With Harassment: A Systems Approach

MARY P. ROWE

People who are concerned about harassment often feel they "know what is best" for a person who has been harassed. But those who have actually been harassed often have very strong—and different—points of view about what they are willing to do. Thus, procedures for dealing with harassment must first take into account the wide range of interests of various complainants—or complainants will not take action. This chapter explores the pros and cons of many possible elements of a complaint system. I conclude by recommending an integrated dispute resolution systems approach, which provides options for complainants, respondents, bystanders, and supervisors.

DESIGNING AND REVIEWING HARASSMENT POLICIES AND PROCEDURES

Employers large and small are designing and reviewing harassment olicies and procedures—and are surprised by the difficulty of the task. uch review is in fact objectively difficult, because there is no ideal way o resolve the complex and painful problem of harassment. It *is* possible o deal better with harassment now than in the past. I recommend an ntegrated, systems approach to conflict management—especially for large enterprises but also for small ones. A systems approach provides options and choices for complainants and, to some degree, for supervisors and respondents.

An integrated conflict management system, in my view, has a number of specific characteristics. In the language of dispute resolution systems design, there should be "multiple access points" for people with concerns and grievances. These gatekeepers should include people of different races and genders. The gatekeepers should include resource people who concentrate on providing interest-based options as well as those who handle rights-based options. For example, a medium- or large-sized organization might have an ombudsperson as one of the options for managing conflict. Some options should be interest-based and some rights-based (or based on rights and power). A complainant may in many circumstances either loop *forward* from an interest-based option to a rights-based option, or loop *back* from a rights-based option to an interest-based option. Options are often available in parallel, rather than designated as steps of a grievance procedure. Options in the system are initially available for *complainant* choice for most problems—rather than solely at *complaint handler's* choice, which used to be the common mode for a nonunion environment, and rather than a *single grievance channel,* which is the classic mode in a unionized environment. At the end of the line, there is an option that takes investigation or decision making, or both, out of the line of supervision. The system is open to managers with concerns, as well as employees. It takes virtually every kind of concern that is of interest to people in the organization, including, for example, disputes between coworkers and between fellow managers, teammates, and groups, as well as classic concerns about discrimination, conditions of employment, and termination. There is an overall value system with respect to conflict management derived from the core values and human resource strategy of the organization, which is backed by top managers and taught to both employees and managers. With respect to harassment and discrimination, there is explicit recognition of the rights and responsibilities of four groups: complainants, respondents, supervisors, and bystanders.

This chapter first states why I believe that there is no single correct policy or procedure for harassment, and suggests why the process of conflict management systems design is difficult for employers. I discuss the rationale for a systems approach. I set forth major issues that must be addressed in taking this path as well as some pros and cons attached to major issues in harassment system design—which are excellent topics for research.

Since 1973, I have been an ombudsperson,[1] working and teaching within a research university, and also consulting to corporations, academic institutions, and government agencies. (An ombudsperson is a conflict management professional, designated as neutral, who has all the functions of any complaint handler, except those of formal investigation and adjudication, and who offers confidentiality under all but potentially catastrophic circumstances.) I am a general ombudsperson, but about half of the concerns that come to me deal with harassment, discrimination, or some other kind of workplace mistreatment. Counting many calls from outside my own institution, I estimate that in the last 23 years I have helped with or consulted on some 8,000-9,000 complaints, concerns, and questions about various kinds of harassment, discrimination, and workplace mistreatment[2]—and about how an employer should deal with these problems. I have also helped hundreds of institutions and government agencies to design and set up complaint systems to help deal with harassment. This chapter is drawn from analysis of this experience. From a scholarly point of view, the points made in this chapter may be considered hypotheses in a field with virtually no large-scale research.

THERE IS NO PERFECT POLICY OR PROCEDURE

Many writers have attempted to describe "the right" policy and procedure for dealing with harassment. I believe that there is no perfect policy or procedure. This is true for at least three reasons. First, it is nearly impossible to design a complaint system that users will think is satisfactory. Once harassment has occurred, it is difficult to bring about any resolution that is wholly positive. This virtually guarantees that harassment policies and complaint systems have an unsatisfactory reputation. In an ideal system, a high proportion of complainants would feel satisfied, most respondents would feel fairly treated, and most complaint handlers would feel they acted fairly. In actuality, the complainant's pain is often long lasting. *Any* steps that can be taken after harassment has occurred may lead to feelings of more injury. The evidence is often only one person's word against another, so one party may feel mistreated and the complaint handler unsure about what is fair. Often, the best that an employer feels it can do is to minimize pain and loss—for the harassed person and for others who have been affected—and perhaps learn how to do better in the future.

The second reason there is no perfect system is that institutions differ. They have different missions, for example, "readiness" in the armed forces, education and research in a university. They are subject to different laws and rules and traditions, in different industries, different states and countries.

The third reason is that different people have very different ideas about what constitutes a good system. It is therefore not possible to design a policy or procedure, even within a single workplace, that everybody will find acceptable. One might, for example, think that most people could at least agree about prevention programs—almost everyone believes in prevention—but even here there is sharp disagreement about whether to take a legalistic approach or an educational approach, a narrow punitive approach or a broad positive approach. Controversy is even more fierce with respect to complaint handling. As we shall see, people disagree about how broad a harassment policy should be and whether there should be a central office or EEO function for dealing with all complaints.

In particular, responsible people disagree about how much choice a complainant should have—of resource persons and of options—for dealing with harassment. Probably the most serious differences occur between those who believe in offering *interest-based options* for most noncriminal harassment (a direct approach from the offended person to the offender, a go-between, classic mediation, a generic approach, systems change, or even avoidance) and those who believe in options based on *rights* or *rights and power* (investigation and adjudication; complaint to a government agency, the security department, police, a court; or even "just firing people" who are alleged to have harassed). Consider the following true story.

> "Can I tell you my story?" asks a caller from out of state. "I came in early to the office and I overheard a secretary talking on the phone, about a colleague of mine. I could hear her saying that she was being brushed against, crowded, and stared at. She said that my colleague is deliberately trying to make her blush with many kinds of sexual comments. He laughs at her, trying to get a rise out of her. She said that he is very careful to do

it only when they are alone together. She keeps asking him to stop it. But yesterday he put out his hand to take a paper from her—and then put his hands up under her breasts and held them there. She was crying on the phone. She told her friend that she was going to try for a transfer.

"I walked quietly to my own office without saying anything to this secretary because she was crying so hard and seemed so upset. At nine o'clock I called our General Counsel's office. Fortunately I did not mention anybody's name though they tried to find out who I am. They said I am required immediately to call the EEO Office and that EEO in turn is required to institute a fair, prompt, and thorough investigation. So I went back to the secretary to talk with her. She was stunned to think that I had overheard her. She pleaded with me to keep my mouth shut. She said it would be 'his word against hers.' She is afraid that somehow he will get back at her covertly. She is desperately worried about not having anyone else know the story—she is especially concerned that her husband must never hear about this.

"We talked it over at lunchtime. She said she did not want to get anyone in trouble, she did not want an investigation, all she ever wanted was for the behavior to stop. She was *extremely* upset with me for eavesdropping. She says there is absolutely nothing that anyone can do, and that I have to keep quiet about this until she can get a transfer. She is working on a degree and does not want anything to derail her—especially in this economic climate. She is worried about her references, and she is beside herself about what her husband—and his family—might do.

"Our Total Quality Management training program says that I am supposed to think of our employees as one group of 'customers.' So here I am required by company policy to ignore the wishes of a 'customer' and—so to speak—to turn her in—in a circumstance where she feels that the personal and professional consequences might be really terrible for her. I cannot believe this is happening. Can you help me?"

As this case makes clear, harassment can raise agonizing dilemmas. In this example, a staff person believes that her employer cannot protect her from personal or professional injury if the eavesdropping manager "turns her in." On the other hand, taking no action in a harassment case may lead to continued abuse by a grossly irresponsible supervisor, serious damage of persons thereby abused, and a costly suit against the employer. It may also lead to loss of image for the company, agency, or university as a responsible institution. It is therefore essential to start with the premise that harassment issues are complex. This means listening to those who will be affected.

IDENTIFY THE STAKEHOLDERS

An institution that is reviewing complaint procedures or designing a system may inadvertently have the interests of just one or another group clearly in mind. It is important to identify *all* those whose interests are at stake.

Groups Focused on a Rights-Based Procedure

There may be institutional lawyers whose interest, by their ethics, lies in protecting the employer and who lobby for mandatory reporting, formal investigation, and careful record keeping with respect to harassment concerns. In addition, there may be others in the institution—some of whom have been harassed—who also want mandatory investigation and adjudication of all complaints. Their focus is often on punishment, on defining and announcing sanctions against those who harass. These two sets of stakeholders are likely to use quite broad definitions of harassment, which include offensive speech and expression, although they are often focused only on sexual harassment. There are also men and women who are primarily concerned for the rights of alleged offenders. The focus of this group is likely to be defined as "justice for all disputants." They typically prefer rather narrowly written policies. In addition, for most organizations, there are regulatory agencies and external constituencies whose guidelines and outlook must be considered and whose primary focus is on adjudicating rights.

Groups Primarily Focused on Interest-Based Procedures

There is always a great silent pool of women and men who have been or will be harassed whose interests lie, at least in the beginning, in having choices about what to do—including having choices that do not involve investigation or at least do not involve punishment. There are usually people of different nationalities, colors, and religions who want to have a broadly defined harassment policy that includes harassment and discrimination against all legally protected groups but that provides interest-based options for different subcultures. There frequently are people who feel strongly about free speech who insist on interest-based options, because they feel that harassment by means of speech, graffiti, and posters should never be punished.

Groups Focused on Power-Based Procedures

There may be senior managers who believe that sexualization and harassment in the workplace must be eliminated by any means necessary—including simply firing people about whom such a concern is raised, or by getting rid of complainants, or by making settlements even if they are inappropriate. In addition, there may be managers who do not care about harassment and want to ignore the subject. These groups typically just want options based on management power. Finally, there may be security personnel or police who want to discuss power-based procedures that increase safety, as well as rights-based procedures.

Some of the points of view discussed in this chapter may not be acceptable to a committee that is reviewing harassment procedures or designing a system. Discussion of the questions below will, however, at least permit better informed policy making.

SPECIFIC OR GENERAL POLICY AND PROCEDURES

Specific Policies

Those who argue for specific policies (for example, solely about sexual harassment or racial harassment) often note that there are differences with respect to the origins, manifestations, and effects of sexism, racism, and other kinds of mistreatment—and therefore each kind of harassment should be dealt with separately. They may argue that specific policies convey more of a sense of urgency about one particular kind of harassment. Narrow definitions of proscribed behavior are sometimes thought to be more easily understood. Policies that deal with all types of harassment and policies that deal with a wide range of severity of offense may be attacked as "too vague." Sometimes senior management cares most about just one kind of harassment and would prefer to concentrate on the issue of most concern to them. Sometimes stakeholders such as lesbians, gays and bisexuals, or men and women of color are incensed about their particular issue, usually because there has been a recent crisis. These people may not want institutional effort, airtime, or their own scarce resources dissipated over a wide range of problems. Finally, some managers who want to limit complaints will oppose having "plain workplace mistreatment" included in a harassment policy.

General Policies

Those who argue for general policies often point out that general policies are used by more complainants and therefore are likely to be more widely understood. They may note the recent emphasis of the U.S. Equal Employment Opportunity Commission (EEOC) on addressing harassment against all legally protected groups. General policies may be seen as fairer and less invidious in coverage. There is less backlash from white males where employer policies protect everyone against all workplace abuse and mistreatment, in addition to specific protections with respect to race, age, religion, gender, and so on. A general harassment policy also provides for more choice for individuals. For example, a woman of color may ask that persistent questions about her sexuality or an indecent assault be seen as racism—rather than sexism—for the purpose of devising an appropriate remedy. Having a general policy may avoid certain semantic disagreements ("This is not sexual harassment, this is homophobia") and help focus attention on unreasonably offensive behavior rather than permitting people to avoid a problem by quarreling over terms. General policies appear more appropriate for small enterprises that would not want to have separate policies about each form of abuse. Having a general policy has also proved helpful in certain institutions in providing coverage to emergent groups such as gays, lesbians and bisexuals, and Muslims.

All Policies

All policies should define harassment. All policies should provide examples of the discrimination that will be covered, such as cultural, religious, racial, sexual, age, sexual orientation, and disability harassment. All policies should describe management responsibilities that per se are not harassment, such as negative performance evaluations and work assignments. All policies should proscribe reprisal for bringing a complaint in good faith. Helpful resource personnel and their characteristics—that is, who can keep the complainant's confidence, who must act if notified—and the options available for dealing with harassment should be listed specifically. All policies should be addressed explicitly to at least four groups: complainants, respondents, supervisors, and bystanders.

WHAT OPTIONS SHOULD BE PROVIDED?

Providing Only Investigation and Adjudication

In some workplaces, there is only one option for a complainant—rights-based, win-lose investigation and adjudication. In some workplaces, such as the one in the opening story, this option is mandatory, meaning that anyone who hears of harassment must report it, and all reports must be investigated. Rights-based procedures usually follow specified steps. The complaint and outcome are usually in writing and recorded formally. Some employers insist on a finding—either the complaint is substantiated or it is not. And in some workplaces, there are only two possible outcomes—the alleged offender is guilty or innocent. Some employers provide for degrees of substantiation—that is, a concern may be affirmed in whole or in part or not affirmed. Other employers also provide for the possibility that there is simply not enough evidence to come to a conclusion, in which case some keep records of the case and some do not. Some keep harassment complaint records in the files of the alleged offender. Some keep them in the file of the complainant—a practice sharply criticized by some observers and seen as fair by others.

The rationale for providing a single, rights-based option includes the following points: It will be easily understood; it will provide justice; repeat offenders can be tracked; the process is easily monitored by senior administrators; and managers are more easily held accountable.

There are a number of problems with providing only a win-lose, rights-based procedure. Many people (e.g., Gadlin, 1991; Rowe, 1990b)—especially those of certain cultural backgrounds and especially women (e.g., Gwartney-Gibbs, & Lach, 1991, 1992; Lewin, 1990; Riger, 1991)—deeply dislike win-lose procedures. I believe that a major reason is that rights-based procedures are thought to polarize issues and affect workplace harmony and career relationships. In addition, an adjudicatory option may not be adequate for subtle or covert discrimination, free speech issues, and the fear of reprisal.

Rights based not good for subtle stuff

A rights-based procedure will not deal well with subtle or covert discrimination (see Gwartney-Gibbs & Lach, 1991; Rowe, 1990a)—which in my experience is often as damaging as other forms of harassment, especially on a cumulative basis—because of the problem of inadequate evidence. And even though the EEOC guidelines do include matters of speech in the definition of harassment, some complainants and some employers do not believe in using formal procedures with respect to offenses that are matters of speech and expression. Finally, although many institutions try hard to prevent reprisal, it is in fact impossible for an employer to prevent many forms of reprisal. Examples include covert repercussions and cold shouldering or abuse from peers, family, and colleagues in other institutions.

For these and other reasons, formal grievance procedures are used only rarely by comparison with the proportions of women and men who report on anonymous surveys that they have been harassed. It is not unusual, however, to find employers who offer only win-lose, rights-based procedures, despite the fact that it is widely understood that such procedures are used comparatively rarely. (Some employers have told me that they prefer offering only a rights-based procedure to discourage concerns about harassment.)

Providing Only Interest-Based Procedures

Most employers deal relatively informally with virtually all non-criminal harassment and with some harassment that might be criminal in nature. In many small enterprises, there is no tradition of rights-based, win-lose grievance handling, and harassment is dealt with informally, as are all other issues. Many problems are addressed by discussion or reassigning job responsibilities. Interest-based procedures, such as discussion with or between the parties, usually depend on local management style and skill, and often there are no records. The usual rationale for such a model is that many harassment concerns derive from misunderstandings or ignorance and many offenders will straighten up if they are told to do so. Moreover, it is often impossible to know who is telling the truth.

For many reasons, it is unsatisfactory to provide only interest-based options. A small but significant percentage of complainants are only satisfied with win-lose, rights-based processes. In addition, some respondents prefer a rights-based process, when they think this provides the best chance to clear their reputations. Many people believe that all civil rights offenses or at least egregious offenses should be dealt with on the basis of rights (Edelman, Erlanger, & Lande, 1993). In addition, many people believe in having a rights-based, adjudicatory option available, even if they personally would never use it, because this "conveys a message" about the commitment of the employer to deal with harassment. Finally, exclusive reliance on interest-based procedures may contribute to the invisibility of harassment, and complaints of harassment may be discouraged when each offended person thinks she or he is "the only one."

In sum, no single option is right for most complainants. Without a choice of options, many complainants either do nothing about harassment—some suffer acutely in silence—or leave the situation they are in by quitting or transfer. Where there are options, complainants' choices will depend on their perceptions of their evidence, their perceptions of the employer's commitment to maintain a harassment-free and reprisal-free environment, their judgment of the integrity and impartiality of the gatekeepers (Gwartney-Gibbs & Lach, 1991), their wish to safeguard their privacy, their cultural background, the nature of their family and career relationships, their personal histories of abuse or efficacy, their best alternatives to dispute resolution, and other factors.

AN INTEGRATED DISPUTE RESOLUTION SYSTEM

Many employers, both large and small, have turned to providing multiple options within a system. There are five common modes for harassment dispute resolution: (a) direct approach from complainant to respondent in person or on paper; (b) informal third-party intervention; (c) generic (interest-based) approaches and system change; (d) classic (formal) mediation by a designated neutral third party; and (e) rights-based investigation and adjudication (and appeals).

The Direct Approach

Where the complainant particularly wishes to protect her or his relationships and/or privacy, feels that there is little evidence beyond her or his personal testimony, thinks that there may have been misunderstanding, or otherwise simply prefers this option, the complainant may decide to raise the matter directly to the offender. This may happen whether or not the employer "provides" this option. It is a great deal easier, however, for most harassed people and for bystanders to use a direct approach where the employer specifically approves of and encourages such action. It also helps if the employer expects respondents who are approached responsibly to respond responsibly. Large employers should provide off-the-record counseling for complainants to support this option. Counseling is useful both to be sure the complainant knows about all her or his options before choosing this one—and to prepare for this option.

The direct approach often works well with matters of speech and expression and with subtle harassment—possibly because many offenses of this type really do derive from failure by offenders to understand the importance of the offenses. This option usually safeguards the rights and interests of respondents, as well as those of complainants, because miscommunications may be resolved and no employer record will be made of the complaint.

The direct approach is often effective in North America but is not universally helpful. It does not necessarily appeal to people of every background. For example, some cultures expect use of a go-between. In some milieus, only one version of this option may work well—some traditions favor communications in writing, some favor face-to-face contact.

Informal Third-Party Intervention

Where the complainant wishes help, she or he may turn to a trusted mentor, an immediate supervisor, an ombudsperson, a human resource manager, even a family friend or member of the family to intervene informally. Here the goal is not to establish right or wrong, or to punish wrongdoing, but simply to resolve the problem on the basis of the interests of the parties. The third party may sit down with first one and then the other party. The intermediary might agree, if asked, to separate the work of the parties—or might just have a heart-to-heart talk with the offender. This mode is preferred in many cultural traditions. The option is widely used in blue-, pink-, and white-collar employment and is common in small as well as large work units.

If the informal third party is a supervisor or human resource manager, then informal third-party intervention should have the explicit approval of the employer. It will work best where the complaint handler has had adequate training. Such training should include specification of the main goals: Complaint handlers should be explicitly held to a standard (a) that any alleged harassment must stop and (b) that there may be no reprisal for complaints made in good faith. It will also help the institution to monitor the workplace if complaint handlers get training on how to report identity-free, statistical records on informal harassment complaints. Complaint handlers should also be taught about safeguarding the rights and interests of both parties. For example, although it should be possible for a supervisor to solve a problem informally by taking corrective action that is not disciplinary in nature, I believe that no disciplinary action should be taken against an alleged offender without a fair investigation. In addition, complainants should not be transferred to alleviate tension—unless they ask for a transfer or the situation is an emergency—without a fair investigation.

Generic Approaches and Systems Change

Where a complainant especially dreads reprisal, or loss of relationships and privacy, is concerned about not being able to prove that harassment took place, is concerned about a group of offenders, wants to protect others in the future, believes in education of offenders, or otherwise simply prefers this option, an employer can provide a generic option. Here the relevant department head need not necessarily know the identities of the complainant or the alleged offender(s) but is informed in some responsible way—as, for example, by an ombudsperson—that there is a concern in a certain work area. The department head might then bring in a film or workshop or skit or posters, or might talk about the employer's harassment policy (with some generic examples) at the next department meeting. Whoever knows about the original concern would follow up to see that the alleged harassment had stopped and that there was no reported reprisal, and would keep a statistical record, without names, for an annual report. This option often works well with matters of speech and with subtle harassment. It is a good addition to other prevention programs in the workplace, and usually protects the rights and interests of both complainant and respondent.

In addition, an employer may make changes in the workplace in response to an individual complaint. Examples include increasing the number of women and/or people of color assigned in a certain workplace, successfully recruiting a senior woman manager or a senior black manager for the area, stating clear expectations about professional behavior on business trips, curtailing the use of alcohol at workplace parties, and so on.

Classic Mediation

A number of employers provide for the possibility of classic formal mediation by a professional neutral who is following a publicly available set of ground rules. Typically, this option is purely voluntary for all parties to the complaint. The settlement, if any, is agreed to and belongs to the parties. It is not dictated, monitored, or enforced by the mediator—who typically asks at the beginning for a formal agreement that the mediator and his or her records will not be called if the case is later reopened. The settlement is usually not kept or enforced by the employer—unless such an agreement is part of the settlement reached by the parties. The employer in fact may not even know of the existence of the complaint if the parties choose an in-house mediator. Exceptions occur where employers offer this option only after formal investigation of the facts of the case, or after termination.

This option is sometimes initiated by complainants who particularly wish to safeguard the relationship, and safeguard their privacy, who believe that they do not have enough evidence to prevail in a formal grievance, or simply believe in classic mediation as a form of dispute resolution. Sometimes a complainant asks for mediation because it seems the most likely mode to get a harasser to agree to stop offending in general as well as in the specific case. Both parties may agree to mediate, and comply with a mediated settlement, if they see all other options as worse alternatives. This option is likely to protect the rights and interests of both parties, if it is maintained by the employer as a purely voluntary option, because either party may later choose a different option if mediation proves unsatisfactory.

Formal Investigation and Adjudication

A rights-based option (a formal grievance procedure) should offer investigation, adjudication, and the possibility of appeal. Some grievance procedures separate investigation from decision making, to provide more objectivity, so different people perform each of these tasks. Some grievance procedures use an outside arbitrator, peer review, or a board of appeal to decide cases in the last stage of appeal.

Some organizations that have their own security or sworn police force also offer a second alternative that is based on rights (and on power). A complainant who fears for her or his safety, for example, may approach a police or security officer at the workplace to ask that a harasser be called in for questioning, for a warning, for investigation, or for other appropriate action. Some workplace police and security departments will support employees in seeking a restraining order, enforce trespassing orders, and so forth. Except for emergency action, workplace security and police departments ordinarily coordinate with the employer's interest and rights-based procedures.

A fair investigation is required if the employer is to take disciplinary action against an offender. Typically, a rights-based option is used for the most serious offenses (including allegations of reprisal) and for repeat offenses. It may also be used as the last step in a complaint process. I believe, however, that this option should also be available as a first step to any complainant or respondent who can demonstrate reasonable cause and who prefers an investigative approach. This is because there is a small but significant group of complainants who do not believe in interest-based approaches for harassment, because respondents may wish to have their names formally cleared, because society has an interest in having some allegations of illegal behavior investigated formally to provide a publicly available record, and because most criminal offenses warrant a formal approach.

There are a number of controversial issues that need to be addressed in developing this option. The first deals with the standard of proof used in the judgment of whether or not harassment took place. Some employers say they rely on the civil standard of preponderance of the evidence, and thus determine whether it is "more likely than not" that harassment took place. This standard permits judgments to be made on the basis of "he said/she said" evidence; the decision maker simply decides who is the more credible disputant. Theoretically, this standard—because it sets a low requirement for proof—should lead to more mistakes in judgment, especially in workplaces where the employer insists that a finding be made one way or the other. This standard is therefore sometimes thought to be unfair to complainants and sometimes to respondents. It is, however, the standard used by courts in most harassment cases, and is thought by most observers to be the most appropriate for employers. Employers, however, often use higher standards, closer to clear and convincing evidence. Employers sometimes explain this behavior in terms of not wishing to put anyone's job at risk on the basis of lesser proof. Some employers even use the criminal standard—that is, "beyond a reasonable doubt"—for harassment that would not be considered criminal in nature. In time, legislatures may specify the standard for employers.

Some employers de facto use a different standard of proof where the alleged offender is seen as particularly valuable to the institution—a practice open to sharp criticism. And many employers mix together the issue of how much evidence should decide if harassment actually took place with the issue of how much evidence should result in serious sanctions. Thus a complaint of serious harassment may be lightly punished if the evidence is considered weak but may be more seriously punished if the evidence is strong. This practice may seem to be reasonable—but to many it appears unjust, especially with respect to offenders who admit to the behavior that was the subject of a complaint. This practice may also foster dishonesty on the part of offenders.

How an adjudicatory procedure will deal with concerns of harassment will also depend on how thoroughly the employer investigates a complaint. It is common for employers simply to talk with complainant and respondent, to evaluate the evidence brought by each, and decide the matter on the basis of this investigation. This is sometimes appropriate and sometimes not. Because the complainant and the institution often do not know whether there have been other people offended by the same offender—and because some investigators are very skeptical of complainants or of respondents—the thoroughness of investigations is important to findings of guilt or innocence. On the other hand, the employer who investigates very thoroughly—a really thorough investigation might even require calling former employees and clients or alumni—risks endangering the privacy and reputations of the complainant and respondent and also risks serious upset in the workplace and more suits by respondents.

The potential effects of the standard of proof and the thoroughness of investigations matter enormously to a complainant. They also matter to the respondent; however, the effect on the complainant may determine whether an offense gets surfaced and, therefore, is of first priority for systems design. A complainant whose only option is a rights-based procedure with a de facto high standard of proof typically will not wish to come forward at all—unless it is the rare case where he or she happens to have a great deal of evidence in addition to his or her word. (In my experience, complainants with a great deal of evidence are more willing to use rights-based procedures.) In the common situation where there is only "he said/she said" evidence, some complainants who decide that they must make a complaint will prefer very thorough investigations that look determinedly for other persons who have been offended. On the other hand, because they fear losing their privacy, some complainants avoid bringing a complaint where the employer is known to do thorough investigations in every case. The thoroughness question therefore needs evaluation on a case-by-case basis, preferably including discussion at least with the complainant.

Another issue, especially important in a rights-based option, is that of accompaniment, that is, the possibility for any party in a dispute to be accompanied by another member of the organization. I believe that people who are harassed recover faster and do better if they are assisted by a sympathetic, responsible, and knowledgeable person. This is also true in my experience for respondents. Some employers permit attorneys to be present in internal procedures; most do not. Some employers have an advocacy program or designate a trained manager to assist each disputant. Some employers permit the advocate or assistant to represent the disputant, although many do not. Many permit an "accompanying person" who typically does not represent the disputant but is available for support and advice. It is essential with advocacy and assistance programs that roles are clearly defined, that staff are well trained with respect to policy, procedures, and law, and that they know about various kinds of harassment and their effects, understand the possible effects of any prior abuse of the complainant, and understand their own legal position and possible vulnerability. If advocates are made available by the employer, many people feel that they should be made available to both sides.

CENTRALIZED OR DECENTRALIZED STRUCTURES

Centralized Responsibility

Many employers have addressed discrimination and harassment complaints by setting up a centralized office or EEO function with trained counselor/investigators. This model is often associated with mandatory investigation and mandatory adjudication of all complaints. Skillful, central EEO staff, however, also can provide some informal options for complaint resolution.

A centralized structure has several advantages. It is easy to find for those in trouble. Those who staff the office usually acquire a good deal of experience. Complaints are generally treated in a consistent fashion, which is a virtue for adjudicatory procedures. People who seek help from a central office usually will not have to be referred elsewhere and therefore need not tell their story over and over. Central record keeping provides one way to identify repeat offenders. In addition, a central office can help to interact constructively with repeat complainers. Records are easily compared from year to year. People with serious harassment complaints often feel there will be less conflict of interest if their concerns are dealt with outside ordinary lines of supervision.

Some employers consider it an advantage of the centralized EEO structure that supervisors do not have to spend time thinking about discrimination and harassment because responsibility has been delegated to specialists. The complexities of dealing with complainants and respondents, especially in the context of proliferating harassment laws and regulation, need not be learned by supervisors or other human resource staff. On the other hand, the same points are seen as serious disadvantages by those who feel that a true equal opportunity world requires skill and commitment from everyone in the workplace.

Other shortcomings of centralization include the fact that where EEO staff perform variously as confidential counselors, quasi-mediators, and investigators who are also compliance officers, complainants may be misled about the degree of impartiality and confidentiality that is being offered (see Edelman, Petterson, Chambliss, & Erlanger, 1991; Edelman et al., 1993). It also may be impossible for the complainant who goes to a central office with rigid rules to obtain her or his own choice of option for dealing with the complaint. Over time, central office staff may be tagged as advocates for complainants, or as advocates for one protected group, or as advocates for management, under circumstances that provide no alternatives.

Centralized offices and EEO staff usually work to protect the privacy of those who have contact with the office, as much as possible. A system with a centralized office, however, typically cannot guarantee confidentiality to any complainant or respondent for at least two reasons. First, the office is usually required to respond to any concerns it hears about, whether or not the offended person wants the office involved. In addition, the central office is generally expected to keep records with names, and these records may be subject to review inside and outside the institution.

Public access to harassment records is seen by some people as an asset and therefore an important reason to have a central office. Proponents of record keeping believe that employer accountability requires court and agency access to information on all harassment concerns. Opponents tend to believe that no records with names should be kept by an employer when a complaint is settled on the basis of interests, and some feel that no records should be kept if an investigated complaint is found to be without merit. Opponents therefore may not favor a centralized EEO function.

Decentralized Responsibility

A decentralized system—where all supervisors and human resource staff are explicitly held accountable for preventing and dealing with harassment problems—also has advantages. Many people believe that discrimination and harassment are management responsibilities that ought not be completely delegated—at least not in the initial phases of concern or complaint. In the increasingly diverse workplaces of the future, every worker and manager will need to acquire a basic understanding of discrimination law and human sensibilities with respect to race, gender, religion, disability, color, age, nationality, sexual orientation, and other differences. This point of view is consonant with contemporary management theories of decentralization of responsibility. Those who hold this view often point out that it is impossible to centrally monitor all the perfidies and meanness that can happen in a workplace—so even if all supervisors do not manage harassment perfectly, and keep only statistical records of complaints settled on the basis of interests, it is better to hold responsible as many people as possible.

A decentralized model is capable of dealing with many more offenses than are central offices because supervisors and human resource managers are available as complaint handlers. Moreover, my experience suggests that many people who feel harassed initially prefer to go to someone they know. Some resent being told they only have a single option; they may want a local supervisor, local-area human resource specialist, employee assistance practitioner, or ombudsperson. This is especially true when the only evidence is of a "he said/she said" variety, or the problem is subtle or embarrassing or a matter of free speech in an institution that emphasizes free speech. There also may be resistance to a central office if the office staff are of just one race or gender or religion. Finally, two common problems with centralization—the perception that the central staff are management flunkies or that they do not have much power vis-à-vis senior supervisors—may disappear in a decentralized model.

Typically, the decentralized model provides a range of interest-based options for the complainant. Many complainants precisely do not want a "similar and consistent approach" to be taken to their unique concern. Custom-tailored solutions are more easily provided within the line of supervision than by a central office. A local supervisor may provide the best protection from reprisal. In addition, many people who feel harassed will not report the matter at all if a central record with their name will be made of their concern, so they prefer the possibility of local-area, interest-based resolution that may stay off the record.

On the other hand, in a decentralized model, it can be confusing to find out who has what responsibility, and record keeping may not be complete. Different supervisors have different levels of skill in dealing with harassment and may not acquire enough experience—or may just not want to spend the time that is needed—to do well. People who feel that all complaints should be dealt with in exactly the same way, whatever the severity of the offense, will dislike decentralization of responsibility. And decentralized structures are open to the perception of conflict of interest ("my supervisor will not take action against his friend") whether or not real conflicts of interest exist.

A Decentralized Model With a Central Office

An employer can combine advantages of both models in a systems approach. Most complainants will then have a choice of options, especially with offenses that are not egregious and where there has been no known repetition of offenses. The central office may gather name-free statistics about interest-based problem resolution from supervisors, may coordinate or handle formal investigations and appeals, and may keep records of rights-based actions. In addition, the central office can coordinate AA/EEO compliance requirements, provide training and advice for other complaint handlers, disseminate clear and detailed information about policy and procedures, and advise on policy.

INCREASING THE REPORTING RATE

Respect the Wishes of the Complainant When Possible

Employers commonly wish that people who are harassed would come forward within the workplace, rather than going outside, and that they would do so more promptly than is often the case. These employers must provide complainants not just with options but with a *choice* of options, except in the most serious cases, such as criminal assault, reprisal, or repeat offense. Too often, employers say they are "providing options" when in fact the options exist for complaint handlers rather than for complainants. For example, in a system with mandatory investigation of all harassment concerns, the complaint handler not only investigates, with or without the permission of the complainant, but then may decide, after the investigation, whether there will be an attempt at reconciliation. I believe, by contrast, that even in egregious cases such as criminal behavior, when an investigation must go forward despite the complainant's wishes, the employer should at least offer options about how this will be done—for example, the steps that will be taken to protect privacy, or the nature of further contact between the parties.

Deal With Fear of Reprisal in Policy and Procedures

Managers who are dealing for the first time with the topic of harassment may very much underestimate concerns about reprisal. Sometimes there is hesitation about adding this issue to policies on harassment ("Reprisal is a different topic and does not belong in the harassment policy"). In my experience, almost all complainants and potential witnesses consider and fear reprisal. I believe more people will come forward with concerns about harassment—or be a witness in a formal hearing—if the policy defines reprisal to be as serious an offense as harassment. It can also be argued that harassment and reprisal are similar, in being offensive, hostile, intimidating, and unreasonably disruptive, which makes such a definition reasonable. On the other hand, it is ultimately not possible to protect complainants or witnesses—or respondents—against every kind of reprisal (see Coles, 1986; Gadlin, 1991; Gutek, 1985; Gwartney-Gibbs & Lach, 1991; Lewin, 1990; Riger, 1991; Rowe, 1990b). Reprisal is often very subtle and may simply lie in support not given or opportunities not provided rather than in provable injury. An institution therefore should not "guarantee freedom from all reprisal" in its policy, because doing so may mislead a complainant.

Fear of reprisal may depend in part on the complainant's view of her or his evidence. Complainants who have convincing proof of offenses against them are often less worried about reprisal than are complainants in a "he said/she said" situation. Totally convincing proof is, however, quite rare, which means that an employer that wants complainants to come forward must also keep in mind fear of reprisal as it designs its procedures. An employer should proscribe reprisal whether a complaint is handled on the basis of rights or interests—and whether a formal grievance is found to have been justified or unjustified or not proven—so long as the complaint is not found to have been malicious.

In particular, the employer should take very seriously the need to educate its supervisors about reprisal as well as harassment. It should require its supervisors to have an explicit plan to prevent reprisal before dealing with a complaint of harassment—at least by warning all concerned against retaliation. Supervisors should treat reprisal in the same way that they are required to deal with harassment, should follow up after intervention to ask if there has been reprisal, and should take serious action against those proven to have retaliated against a complainant, a witness, or an alleged offender.

The importance of perceived and real reprisal is a major reason an institution should provide interest-based options, because classic mediation, the generic approach, and systems change appear least likely to provoke reprisal, and the direct approach and informal intervention usually are reported to be safe and effective.

Provide Confidential Advice

Many people want a resource person who will not talk or take action without permission. One way to increase the reporting rate in every kind of system is to provide an ombudsperson who has been trained with respect to harassment. Ombudspeople should be designated as neutrals. There should be a formal agreement that the ombudsperson will not be called on the employer's behalf in any formal hearing in or outside the organization, and that the employer will attempt to quash any subpoena against the ombuds office.

Line managers typically are not permitted to keep harassment discussions completely confidential. Moreover, many people believe that supervisors and human resource managers in fact should be required to act, at least where serious offenses, threats, reprisal, and repeated offenses are alleged—even if the complainant demurs—and that they should not be required to maintain complete confidentiality. But many people also believe that there should be a designated person who will keep confidence in all but catastrophic cases—hence the need for an ombudsperson.

In addition, an employer may provide a hot line for anonymous callers. In ordinary circumstances, persons staffing the hot line should not accept complaints about individuals but simply offer options. Experience indicates that hot lines are used by persons in all four roles—complainants, respondents, bystanders, and supervisors—and can provide essential support to people in great distress. Hot lines and ombudspeople who accept anonymous calls often hear of serious events from people who greatly fear loss of privacy. These callers may then learn of a responsible option they can use.

SPECIAL ISSUES

Privacy Versus Right to Know

A difficult question faced by all employers is how much, if at all, to publicize actions taken in response to harassment. Many employers never speak in public about individual personnel matters. These employers will not wish to do so about harassment matters either. There is an argument that it is hard for a harassed person to come forward if she or he does not know of any case that appeared to be settled fairly and with appropriate action taken against the harasser (see Edelman et al., 1993). If the employer publicizes a case where someone is punished, however, many other people will refuse to come forward, not wishing to be the cause of someone's punishment or not wishing to lose their privacy in the same way.

In any case, an employer should be straightforward about its policies, be forthcoming about its procedures, and publicize aggregate statistics. It may let the community know in general that people can be and are fired for harassment. It may also give the proportions of known concerns and complaints that get settled through rights-based or interest-based options.

Free Speech

In my experience, harassment by means of speech is frequently as disruptive and damaging to targets and bystanders as are forms of harassment like touching. The EEOC specifically mentions offensive expression as potential harassment and has indicated concern about protection of bystanders as well as targets. However, controversies about free speech are far from settled in the United States. Many specific questions have not yet been answered. Will private employers be brought under the same rules as public employers? After a person has been reasonably put on notice about her or his offensive speech, is it then acceptable to bring charges of harassment if the offending person repeats the behavior? Can a bystander bring a charge? Is the situation different if the offensive speaker is a supervisor, or a person of the same race or religion?

Until there is clearer consensus from the courts, I believe that institutions should explicitly ask members of their communities to avoid putting the essential rights of free expression and freedom from harassment to a balancing test. Those who are concerned about free speech should be asked not to test the issue by gratuitous insult. And those who are offended by speech should be encouraged to try interest-based options—at least until it is clear that informal options have failed.

Consensual Relationships Between Supervisor and Supervisee

A consensual sexual relationship between a supervisor and supervisee can give rise to harassment complaints in several different ways. The most important is where the relationship was in fact not completely welcome to one party. In addition, a consensual relationship may become distasteful to one party and not to the other, who may continue to pursue—and thereby harass—the person who has lost interest. Third parties may complain of favoritism and may sometimes claim sexual harassment if a party in the relationship appears to benefit in an unfair way. Consensual relationships may also give rise to complaints of harassment if the behavior between the parties—such as making love indiscreetly in the office—is considered unreasonably disruptive and offensive by third parties. Thus, while some employers decline to have any policy with respect to this situation—usually on grounds of not wishing to invade the privacy of anyone in the workplace—it makes sense for all employers at least to consider the issue.

Some employers deal with the question of supervisor-supervisee consensual relationships as a form of harassment, or proscribe all senior-junior relationships in their harassment policies whether the senior supervises the junior person or not. The usual rationale for doing so is that there can be no such thing as a truly consensual relationship between people of unequal power. This possibility is often discussed where there are trainees, or students, or other young people reporting to older people of different status. There are shortcomings in such policies. The first is that, although the general public often disapproves of dating relationships at work, the public usually does not think of consensual relationships as harassment and may also resent implicit invasions of privacy and free expression. In addition, *universal* no-dating policies may appear to protect the employer but cannot be effectively implemented—and they encourage dishonesty.

Another option is to deal with consensual, supervisee-supervisor sexual relationships in a conflict of interest policy. An emergent question is whether dotted-line supervision—for example, where there are cross-functional teams, and people work for more than one team leader—should be included in such policies. The logic for suggesting that personal relationships pose the potential for conflict of interest, when they occur within any type of supervision, is that favoritism distorts meritocratic relationships. In addition, there may be less tension and backlash when supervisor-supervisee consensual relationships are dealt with in a conflict of interest policy, because almost everybody is against conflicts of interest.

Under a conflict of interest policy, a typical employer will not punish supervisors and supervisees who fall in love with each other but will, instead, help find alternative supervision for the junior party over a reasonable period of time. The rationale is that the personal relationship is not a problem per se but that the problem lies with the existence of a personal relationship within a supervisory relationship. A conflict of interest policy should require both parties to seek advice if a conflict of interest of this sort arises.

Vendors and Clients, Patients, Donors, and Visitors

Harassment by outsiders is a serious problem. In some institutions, the majority of serious harassment is thought to originate with people who do not work for the employer. Managers and employees typically feel very uncomfortable complaining against those on whom the institution depends, such as clients, customers, and donors. The employer might consider brainstorming with employees at various levels to identify the kinds of harassment received from outsiders and to elicit suggestions for how to prevent and deal with such harassment. The employer will not necessarily be able to prevent reprisal by an outside offender, against a complainant, or against the institution itself. These problems need to be discussed openly. It is important to include examples of outsider harassment in policy and in training programs. It is essential to train supervisors about the importance of listening sympathetically to those who speak up in this situation.

Cross-Cultural Miscommunication and Intragroup Harassment

Globalization of the economy, and increasing diversity in the labor force of virtually every country, guarantees that employers, especially multinational employers, will encounter cross-cultural harassment—including complicated harassment where religion, gender, class, race, and nationality are all involved. I recommend thorough discussion of local norms with respect to male-female and cross-cultural relations in each country where a United States institution employs people. Variations from any U.S. norms, and the laws governing U.S. companies overseas, need to be discussed explicitly. Unless thorough discussions produce agreed-upon local policy within each country, a U.S. employer should, courteously, try to follow U.S. law and custom.

In any situation where intragroup harassment is alleged, and the employer does not have appropriate experts among its complaint handlers, such expertise should be sought, at least on a consulting basis. Great harm can be caused to complainants and others attached to a case if the employer takes the wrong step—especially in a case involving strong traditionalist or fundamentalist beliefs and practices. Where intragroup harassment can be anticipated, the employer should plan explicitly for interest-based options, appropriate complaint handlers, training, case examples for discussion, and local language materials

Explicit consideration should be given to prevention of reprisal with respect to intragroup harassment.

Cross-Complaints, Countercharges, Multiple Concerns, and Criminal Behavior

People accused of harassment often bring countercharges. It may seem appropriate to deal with both complaints together, and occasionally the circumstances of the case—for example, an allegation of reprisal—may make it sensible to deal with such charges simultaneously. This is especially true if both sets of concerns have been raised informally to a supervisor or to a peer for that person's recommendation or disposition. It is important for the employer to recognize, however, that one instance of unacceptable behavior does not justify another. Thus an employer should in each case consider dealing separately with formal charges and countercharges. On the other hand, multiple, simultaneous complaints against the same person usually should be dealt with together.

A substantial number of concerns about harassment are raised together with serious concerns of other types—for example, with concerns about conflict of interest, favoritism, threats, theft of intellectual property, academic misconduct, fraud, defamation, invasion of privacy, or the like. The employer that only has a specific policy about one or another form of harassment will probably not wish to deal with multiple kinds of concerns together. But it is sometimes easier to resolve all allegations of unacceptable behavior together, especially if the issues are linked.

The question of how to deal with criminal behavior needs to be reviewed explicitly. Some institutions refer all concerns about criminal behavior to law enforcement authorities. Other employers handle a wide variety of behaviors that might be construed as criminal. If this question has not been thought through, then the review of harassment policy should be used as an opportunity to review policy about criminal behavior.

Difficult and Dangerous Situations

Harassment of a difficult and/or dangerous nature is being reported more frequently. Such harassment includes stalking, people who "won't let go of a grievance" and are vengeful and disruptive, people who are followed to work by frightening strangers or estranged friends or family members, assaults, repeated obscene calls, threats, and the like. Complaint handlers should call security experts or others with special expertise in these areas—protecting privacy where possible.

All employers including small ones should consider having a plan for dealing with difficult cases. Larger institutions need an ongoing "problem assessment group" for a number of reasons. Exceptionally difficult harassment problems are becoming more common. The most difficult problems need various different kinds of expertise—for example, from human resource managers, ombudspeople, security, equal opportunity specialists, employee assistance and other health care practitioners, legal counsel, and senior line managers. In academic and other residential institutions, this list might include persons responsible for housing. Just recognizing the most difficult problems may require information from various functions in the organization, each of which has picked up a fragment of data. Dealing with the most difficult problems will often need the involvement of various functions inside the organization, and sometimes their professional contacts outside the organization. It is helpful in a crisis if the relevant group of managers has been meeting together regularly and is used to working with each other and learning from each other.

Monitoring

Yet another reason for an ongoing group is that the managers in a given workplace who have an interest in harassment need to be up to date about the problems the employer is facing, and they need to know if new kinds of problems are occurring. This group should monitor the conflict management system, receive regular statistical reports, design training, and work on continuous improvement.

PREVENTION PROGRAMS

The most important function of a dispute resolution system is prevention. Here, too, there are different views about implementation. Some employers train everyone regularly with respect to the employer's definition of harassment and complaint system options; some train only a few. Some such programs concentrate on consciousness-raising and sensitivity training; some focus on the law. Some are led by EEO specialists and some are led by the CEO or other senior managers. Some programs concentrate on team building with people of different race and genders dependent on each other for their success—where one person cannot succeed as an individual but only as a member of a diverse group. Some encourage bystanders as well as supervisors to intervene against harassment, if they can do so appropriately. Some programs sandwich diversity issues in with general management issues. Some are intentionally funny and upbeat about diversity; some are earnest. Some programs are oriented positively (the gains from diversity) and others negatively (do not harass or you will be punished).

Having observed programs in a variety of settings with diverse policies and complaint systems, I believe that we know very little about "what works" in even one setting, let alone whether an apparently successful program can be successfully transplanted elsewhere. For example, what is success? It clearly is possible to reduce the number of reports of harassment, especially in a draconian, single-option system; but does this mean there is less harassment? Could a program stop most harassment but produce a hidden backlash such that many whites and many males stop affirmative action recruitment and mentoring?

I believe employers should consider broadly focused, positively oriented diversity programs and specific training about harassment. I believe in regular programming constructed around a variety of workshops, films, discussion groups, posters, skits, and so on that occur in a wide assortment of settings—so that people do not get bored. Good settings include department meetings, optional lunch meetings for secretaries, retreats, orientation programs, and training for those to be promoted. It helps if senior managers frequently talk about "diversity on the team," recruitment, networks, mentoring, and harassment, in many settings. Respectful humor definitely helps.

I believe that the employer's written materials on harassment should be addressed explicitly and simultaneously to four roles in a workplace—*the complainant, the respondent, the bystander, and the supervisor*—not just to one of these roles. It is common for people in one role not to know the rights and options of people in other roles, and people may find themselves in any of these four positions. Bystanders should not be overlooked; they are frequently effective in stopping both harassment and reprisal.

CONCLUSION

The employer who sets up an integrated dispute resolution system, with ongoing prevention efforts, should expect a relatively high reporting rate of relatively low-level concerns that can be settled satisfactorily on the basis of the interests of those involved. There will be a few serious complaints that require a rights-based procedure—investigation and adjudication. There will be a few difficult and/or dangerous cases—that cannot easily be prevented by training programs—which may be brought to light at an early stage, and dealt with more effectively, than would be the case without an integrated system.

I believe in providing options. In the case cited at the beginning of the chapter, the support staff person should have been able to seek help off the record, for example, from an ombudsperson. A generic approach—for example, a departmental training program proposed by the ombudsperson—might have helped stop the problem, at less cost to the woman's peace of mind and at no cost to the rights of the alleged offender. Alternatively, an early informal discussion by the ombudsperson with the offender might have stopped the harassment, if the complainant had requested such an option. An ombudsperson might have helped provide support to the complainant until she could transfer, if she insisted on transfer. A trusted HR manager might have been able to expedite a transfer. After the transfer, the complainant might have agreed to permit a discussion with the alleged offender or might have agreed to a formal complaint and investigation. There may have been custom-tailored options available.

I sympathize with those who believe that the rights of all parties are often best served by investigation and adjudication, especially where there are allegations of unwanted assault and repeated offenses. However, the first issue—both for society and for employers—is to persuade those who feel harassed to decide to take action. To persuade the majority of those who are harassed actually to take effective action, employers must respect the wishes of complainants and provide multiple access points and many options. I believe this is best done within a comprehensive systems approach.

NOTES

1. Many male and female ombudspeople in North America have changed to the use o the terms *ombud* or *ombuds* or *ombudsperson* rather than the term *ombudsman* (see Rowe M. P., Options, functions, and skills: What an organizational ombudsman might want t know, *Negotiation Journal, Vol. 11*(2), 1995).

2. MIT may have been the first major institution—starting in 1973—to design policies and procedures with respect to sexual harassment.

REFERENCES

Coles, F. S. (1986). Forced to quit: Sexual harassment complaints and agency response. *Sex Roles, 14,* 81-95.

Edelman, L. B., Erlanger, H. S., & Lande, J. (1993). Internal dispute resolution: The transformation of civil rights in the workplace. *Law and Society Review, 27*(3), 497-534.

Edelman, L. B., Petterson, S., Chambliss, E., & Erlanger, H. S. (1991). Legal ambiguity and the politics of compliance: Affirmative action officers' dilemma. *Law and Policy, 13,* 73.

Gadlin, H. (1991). Careful maneuvers. *Negotiation Journal, 7*(2), 139-153.

Gutek, B. A. (1985). *Sex and the workplace: Impact of sexual behaviors and harassment on women, men and organizations.* San Francisco: Jossey-Bass.

Gwartney-Gibbs, P. A., & Lach, D. H. (1991). Workplace dispute resolution and gender inequality. *Negotiation Journal, 7*(2), 187-200.

Gwartney-Gibbs, P. A., & Lach, D. H. (1992, Summer). Sociological explanations for failure to seek sexual harassment remedies. *Mediation Quarterly, 9*(4), 365-373.

Lewin, D. (1990). Grievance procedures in nonunion workplaces: An empirical analysis of usage, dynamics and outcomes. *Chicago-Kent Law Review, 66,* 817, 823-844.

Riger, S. (1991). Gender dilemmas in sexual harassment policies and procedures. *American Psychologist, 46,* 497-505.

Rowe, M. P. (1990a). Barriers to equality: The power of subtle discrimination to maintain unequal opportunity. *Employee Responsibilities and Rights Journal, 3*(2), 153-162.

Rowe, M. P. (1990b). People who feel harassed need a complaint system with both formal and informal options. *Negotiation Journal, 6*(2), 161-172.

Rowe, M. P. (1995). Options, functions, and skills: What an organizational ombudsman might want to know, *Negotiation Journal, Vol. 11*(2). *Negotiation Journal, Vol. 11*(2), pp. 103-114..

13

Sexual Harassment at Work: When an Organization Fails to Respond

BARBARA A. GUTEK

Few organizations are well equipped to handle allegations of sexual harassment. This chapter describes one organization's experience with an allegation of harassment and my involvement as a consultant to the organization. The chapter focuses on my analysis of the problem and the organization's proposed solution to it, at the same time illustrating some of the principles, findings, and concepts discussed in the other chapters in the book. Almost two years after the original investigation, the organization is still dealing with the consequences of the allegations. The identity of the organization, the law firm, and all others involved with the case are disguised so they may remain anonymous.

In the past, sexual harassment was an invisible problem. Sexual harassment had no name and organizations were not responsible for it if it occurred. Today, it not only is visible but has achieved a certain amount of notoriety because of several very prominent cases, notably the allegations made in fall 1991 by Professor Anita Hill against then-Supreme Court nominee Clarence Thomas.

Various public and private agencies as well as the courts have seen a steady if uneven increase in sexual harassment complaints since the early 1980s (e.g., "Sexual Harassment," 1992). For example, in the years between 1984 and 1988, the number of sexual harassment complaints filed with the Equal Employment Opportunity Commission (EEOC) generally rose, and dropped only twice (from 4,953 in 1985 to 4,431 in 1986 and from 5,336 in 1987 to 5,215 in 1988; Budhos, 1995). A total of 5,557 complaints were filed in 1990 (Clark, 1991, p. 541) but there are now over 10,000 cases filed with the EEOC annually, and there is every reason to think that the number will continue to increase. In many large organizations in North America today, one or more human resource specialists have become knowledgeable about the legal guidelines and their company's legal liability. All too often, even in the more enlightened organizations, too few human resource specialists, not to mention general managers, have much of an understanding of the origins of sexual harassment and the workplace factors that contribute to it. Thus they are ill-prepared for preventing sexual harassment from occurring in the future, although they may be able to handle allegations when they arise.

Smaller organizations often have much less knowledge about sexual harassment. Sexual harassment may be one of dozens of human resource responsibilities of the managers. Sexual harassment is common; about one of every two women is likely to be sexually harassed at work sometime during her working life (Gutek, 1985) and about two in five have been harassed within the previous two years (U.S. Merit Systems Protection Board, 1981, 1988). Most instances of sexual harassment are not reported, however, and many organizations with under 100 employees (where about 42% of the labor force works; Schor, 1994) still have had little experience with it.

In this chapter, I describe one organization's experience with an allegation of harassment and my involvement with that organization as an external consultant. The chapter focuses on my analysis of the problem and the organization's proposed solution to it, at the same time illustrating some of the principles, findings, and concepts discussed in the other chapters in the book.

The case around which this chapter is built depicts a small organization of mostly professional people with a high level of commitment to the organization, which is torn apart by a sharp division among employees and students. At the center of this division lies a charge of sexual harassment.

THE CASE[1]

Pleasant Oaks is a small music college on the West Coast. A private college, it has just one major, music, a small budget, high tuition, and very committed faculty and students. Its faculty are drawn from practicing musicians, so "full-time" faculty are actually often away from the campus touring or giving concerts, and salaries are relatively low. The college views the fact that faculty are practicing musicians in a positive light, and the "real world" experience of the faculty draws many of the students to the college.

The college was started by three musicians who wanted an alternative to traditional academic musical education. Two of the three are still with the school and one is its current director. The college has been in existence for 25 years now, and they have 250 undergraduate and graduate students. Although the college has achieved a reputation as a unique, high-quality nontraditional institution, its financial base continues to be weak. Several years ago, the collective faculty and the board of directors of the college together decided the college could better achieve fiscal stability by hiring a full-time professional finance officer. Up until that time, the faculty had performed all administrative functions with the assistance of mostly part-time clerical workers who, more often than not, were students at the college. Thus the work of the college was handled primarily by faculty and work-study students who performed various clerical activities. Human resources responsibilities were divided among one clerical worker and two faculty members. Neither the clerical worker nor the two faculty members had any training on the topic of sexual harassment or any other equal employment opportunity issue. None had encountered any formal allegations of sexual harassment, although there had been some very visible (and several messy) personal and apparently sexual relationships between (male) faculty members and (female) students or staff. A significant feature of the organization was the gender distribution: All of the board of directors and 85% of the faculty were male; 90% of the staff and 65% of the students were female. Although it is not uncommon to find that men tend to be in the higher-status positions and women in the lower status ones (see Grauerholz, this volume), the degree to which status was associated with gender at Pleasant Oaks was especially pronounced. And as Cleveland and Kerst (1993) point out, power inequities can undermine trust.

In 1988, for the first time, a financial officer was hired by the college. Although the college was financially strapped and the offer they were able to make was not especially competitive, the board of directors were pleased with the person they hired. He was experienced, came with a good recommendation, and showed lots of enthusiasm for putting the college on a sound fiscal footing. The board of directors and director of the college gave the new financial officer free reign in making changes for the college. He immediately hired two associates and began to make many changes in the way money was handled in the college. A variety of cost-cutting measures were implemented and more accountability was built into many of the procedures. The financial officer made decisions easily and soon assumed control over many of the decisions formerly made by the director of the school, who seemed relieved to have more time to devote to activities at which he excelled: external relations, teaching, and professional affairs. Within six months of being hired, the financial officer was, in effect, the day-to-day chief operating officer for the organization.

Although the board of directors was pleased with the progress the financial officer was making, a variety of complaints began surfacing. The new financial officer was apparently not the most tactful person, did not understand or appreciate music, and began making enemies, mostly among the clerical workers, some of whom were tuition-paying students at the college as well. About nine months after he arrived, one of the part-time workers in his employ complained to one of the female faculty members that she was being sexually harassed by the financial officer. The faculty member was not sure what to do with the allegation—the school had no sexual harassment policy or any procedures for handling complaints—so she did nothing. Several months later, a second complaint surfaced. This time a student complained to a faculty member (not the same faculty member who heard the first complaint) about inappropriate sexual comments and pressures for dates from the financial officer. She, too, was not sure what to do, but discussed it with the director of the school, who also was not sure what to do. He agreed to discuss it with the financial officer, but forgot about it in the press of other responsibilities.

Within 18 months of being hired, the financial officer was embroiled in a very messy allegation of sexual harassment. When a third woman, Nancy, felt the financial officer was making inappropriate sexual comments to her—telling her about his sexual preferences and inquiring about hers—she began talking to other female students and then male students. Once it was determined that, by then, at least three people had been harassed—by their judgment—and two of them had complained to no avail, they were angry. A small committee was formed; the aid of a female faculty member was solicited; and together they drafted a complaint to the board of directors, calling for the immediate dismissal of the financial officer. They demanded that the college adopt a sexual harassment policy, and drafted one that they liked.

The board of directors, meanwhile, was pleased with the progress made by the new financial officer: The college was fiscally stronger than any time in the past 10 years and the projections for further fiscal stability were encouraging. The last thing they wanted to hear was that the financial officer, who had seemed like a bargain and savior, was charged with sexual harassment by one full-time student and two employee-students. The board of directors heard the complaint that was drafted by a group that became known as "the woman's group" and saw the draft of the sexual harassment policy. These were presented to the board by the third woman, Nancy, who was quickly viewed as the leader of the group.

Nancy had moved across the country to attend Pleasant Oaks. She was passionately committed to the goals of the college and volunteered to be on several student committees. She suggested the school design new promotional materials to attract more students from other countries and soon knew more about strategies for increasing admissions than the faculty member who was in charge of admissions. At the encouragement of several faculty, in her third year Nancy began working as the college's part-time admissions officer.

By all accounts, she and the financial officer did not "hit it off well." They worked in adjacent offices and needed to interact fairly regularly. The financial officer was the higher-ranking person and he controlled all matters pertaining to spending. Thus Nancy needed approval from the financial officer to implement the admissions strategies she devised. She asked for a fixed budget but the financial officer declined, saying that until the college was fiscally stronger, he intended to retain control over each and every financial decision.

When the board of directors heard the report from Nancy, they were distressed but were still reluctant to confront the financial officer, with whom they were pleased. So they consulted the college's legal counsel. Eventually, the board agreed to ask the financial officer about the allegations. When they did so, the financial officer responded indignantly saying that Nancy was a troublemaker and that naturally people were unhappy with him. He was the person who was putting the brakes on spending. He had implemented a firm fiscal policy over which he exercised strict control and all of this was done with the board's approval. The charge of sexual harassment was, he said, ridiculous. He let the board know he was very dissatisfied with their accusation, he had worked diligently and responsibly at a substandard wage, and had worked hard to gain the board's trust, which, he believed, was crucial to obtaining fiscal stability at the college. He pointed out that he liked women, got along with them well, and had three daughters. Finally, he let the board know that if he was discharged because of an unfounded accusation, he would show no hesitation in filing a suit against the school. This would be necessary, he said, to protect his reputation.

The board, feeling some anguish and unsure how to ferret out "the truth," decided to move Nancy to another part of the building and have her report directly to the director of the school rather than to the financial officer. In the meantime, they contacted their legal counsel about the sexual harassment policy drafted by the group of women faculty, students, and staff known as "the women's group."

The school's attorney, when apprised of the situation and the existence of sexual harassment guidelines, acknowledged that the organization was in a delicate situation. She opined that the school possibly could be sued for both sexual harassment and defamation of character or unlawful discharge. She also recommended some changes in the wording of the sexual harassment policy.

The dilemma faced by the school at this point was, of course, to resolve the situation to everyone's satisfaction and avoid any lawsuits. The school could not afford a lawsuit and any lawsuit would more than undo the fiscal progress made during the financial officer's tenure at the school.

Unfortunately for the school, Nancy was not satisfied with their response, namely, to physically move her and change her line of reporting. The financial officer still controlled all financial decisions regarding admissions; thus, although Nancy no longer directly reported to the financial officer, her job was highly dependent on his approval. In addition, the women's group felt that the wording changes made by the school's counsel significantly reduced the impact of their policy. "The policy is now toothless," complained one of the women faculty.

To show their dissatisfaction, the women's group and other dissatisfied students and staff organized a petition campaign to have the financial officer discharged. The financial officer also organized a petition campaign, the opposition later reported, but they said he was able to garner only a few signatures. When the director and the board did not take further action against the financial officer, some people took more direct actions. One day he found that the tires on his car were slashed; another day, he found disparaging comments written about him in one of the men's bathrooms. About the same time, the financial officer fired one of the women staff members. This was one of the first firings in the school's 25-year history, and many of the people who were dissatisfied with the financial officer rallied around the woman who was fired. She too said the financial officer had made passes at her and others said her firing was retaliation for failure to go along with his requests for dates. Armed with the petition asking for the financial officer's discharge, the student representative to the board went before the board to express the collective dissatisfaction of what was now a broad constituency of students, staff, and some faculty. She told the board that they had not been sufficiently responsive to severe violations of professional conduct by the financial officer and reminded the board that over half of the students and over 90% of the staff were women. The students were paying very high tuition and the staff members were working for substandard wages; they all were committed to the school and its ideology, and they felt their care and concern was being repaid with indifference or downright contempt. Surely, it must be easy to find a finance person who would be a better fit with the unique characteristics of the school and would treat women with respect and dignity, they argued.

The board, realizing that their attempts to diffuse the situation had failed, once again turned to their legal counsel. Now what? Morale was low; the school was thoroughly divided and faced with several potential lawsuits, one or more alleging sexual harassment that was reported to the school and about which the school had done little—or nothing in at least one case—and one potential unlawful discharge or defamation of character suit.

SOLVING THE PROBLEM?

The board, together with the school's legal counsel, decided to call in an expert on sexual harassment. This was the point at which I became involved. I had worked with the organization's legal counsel on several cases of sexual harassment, and she suggested me to the board of directors. By this time, the organization was so divided it was impossible to find anyone in the organization who was viewed as a neutral party; thus they sought outside help. I received a phone call from Pleasant Oaks's legal counsel, who inquired if I would be interested and would have the time to investigate the situation. Pleasant Oaks's attorney thought I had both the experience and the academic credentials to be accepted both by the board and administration of the school and by the students and staff. Needless to say, I would have preferred to have been consulted much earlier before a crisis had developed.

I had two roles in my consulting at Pleasant Oaks: The first role was to sort out the facts of the case; the second role was to make some recommendations for both solving the problem and preventing it from recurring. In particular, the board wanted to know if any of the women alleging sexual harassment had a legally defensible case. As time progressed, it became obvious that the first role was more important to the board than the second one. Thus my involvement was rather limited.

The organization's attorney circulated my CV among the board, the financial officer, and various student and faculty groups, and the school decided to retain me as a consultant in the case. I first had a lengthy discussion with the school's legal counsel, followed by discussions with the two faculty members who were responsible for some of the school's human resources functions. I agreed to meet with people privately to discuss the issues. These interviews were set up at a nearby hotel by one of the school's two human resources faculty members. When I arrived at the hotel, I first met with that faculty member and one of the members of the board of directors. They supplied additional background information. I spent the remainder of the day talking individually in one-half to one-hour meetings with students, staff, and faculty, including the key parties in the dispute, Nancy and the financial officer. At his request, the financial officer was scheduled to be interviewed last because he thought he could defend his actions better knowing of what he was accused.

The interviews with faculty, staff, and students made it clear that the financial officer had engendered a lot of distrust and hostility. Many people simply did not like him or his management style. They described him variously as overbearing, condescending, contemptuous of artists including musicians, domineering, controlling, argumentative, and unprofessional. Two people sent letters to me rather than appearing at the interviews; both expressed concern that they would be identified as troublemakers and feared they would lose their jobs if they were seen at the hotel where the interviews were conducted. The financial officer, they wrote, had "spies" checking on everyone who came and left the hotel where the interviews were being conducted.

When he was interviewed, the financial officer said he felt grievously wronged; he did not know the identity of all of his accusers. He said he was doing exactly that for which he was hired, to put the school on a good financial footing, and that a small group of troublemakers objected to his management style, which he described as forthright and "no-nonsense." He denied ever asking an employee or student for a date and denied having told anyone his sexual preferences or pressing them for details of their sex lives.

Although there were a variety of complaints made against the financial officer, only Nancy's complaints appeared to me to fit clearly within the legal guidelines of sexual harassment. In fact, it appeared that Nancy might have not only a case but a case that she could win. Less than half the cases of sexual harassment that go to court are won by the plaintiff (e.g., Terpstra & Baker, 1992), but the probability of winning goes up when the plaintiff has witnesses or other evidence; has informed the organization, which, in turn, retaliates against the complainant, does nothing, or does not respond satisfactorily; and experiences work-related or other consequences that can be *clearly* tied to the harassment including physical or mental health consequences. People who are harassed but cannot "prove" it do not have a good court case regardless of the personal anguish or negative job effects they may have experienced.

In this case, Nancy had kept a detailed diary of events, could offer witnesses who were present when the financial officer made some offensive sexual remarks, albeit the less offensive ones, and although she had informed the organization that she was being harassed, the organization failed to respond. I read some of the diary. When I asked if she had shown it to any of the faculty or members of the board, she said she had not and that her attorney advised her against giving the diary to me. During the interviews, two people volunteered that they had heard the financial officer scream at Nancy and/or make sexually inappropriate comments, and when I asked them if they would repeat that information in public or in court, both said they would. In addition Nancy had informed the organization, and she was not the first person to complain of sexual harassment against the financial officer. The organization's response was not satisfactory to Nancy.

Another point that might operate in Nancy's favor should she take her case to court was the fact that she had been seeing a therapist, a consequence, she said, of the harassment she had experienced from the financial officer. The financial officer countered that Nancy had problems, particularly in relationships with men; seeing a therapist was a result of the breakup in her last relationship and had nothing to do with working at the school, he said.

It is worth noting that this last issue, physical and psychological consequences, is often a double-edged sword for a person alleging sexual harassment. To show that the harassment was severe, a judge and jury want some evidence of negative consequences. If the sexual harassment did not negatively affect a woman's physical or mental health, it may be regarded as inconsequential and not severe. It is important to note that the U.S. Supreme Court ruled in 1993 (*Harris v. Forklift Systems,* 1993) that it is not necessary to show physical or psychological consequences to prove sexual harassment. In addition, if the person alleging sexual harassment is a physical or emotional wreck as a consequence of the harassment, she runs the charge of being labeled a crazy, sick, or hypochondriacal woman who was always like that. And, of course, who would believe the allegations of a crazy woman? Thus the consequences of the harassment can themselves undermine the complainant's case.

As far as Pleasant Oaks was concerned, the cost of a court case would be substantial even if the school won in court, not to mention the negative publicity that goes along with a sexual harassment case. Thus the board was not so much interested in whether the school could win a case should one materialize, but wanted to know how strong a case the relevant parties might have under the assumption that the greater the likelihood of Nancy's winning a case, the greater her likelihood of pressing charges against the school.

After I met with the various school faculty and staff, I called the two people who wished to remain anonymous and then put together the "facts" of the case. I then met with the school's director and several members of the board of directors to discuss "facts," options, and strategies. The school was so polarized that, regardless of what I concluded, I surmised one side would view my conclusions as biased. I concluded that although many of the complaints against the financial officer were opportunistic attempts to remove a very unpopular person, there was at least one legally defensible case of hostile environment sexual harassment (see Paetzold & O'Leary-Kelly, this volume). In addition, regardless of whether anyone had been sexually harassed, it was worth noting that many people were very unhappy with the financial officer, and their complaints had some legitimacy. Even if every person who was dissatisfied showed up that day, it was evident that a substantial number of people regarded the financial officer as arrogant, power hungry, and rude to staff and students. If the financial officer had strong supporters who thought his treatment of people was justified, they did not materialize the day of the interviews.

After lengthy discussion, the head of the board of directors and the director of the school decided to do the following:

1. They would reorganize the administration such that professional musicians would again run the school. So that the director could devote the time he wanted to external relations and professional affairs, an academic vice president would be hired to "run the school," leaving the director free to use his considerable influence and reputation to influence external relations. They decided that giving so much authority to someone who was not a musician was a mistake.
2. The board would eliminate the position of financial officer and create a new position, director of accounting. The new position is still a professional position but below director and the new academic vice president. The director of accounting would be subject to the board of directors, the director of the school, and the academic vice president. In addition, the current financial officer's contract would not be renewed when it expired on the grounds that his position was no longer needed and the new position no longer required a person of his level.
3. Although it appeared that he did sexually harass at least one person, he would not be charged with harassment and nothing would be mentioned in his personnel record, leaving him free to pursue another job without the stigma of harassment. The school would not pursue the sexual harassment allegations further given that they were going to eliminate the financial officer's position.
4. Separate from the reorganization of the administration of the school, the board and the school's attorney would try to negotiate a settlement with Nancy.

The decision to fail to renew the contract of the financial officer when his expired, was, in essence, a decision to call his bluff about suing the school. The director would confront him with the possibility of his being party to a sexual harassment lawsuit and the possibility that the school would not support him in the case. The offer, to not mention the harassment in his file and to provide a legitimate reason to hire a lower-level financial person, would free him to find another job while appearing to be a success at Pleasant Oaks. The board members agreed that they would remain mum about the allegations of harassment.

In turn, the failure to renew the financial officer's contract was a decision that, the board hoped, would mollify Nancy and the disgruntled faculty, staff, and students. The board hoped too that the financial officer's departure would be interpreted as their being responsive to the concerns of their female students and staff, and the replacement of the financial officer would return the school's faculty, staff, and students to their former higher level of morale. They would implement a sexual harassment policy that they hoped would prevent future problems.

AN ANALYSIS OF THE DEVELOPMENT OF THE PROBLEM

Pleasant Oaks had in the past depended on commitment to the school to keep problems from developing and to facilitate a speedy resolution should a disagreement develop. In this case, commitment was not enough. Why? Perhaps because several other factors contributed to the escalation of the problem. Without them, commitment might have been enough.

The first contributor was a lack of knowledge about sexual harassment. None of the faculty charged with human resources issues knew much about sexual harassment, its definition, the conditions under which organizations incur legal liability, the conditions that facilitate harassment, and the like. Pleasant Oaks did not have a sexual harassment policy or guidelines. Thus, confronted with an allegation of harassment, they did not know what to do or even if the allegation represented a problem. There was no easily accessible source of knowledge for the people who received the complaints. Eventually, the board of directors turned to the school's legal counsel for knowledge. The complainants and the woman's group in general also lacked knowledge that good human resources policies would have provided. For example, their call for the immediate dismissal of the financial officer was unrealistic.

A second contributor was the fact that the issue was not regarded or defined as a problem until it had already escalated considerably. The first two complaints were received by different people, who were not sure whether the complaint represented a problem, in part because they lacked knowledge about sexual harassment and in part because they lacked complete information about the issue. Neither knew about the other complaint. If either had known that there was another complaint, both receivers of the information might have responded with a bit more urgency. But the school lacked both a formal and an informal complaint mechanism (see Rowe, this volume) and it was not clear if any (but especially the first two) of the complaints should have been regarded as a formal complaint or an informal attempt to solve the problem.

A third contributor was the lack of clearly specified human resources responsibilities. These functions were divided among three people: two faculty members and one clerical person. For each of these people, human resources was a part-time activity. Although some specific responsibilities were allocated to one of the three, others were diffused across the three people. Thus the women who felt they were being sexually harassed could not identify a single person to whom to take their complaints. As Rowe (this volume) points out, it is helpful to have multiple places or people to whom one can complain, but someone needs to be responsible for finding out if complaints have been made.

A fourth contributor was the lack of clearly defined role relationships among organizational members, including students, staff, and faculty, combined with unequal levels of power (see Cleveland & McNamara, this volume). Indeed, many people held several different formal roles at once. In particular, many students were also employees. Because of the nature of their work, students and faculty were often together in the evenings. In one situation, two people might be interacting as two employees of Pleasant Oaks; in another, the same two might be interacting as a faculty member and a student; and in yet another, the same two might be interacting as two musicians in a musical group. Under some of these circumstances, lines of authority and power differences might be overlooked or minimized, especially by the higher-ranking person, who assumes that the lower-ranking person can and will "speak up" if that person's rights are being violated. In addition, higher-ranking people who do not abuse their power are often unaware that other high-ranking people do subtly or overtly exploit lower-ranking people.

A fifth contributing factor might be called "facilitating conditions." Two such facilitators stand out. One was the distribution of men and women at Pleasant Oaks that was previously mentioned. The board of directors and faculty were mostly male; 90% of the staff and 65% of the students were female. Many interactions between the two sexes at Pleasant Oaks involved a high-status man and a lower-status woman. The lone exceptions would be the interactions of the few female faculty members either with a male student or with one of the few male clerical employees.

The other facilitating condition was the norm about dating and relationships between people at Pleasant Oaks. Dating and affairs between faculty and either students or staff were quite common and, to a newcomer, might well appear to be acceptable or expected. At Pleasant Oaks, there was little social consensus about whether such behavior is evil or good (Bowes-Sperry & Powell, this volume). In several cases, such relationships were "in the open" and well known to faculty, staff, and students. Sexual harassment is more common in sexualized work environments (Gutek, 1985) and in academic departments where faculty-student dating is the norm. The environment at Pleasant Oaks fits the description of an environment that tolerates sexual harassment (Hulin, Fitzgerald, & Drasgow, this volume).

In sum, many factors contributed to the development of this case of sexual harassment at Pleasant Oaks: lack of knowledge about sexual harassment; failure to define the budding situation as a problem; diffusion of human resources responsibilities; lack of clearly defined relationships among faculty, staff, and student roles at Pleasant Oaks; distribution of men in higher-ranking positions and women in lower-ranking positions; and a history of dating relationships and sexual liaisons between men and women at Pleasant Oaks. Taken together, these factors prevented Pleasant Oaks from responding until a crisis had developed. It is noteworthy that the organization's legal counsel was called before a human resources consultant. By the time I was contacted, the board was already concerned about the possibility of at least one lawsuit.

AN ANALYSIS OF THE PROPOSED SOLUTION

In any situation, the way a problem is defined generally dictates the kind of solution that is proposed; that is, the proposed solution fits the defined problem (see Nieva & Gutek, 1981, chap. 10). In this case, the director and the board selected a strategy that was structural to deal with a problem that, on the face of it at least, appeared to be personal or interpersonal. It seems easy to define the problem as the financial officer or the relationship between the financial officer and Nancy or some small group of Pleasant Oaks staff and students. Was this really a personal problem, and if so, why not a personal or interpersonal solution?

At a more practical level, one might contemplate the outcomes of the board's selected strategy. Do the chosen solutions fit the problem? For example, one might ask why, if the financial officer had harassed at least one person, he was not sanctioned for the harassment and then allowed to continue on with his job if the harassment was not severe enough to warrant discharge from the job. One might also ask why, if the financial officer did in fact harass at least one employee, the board should agree to keep that "fact" silent in recommending the financial officer for another job.

One might also inquire about the probability that the financial officer was being "framed" by spiteful or vindictive students, faculty, and staff who were retaliating against the financial officer for the impositions and budget cuts that he had imposed, or even for sexual attraction or overtures directed at the financial officer, who rebuffed them. Could being rebuffed by the financial officer lead one or more women to counter with charges of sexual harassment against the financial officer?

Is the problem personal or structural? Although the problem can easily be framed as a personal problem, it was no doubt affected by the structure of the organization. The fact that no one person in the school was responsible for human resources and no one had either knowledge or training on issues like sexual harassment might guarantee that sooner or later some human resources issue would reach crisis proportions. In general, the school depended on the collective commitment of the faculty, staff, and students to keep any issue from reaching the crisis stage. But when one contingent felt their commitment was being repaid with indifference or even hostility, consensus quickly broke down. Unfortunately, it took the director and the board a while to comprehend the magnitude of the problem, and when they did recognize it, they had no mechanism or set of mechanisms in place for dealing with it.

In general, any organization could hire a person who makes inappropriate sexual remarks and requests to members of the organization, but organizations having multiple mechanisms in place to handle complaints are, when confronted with an instance of sexual harassment, less likely to reach the crisis stage experienced by Pleasant Oaks (see Rowe, this volume). Because Pleasant Oaks had never seen fit to actively discourage or sanction faculty who got involved with students or staff at the school, the financial officer may have inferred that at Pleasant Oaks, sexual liaisons were acceptable and perhaps even expected. He may have intended to imitate (and perhaps was imitating) the behavior of some of the school's prominent faculty after finding little consensus about such behavior and, based on the experiences of others, a very low probability of any negative effects (Bowes-Sperry & Powell, this volume). An environment that tolerated sexual liaisons and perhaps sexual harassment may have encouraged the financial officer to act on his own proclivities to harass (see Pryor, 1987). In any event, he might have behaved differently had Pleasant Oaks had either strongly held social norms or a strong and visible policy discouraging any behavior that could be viewed as sexual exploitation of students, faculty, or staff.

Thus, although the problem might appear to be purely a problem of the financial officer's personality or the relationship between the financial officer and Nancy, it is obvious on careful examination that structural factors influenced the development of the problem at Pleasant Oaks. There is much that can be done in addition to trying to screen out potential sexual harassers or "easily offended" women.

Is the solution appropriate to the problem? The proposed solution to this problem, like the solutions to many problems, represents a compromise between the practical and the ideal.

For example, if, on the basis of my investigation, I concluded that the financial officer had sexually harassed at least one person at Pleasant Oaks, why not charge him with harassment and apply whatever sanction seems appropriate for the level of his offense? Several factors influenced the board's decision not to press charges of sexual harassment against the financial officer.

Because there is relatively little documentation of sexual harassment in this case and it is clear that the financial officer was disliked by many people who were not harassed, there is a slight possibility that he was simply being framed by disgruntled faculty, staff, and students who wanted him removed and seized upon sexual harassment as a convenient vehicle for doing so. It is also within the realm of possibility that Nancy was particularly unhappy with him because he rejected her sexual overtures, rather than that she rejected his. Although both of these scenarios were possibilities, both were highly unlikely given the preponderance of the evidence. Nevertheless, the remote possibility that either could be operating may have contributed to the board's reluctance to pursue more severe punishment of the financial officer.

Perhaps more important, the director and the board were hesitant to press charges because, in fact, the past behavior of some of the faculty may have been uncomfortably similar to that of the financial officer's. In some of those cases, the faculty member was more popular and, for whatever reasons, the "victims" had not chosen to press charges. Pressing charges now against the financial officer might have the effect of reopening some old incidents, which might further divide the Pleasant Oaks community. Understandably, some faculty expressed reluctance to "cast the first stone."[2] Thus the board chose a conservative strategy of not pressing sexual harassment charges. Furthermore, once they had decided to let the financial officer's contract lapse, they had little incentive to pursue the allegations in more detail, and were somewhat concerned that the financial officer might initiate a lawsuit. Furthermore, they were reluctant to tackle the broader issue of personal and dating relationships among faculty, students, and staff for a variety of reasons, including pride in being "nonbureaucratic" and a history of such relationships among members of the academic community.

All in all, the events surrounding the allegations of harassment influenced the board to rethink the structural changes they had made when they hired the financial officer. For the first time in the school's history, the day-to-day running of the school was not in the hands of musicians. Although hiring the financial officer had some beneficial consequences, it also had some negative ones. The decision to delete the position of financial officer was an attempt not only to handle the allegations of sexual harassment but also to find a structure for the school that yielded a financially stable operation but retained its unique character as a small, highly reputed music school.

In hindsight, the school might have achieved the fiscal stability they sought by hiring a long-term consultant to work with the administration of the school rather than hiring a full-time employee. On the other hand, had the financial officer behaved differently, he might still be in the position and the board and director might have concluded that hiring a nonmusician financial person was "just what the school needed."

The main problem with the solution embraced by the director and head of the board was that it did not address the concerns of the woman's group. There was little in the solution that would make women staff or students feel that the board and the director of the school were responsive to their grievances. As several of the women told me in the meetings at the hotel, they were the majority of the tuition-paying students, and women held most of the staff jobs. They hoped the school would let them know women were valued. But the school never took a strong stand against sexual harassment or, for that matter, rude and arrogant treatment of students and staff. They did, however, negotiate a settlement with Nancy such that she left the school. Since then, however, two other women have also sued the school for sexual harassment. One of those cases has also been settled but the other is ongoing. If the school had taken a stronger stand against sexual harassment, perhaps the other cases might not have materialized. Conversely, more complaints might have surfaced if women thought the school was more supportive—or willing to make a financial settlement with complainants.

At Pleasant Oaks, the division of men and women certainly facilitates the development of sexually exploitative relationships and undermines trust between men and women, staff and faculty. The fact that the group making complaints became known as "the woman's group" served to separate them from the faculty and the board—that is, "the men's group"—and facilitated sex role spillover (see Gutek, 1985; Nieva & Gutek, 1981; Stockdale, this volume). Furthermore, trust between the board and faculty (mostly men) and students and staff (mostly women) is still low (see Hanisch, this volume, on organizational outcomes). Although some board members and faculty believed the settlement with Nancy encouraged others to make charges that would lead to financial settlements, many of the women felt that the school was more concerned about its legal liability than about them. Unless more women are hired or promoted into high-ranking positions and/or more men are hired as clerical workers, the gender division of labor in the school will remain. Thus, in many ways, the school is still vulnerable to another incident of sexual harassment that could be as, or almost as, problematic as this case.

Although the experience has been costly for Pleasant Oaks, as it is for most organizations (Knapp & Kustis, this volume), this case shows just how difficult it is to handle an allegation of sexual harassment in a manner that is fair and satisfactory to all parties. Organizational interventions (Cleveland & McNamara, this volume) and methods of negotiation, mediation, and conflict resolution (Rowe, this volume) might fruitfully be applied to handling complaints of sexual harassment.

NOTES

1. For this case, identities have been changed to protect the organization and the individuals involved. In addition, so have some of the details of the case been modified, although the general statement of the problem is factual.

2. Similar conjecture arose during the Clarence Thomas confirmation hearings. People noted that the behavior of some of the senators sitting in judgment of Clarence Thomas may well have been subject to similar allegations of sexual harassment.

REFERENCES

Budhos, M. (1995). *Sexual harassment: Research and resources* (3rd ed., based on 1st and 2nd eds. by D. Siegel; M. E. Capek, Ed.). (Available from the National Council for Research on Women, 530 Broadway, New York, NY 10012-3920)

Clark, C. S. (1991). The issues. *Congressional Quarterly Researcher, 1*(13), 539-545.

Cleveland, J. N., & Kerst, M. E. (1993). Sexual harassment and perceptions of power: An under-articulated relationship. *Journal of Vocational Behavior, 42,* 49-67.

Gutek, B. A. (1985). *Sex and the workplace.* San Francisco: Jossey-Bass.

Harris v. Forklift Systems, Inc., 114 S.Ct. 367 (1993).

Nieva, V. F., & Gutek, B. A. (1981). *Women and work: A psychological perspective.* New York: Praeger.

Pryor, J. B. (1987). Sexual harassment proclivities in men. *Sex Roles, 17,* 269-290.

Schor, J. (1994, November). Debunking the small-business myth: Big firms still dominate. *Working Woman,* p. 16.

Sexual harassment charges rise. (1992, October 2). *USA Today,* p. 6A.

Terpstra, D. E., & Baker, D. D. (1992). Outcomes of federal court decisions on sexual harassment. *Academy of Management Journal, 35*(1), 181-190.

U.S. Merit Systems Protection Board. (1981). *Sexual harassment in the federal workplace: Is it a problem?* Washington, DC: Office of Merit Systems Review and Studies/ Government Printing Office.

U.S. Merit Systems Protection Board. (1988). *Sexual harassment in the federal government: An update.* Washington, DC: Office of Merit Systems Review and Studies/ Government Printing Office.

Index

Academic environment, 38
Accompaniment, for a party in a dispute, 257
Acknowledging SH, 16
Adjudication. *See* Dispute resolution
Aggressive Sexual Behavior Inventory, 72, 73
Amicus curiae brief, APA, 13
Andrews v. City of Philadelphia, 95, 96
Appraisal of SH, 14. *See also* Acknowledgement of SH
  rape and, 16
  victims (targets), 14
Attitudes:
  leaders, 5
  supervisors, 8
Attractiveness:
  personal, 74
  sexual, 74
Attribution theory and ethical decision making. *See* Ethical
Attributions, 5
Authority factors and ethical decision making. *See* Ethical

Battered women syndrome, 221
Behavior costing, 202
Biological/Natural model of SH, 68
Burns v. McGregor Electronics Industries, Inc., 94, 100
Bystander harassment, 158
Bystander stress, 132

Canadian women, SH of, 161, 162, 163
Categories of SH, 6
Chilly climate, universities, 46, 47
Civil Rights Act, Title VII and SH, 88
Clear and convincing evidence. *See* Standard of proof
Climate:
  organization and appraisal of, 14
  organizational, 19, 129, 131, 132
  work group, 19

workplace, 5

Complaint handling structures:
centralized, 257
decentralized, 259, 260
Complaint mechanisms, formal and informal, problems with lack of, 284
Complaints of sexual harassment, 86
Concentration of effect and moral intensity. *See* Moral intensity
Conflict of interest policy, 265
Consensual relationships, 264
Consenting relationships, norms for, 285
Consequences of SH, 13
by race, 58
individual, 4, 18, 59
magnitude of and moral intensity. *See* Moral intensity
multi-level, 19
organizations, 4, 59
physical and psychological and alleging SH, 281
responsibility for and ethical decision making. *See* Ethical
women of color, 53
Contact, cross-gender, 8
Contextual similarities, domestic violence and SH, 223
Contrapower harassment, 30
Cost of SH, 201
U.S. Army, 208
Costing model of sexual harassment, comprehensive behavioral, 202
Costs of SH:
absenteeism, 205
administrative, 205
comparison of estimates, 189
incident, 204
individual, 175
limitations in studies of, 180
organizational, 20, 175
other, 207
productivity-related, 203
productivity-reduction, 204
replacement, 206
separation, 205
transfer, 206
victim, 20
Courts, federal appellate, 88
Cross-complaints, countercharges, 267
Cross-cultural harassment, 266
Culture, 5
occupational, 8
organizational, 131, 132
Cycle of violence theory, 224, 225

Definition of SH:
legal, 6
psychological, 6
Dispute resolution:
classic mediation, 254
direct approach, 251
formal investigation and adjudication, 254
generic approaches and systems change, 253
informal third-party intervention, 252
Domestic violence, and SH, 218
Domestic violence interventions:
conciliation, 225
law enforcement, 225
Dominance motives, 9, 10, 12. *See also* power motives

EEOC:
complaints filed with, 273
proposed Guidelines, 101
Ego strength, 116
locus of control, 116
reinforcement contingencies, 117
responsibility for consequences, 117
Ego strength and ethical decision making. *See* Ethical
Ellison V. Brady, 95, 97
Ethical decision making105, 106, 108, 109, 110
attribution theory, 118
authority factors, 117
misperception theory, 117, 118
power theories, 118
European women, SH of, 161, 162, 163
Experience, harassing and nonharassing events, 6

Experiences of SH:
by race/ethnicity, 54
women professors, 32, 33, 34
Explanations of SH, 68

Faculty women:
factors contributing to the SH of, 39
factors inhibiting the SH of, 45
Forms of SH:
environmental, 158
personal, 158
Free speech, 264
Frequencies of SH experiences, appraisal and, 14

Gender harassment, 6, 43, 136, 168
Gender skew, 10, 12. *See also* Work group, gender composition
Grievance channel, single, 242

Hall v. Gus Construction Co., 94
Harassers:
organizational role of, 136
supervisors vs. coworkers, 90
Harassing behavior, type of, 136
Harassment by outsiders, 266
Harris V. Forklift Systems, Inc.87, 97, 99, 100, 101, 103, 158
He said/she said. *See* Standard of proof
Highlander v. K.F.C. National Management Co., 99
Hostile environment harassment, 86, 87, 101, 113. *See also* Hostile work environment
case of, 281
hostile work environment, 6, 136
legal theory, 93
racial implications for defining, 61, 62
Hypermasculinity Scale, 72, 73

ISH sale, 9
Individual consequences of SH. *See* Consequences
Individual-level policy considerations of the behavioral costing model of SH, 210
Integrated conflict management system, 242
Integrated dispute resolution system, 251
Interest-based options for complaint handling242, 244, 246, 250
Intervention, 20
addressing consequences of SH, 235
cognitive-behavioral therapy, 226
linking antecedents and consequences of SH, 234
preventive strategies, 234
Inventory of Sexual Harassment, 154, 168

Jones v. Wesco Investments, Inc., 94
Just-world hypothesis, 14

Knowledge:
actual, 96
constructive, 96
lack of understanding SH and contributions toward SH, 283

Labeling sexual harassment, 121, 122
Lesbians, sexual behavior toward, 42
Liability, employer, 88, 96
Likelihood to Sexually Harass, 9, 12, 79
Likelihood to Sexually Harass Scale, 79, 80
Litigation:
individual outcomes of SH, 186
organizational outcomes of SH, 186
locus of control, and ethical decision making. *See* Ethical

Marginality, cultural and economic, 55
Masculine job gender context, 129
Mediation. *See* Dispute resolution
Meritor Savings Bank v. Vinson, 87, 88, 95, 96, 98
Minority group status, marginality and vulnerability, 55, 56

Misperception theory and ethical decision making. *See* Ethical
Misperception, by men, 42
Misperceptions:
  and sexual harassment, 72
  measuring, 71, 72
  women's friendly behavior, 69, 81
Moral intensity 106, 107, 108, 114
  concentration of effect, 108, 113
  proximity, 108, 111
  magnitude of consequences, 108, 112
  probability of effect, 108
  temporal immediacy, 108
  variables that influence the perception of, 114, 120, 121
Moral issue, steps in recognizing, 107
Morality, 106
Mother role, 42, 43
Multiple-level change: unfreezing, changing, refreezing, 229, 230

Norms permitting SH, 130, 131
Norms, sexual conduct 9

Obscene language, 44
Observer:
  characteristics, 5
  gender role appraisal and, 14
  sensitivity, appraisal and, 14
Occupational characteristics, 7
Occupational culture. *See* Culture
Offender status, 35
Offenders, characteristics of, 8, 9
Options, investigation and adjudication, 249
Organizational:
  characteristics, 7
  climate, appraisal and, 14. *See also* Climate
  conflict and change and SH, 227
  consequences of SH. *See* Consequences
  model of SH, 68, 82
  social systems, 128
  technical systems, 128
  tolerance for SH, 135
Organizational Tolerance for Sexual Harassment Inventory, 135
Organizational-level policy considerations of the behavioral costing model of SH, 209
OTSHI, 135, 141, 144, 147
Outcomes of SH, 177, 179
  and organizational tolerance of SH, 145
  individual, 175
  individual health, 181
  individual, work role attitudes, 182
  organizational, 175
  organizational health, 181
  organizational, work role attitudes, 182
Outcomes of complaints of SH, 137

Patriarchy, 11, 19
Perception of SH, 4, 6
Perceptions, of victim's, 5
Perpetrator:
  similarities, domestic violence and SH, 221
  students, 5
Person X Situation framework, 9
Pervasiveness. *See* Severity
Plaintiff:
  information, 90
  occupation, 91
Policies of SH, designing and reviewing, 241
  all, 248
  general, 248
  racial implications, 63, 64
  specific, 247
Posttraumatic stress disorder, 4, 221
Power, 12, 19, 37, 222
  and misperception, 70, 82
  by students, 37
  motives, 10, 12. *See also* Dominance motives
  organizational conflict and change, 230
  power differentials, 223, 234
  theories and ethical decision making. *See* Ethical

Power-based procedures for complaint handling, 247
Powerlessness, 222
Prevalence of SH, 4
academia, 30
Prevention programs, 268
Prima facie case, 93
Privacy vs. right to know, 263
Probability of effect and moral intensity. *See* Moral intensity
Protected class, 93
Proximity, and moral intensity. *See* Moral intensity
Psychological harm, requirement for SH, 98

Quid pro quo, 6, 11, 86, 87, 113, 136

Rabidue v. Osceola Refining Company, 93, 153
Race discrimination and SH, 58
Race, power and, 11
Racially skewed environments and SH, 62
Rape-supporting belief system, 8. *See also* Sexual-assault supporting belief system
Reasonable:
person 95, 98, 99, 102, 157, 170
victim, 95, 98
woman, 95, 99, 101, 102, 157
Reasonable doubt. *See* Standard of proof
Reasonable woman standard, 236
and race, 62, 63
Reinforcement contingencies and ethical decision making. *See* Ethical
Reporting rate, methods for increasing, 261
Reprisals, dealing with, 261
Response style, 16
active/assertive, 17
externally focused, 17
instrumentality, 17
internally focused, 17
passive/unassertive, 17
Right to know. *See* Privacy
Rights-based options for complaint handling 242, 244, 246, 249
Robinson v. Jacksonville Shipyards 153, 158
Role analysis, 232, 234
Role negotiation, 233, 234

Saxton v. American Telephone and Telegraph, 101, 102
SEQ, 145
Seductress, 40, 41, 43
Severity of SH, 155, 162
appraisal and, 14
enhancing understanding of, 167, 168
vs. frequency, in establishing prima facie case, 95
Severity/pervasiveness, 94, 98, 101
Sex, based on, 94
Sex role spillover 10, 19, 40, 68, 82, 289
Sexual Experiences Questionnaire, 145, 154, 168
Sexual:
arousal, 12
coercion, 6, 136
racism, 52, 53, 57, 58
scripts, 42
Sexual-assault supporting belief system, 9. *See also* rape-supporting belief system
Sexualized work environment, 115
Situational characteristics, 9, 14
Social consensus, and moral intensity, 108, 109, 115
Social isolation, 223
Social systems. *See* Organizational settings
Sociocultural model of SH, 68, 82
Soviets, former, SH of. *See* European women
Stakeholders, complaint handling, 246
Standard of proof, 255
beyond a reasonable doubt, 256
clear and convincing evidence, 255
he said/she said, 255, 257, 259
Staton v. Maries County, 94
Status relationships, perpetrators and targets, 5

Stereotyped roles, 40, 41
Stereotypes, racial/ethnic, 54, 57, 58, 59, 62
Stressors, 20
  multiple, 191
  organizational, 190
Survey of SH in academia, items, 47, 48
Systems approach to conflict management, 241

Tailhook, 86, 122
Target characteristics, 7
Team building, 231, 232
Technical systems. *See* Organizational settings
Temporal immediacy and moral intensity. *See* Moral intensity
Third party intervention. *See* Dispute resolution
Training considerations, 210

Universality:
  of SH severity, 164, 166
  of SH types, 162, 166
  of sexual harassment, 152, 153, 170
Unwanted sexual attention, 6, 136
Unwelcome harassment, 93, 99, 100

Victim:
  characteristics of, 12
  responses, domestic violence and SH, 220
  similarities, domestic violence and SH, 220
Violence against women, 218, 219
Voluntariness, 88

Winning a case of sexual harassment: complainant, 280
Withdrawal, job:
  individual outcomes of SH, 183, 184, 185
  organizational outcomes of SH, 184, 185
  organizational, work, 183
Women of color:
  defined, 52
  definitions of SH, 53, 56
  frequency of SH, 53
  sexual behavior toward, 41
  SH of, 51
Women professors, SH experiences (*see* xperiences of SH
Work group, gender composition, 10
Work relationships with men and black women, 59
Workplace climate. *See* Climate

About the Authors

Lynn Bowes-Sperry is a doctoral candidate in management/organizational behavior at the University of Connecticut. She received her B.A. (1985) in economics from the College of the Holy Cross in Worcester, MA, and her M.B.A. with a concentration in human resource management from the University of New Haven (1990). Her research interests include ethical decision making in organizations, impression management, organizational justice, human resource management, and women in management. Her dissertation examines observers' reactions to sexual harassment from an ethical decision-making perspective.

Jeanette N. Cleveland is Professor of Psychology at Colorado State University. She received her B.A., in psychology from Occidental College and her M.S. and Ph.D. in industrial and organizational psychology from the Pennsylvania State University. She serves on the editorial boards of *Academy of Management Journal* and *Journal of Vocational Behavior*. She is the author of numerous articles and book chapters, and is author or editor of three books. Her research interests focus on contextual factors in performance appraisal and age and gender issues in the workplace.

Fritz Drasgow is Professor of Psychology and of Labor and Industrial Relations at the University of Illinois at Urbana–Champaign. Much of his recent research has focused on computerized tests and assessments. This work uses multimedia computer technology to assess social and interpersonal skills not easily measured by paper-and-pencil tests. He is a former chairperson of the American Psychological Association's Committee on Psychological Tests and Assessments and the U.S. Department of Defense's Advisory Committee on Military Personnel Testing. He is a member of the editorial review board of six journals, including *Journal of Applied Psychology* and *Applied Psychological Measurement.*

Louise F. Fitzgerald is Professor of Psychology and Women's Studies at the University of Illinois at Urbana–Champaign. She received her Ph.D. in Psychology from the Ohio State University and is one of the leading researchers in the United States on the topic of women and work, especially sexual harassment. Her work has been cited to the U.S. Supreme Court, the New Jersey Supreme Court, and in numerous other judicial proceedings. She is a consultant to the Civil Rights Division of the U.S. Department of Justice, is a member of the APA Taskforce on Violence Against Women, and was recently appointed social science consultant to the U.S. Eighth Circuit's Taskforce on Gender Fairness in the Courts. In addition to her research, writing, and consulting activities, Professor Fitzgerald works extensively with victims of harassment and is considered an authority on outcomes of workplace victimization.

Elizabeth Grauerholz is Associate Professor of Sociology at Purdue University. Her research focuses on the intersections between gender and power, especially with respect to sexual violence against women. Her most recent research has explored the experiences that women professors, especially lesbians and women of color, have had with sexual harassment and other forms of sexual assault. She is also interested in differential perceptions of female versus male faculty members. She is the coeditor of *Sexual Coercion: A Sourcebook on Its Nature, Causes, and Prevention* (Lexington).

James E. Gruber is Professor of Sociology at the University of Michigan—Dearborn and has done research in the area of sexual harassment since 1981. His major focus has been on the experiences and responses of women in nontraditional jobs.

Barbara A. Gutek (Ph.D., 1975, University of Michigan) is Professor in the Department of Management and Policy at the University of Arizona, where she currently heads the department. She is an editor for the *Women and Work* series published by Sage. Her publications include *Women and Work* with Veronica Nieva (Praeger, 1981), *Sex and the Workplace: The Impact of Sexual Behavior and Harassment on Women, Men, and Organizations* (Jossey-Bass, 1985), *Women's Career Development* with Laurie Larwood (Sage, 1987), *The Dynamics of Service: Reflections on the Changing Nature of Customer/Provider Interactions* (Jossey-Bass, 1995), and over 70 journal articles and book chapters. Her research has been funded by the National Science Foundation and the National Institute of Mental Health. In 1994, she received two awards from the American Psychological Association and the Academy of Management (Women in Management) Sage Research Award.

Kathy A. Hanisch is Assistant Professor of Industrial and Organizational Psychology at Iowa State University. She received her Ph.D. from the University of Illinois at Urbana-Champaign. Her primary research interests are employees' multiple and patterned behaviors resulting from their attitudes, including work satisfaction and stress. She has identified two employee behavioral families: work and job withdrawal. Her research framework has been generalized to the relations among retirees' attitudes and behaviors. She has written several articles and chapters as well as presented her research results at professional conferences. Her scientific findings have been studied in both private and public organizations.

Charles L. Hulin is Professor of Psychology in Liberal Arts and Sciences and the Institute of Aviation at the University of Illinois at Urbana–Champaign. His research and writings are generally in attitude-behavior relations, with an emphasis on attitudinal antecedents of organizational withdrawal, work motivations, antecedents and consequences of sexual harassment in the workplace, and the effects of anger and gender on supervisory evaluations. He was the associate editor of the *Journal of Applied Psychology* from 1975 to 1982 and has been a masthead editor of *Organizational Behavior and Human Decision Processes* since 1972.

Kaisa Kauppinen-Toropainen is Senior Research Associate at the Institute of Occupational Health in Helsinki, Finland. She has done extensive comparative research on women and work in Scandinavia, the United States, and Russia. Her primary interests are the economic and psychological well-being of working women internationally.

Deborah Erdos Knapp is Visiting Assistant Professor in the Department of Management and Labor Relations at Cleveland State University. She received her Ph.D. degree from Kent State University. Her research interests include sexual harassment, discrimination, and gender-related issues in management.

Gary A. Kustis is a doctoral candidate in the Administrative Sciences Department at Kent State University. He received his M.A. degree in psychology from Cleveland State University. His research interests include sexual harassment, the glass-ceiling phenomenon, employee efficiency, and the effects of new technology on employee performance. His dissertation will focus on why some women break through the glass ceiling and others do not.

Kathleen McNamara (Ph.D.) is Associate Professor of Psychology in the Department of Psychology at Colorado State University. She received her degree in counseling psychology from Pennsylvania State University in 1984. She has taught graduate and undergraduate courses on psychotherapy, women and mental health, clinical interviewing, personality, group psychology, and general psychology. Her research interests focus on women's mental health and psychotherapy evaluation. She is a licensed psychologist in Colorado and maintains a part-time clinical practice.

Audrey J. Murrell received her B.S. from Howard University, magna cum laude, in 1983. She received an M.S. in 1985 and a Ph.D. in 1987 from the University of Delaware. Her major emphasis while at Delaware was in psychology, specifically social psychology. She held an academic position in the Psychology Department at the University of Pittsburgh before joining the faculty of the Katz Graduate School of Business in 1989. Her research interests focus on the process and effect of group identification, or how individuals become effective members of groups and organizations and the impact of this membership for interaction between diverse groups. In addition, she has conducted research on careers in organizations. Specifically, her work has focused on the process of effective career planning and the positive and negative effects of career mobility and transition. She also has served as a consultant in the areas of diversity, teamwork effectiveness, and issues concerning women and work.

Anne M. O'Leary-Kelly is Assistant Professor of Management at the University of Dayton. She received her Ph.D. from Michigan State University in 1990 in organizational behavior and human resource management. Her current research focuses on aggressive behavior in organizational contexts (sexual harassment, organizational violence) and motivational issues in groups. She has published in multiple journals including the *Journal of Applied Psychology*, the *Academy of Management Journal*, the *Journal of Organizational Behavior*, and the *American Business Law Journal*. She is an active member of the Academy of Management, the American Psychological Association, and the Society for Industrial and Organizational Psychology.

Ramona L. Paetzold is Assistant Professor of Management at Texas A & M University. She received her J.D. from the University of Nebraska in 1990 and her D.B.A. from Indiana University in 1979. She has published in the areas of sexual harassment law, employment discrimination law, law and statistics, and feminist jurisprudence. Her current research on sexual harassment involves integration of legal, psychological, and organizational perspectives. She has recently published a book (with Steven L. Willborn) titled *The Statistics of Discrimination: Using Statistical Evidence in Discrimination*. In addition, she has provided expert assistance in a variety of discrimination law cases. She is Senior Articles Editor of the *Journal of Legal Studies Education* and a Staff Editor of the *American Business Law Journal*.

Gary N. Powell is Professor of Management at the University of Connecticut. He is the author of *Women and Men in Management*, currently in its second edition (Sage, 1993), and *Gender and Diversity in the Workplace: Learning Activities and Exercises* (Sage, 1994). He has served as Chairperson of the Women in Management Division of the Academy of Management and is a past President of the Eastern Academy of Management. He has published over 60 articles and presented over 70 papers at professional conferences. He also has served on the editorial boards of the *Academy of Management Review* and the *Academy of Management Executive*.

Mary P. Rowe received her Ph.D. in economics from Columbia University. Since 1973, she has been Special Assistant to three successive presidents of MIT. She is one of two ombudspersons for the faculty, staff, and students of the MIT community. She is also Adjunct Professor at the MIT Sloan School of Management; her teaching, research, and consulting focus on negotiation and conflict management, and on integrated dispute resolution systems design. In 1982, she cofounded the Corporate Ombudsman Association, now The Ombudsman Association. She has written dozens of articles on complaint handling, design of integrated dispute resolution systems, aspects of workplace diversity, and problems of all kinds of harassment. She is currently working on "second generation" problems in harassment: how different people see the issues differently and the need for options in complaint systems.

Frank E. Saal is Department Head and Professor of Psychology at Kansas State University in Manhattan, Kansas, where he is also a member of the Women's Studies and Graduate Faculties. He is author of *Industrial/Organizational Psychology: Science and Practice* (second edition, with Pat Knight, published by Brooks/Cole) and editor of *Psychology in Organizations: Integrating Science and Practice* (with Kevin Murphy, published by Lawrence Erlbaum). He served as Consulting Editor of the *Psychology of Women Quarterly* from 1986 through 1993. He was elected to Sigma Xi in 1980, and received a Faculty Service Award from the National University Continuing Education Association in 1985. His Ph.D. in industrial and organizational psychology is from Pennsylvania State University.

Michael Smith was Professor of Sociology and the Director of the LaMarsh Research Program on Violence and Conflict Resolution at York University, Toronto. His research focused on violence against women, primarily spouse abuse and harassment in public places. He was director of a research project that interviewed a representative, national sample of Canadian women about their experiences with public and workplace sexual harassment. He died in June 1994 after a short illness.

Margaret S. (Peggy) Stockdale (Ph.D., 1990, Kansas State University, Industrial and Organizational Psychology) is Assistant Professor of Psychology at Southern Illinois University at Carbondale. She has maintained an active program of research on women in the workplace with a special emphasis on sexual harassment, and has several publications in peer-reviewed journals. She coedited the 1993 special issue of *Journal of Vocational Behavior* on sexual harassment with Howard E. A. Tinsley, and coedited *Independent Consulting for Evaluators* (1992, Sage). She is coauthor, with J. Cleveland and B. Gutek, of *Women and Men in Organizations: Sex and Gender Issues at Work* (forthcoming, Lawrence Erlbaum). She is also the Director of Applied Research Consultants, a faculty-supervised graduate practicum offering applied experimental psychology consulting services to local, regional, and national organizations.